OWNING OUR VALUES

OWNING OUR VALUES

Understanding Systemic Racism Through the Lens of Property Law

(And Skills to Do Something About It)

NATASHA N. VARYANI
Associate Professor of Law
Roger Williams University School of Law

AP
CAROLINA ACADEMIC PRESS
Durham, North Carolina

Library of Congress Cataloging-in-Publication Data

Names: Varyani, Natasha N., author.
Title: Owning our values : understanding systemic racism through the lens of property law (and skills to do something about it) / Natasha N. Varyani.
Description: Durham, North Carolina : Carolina Academic Press, 2024. | Includes bibliographical references and index.
Identifiers: LCCN 2024015349 | ISBN 9781531025793 (paperback) | ISBN 9781531025809 (ebook)
Subjects: LCSH: Race discrimination—Law and legislation—United States. | Social justice—United States. | Property—United States. | Real property—United States. | Discrimination in housing—Law and legislation—United States.
Classification: LCC KF4755 .V37 2024 | DDC 346.7304089--dc23/eng/20240409
LC record available at https://lccn.loc.gov/2024015349

Carolina Academic Press
700 Kent Street
Durham, North Carolina 27701
(919) 489-7486
www.cap-press.com

Printed in the United States of America

For Nanak, Krish & Kamal
For helping me know what it is to belong.

For Kevin
Without whom I could not do it all.

For Nani & Nana
Who gave everything so I could do anything.

Intellectual work matters.

Love, friendship, community,

the struggle for justice matter.

And increasingly,

I see these all as the same thing.

—Mari Matsuda, August 2021[1]

1. Remarks given (remotely) at the Inaugural Workshop for Asian American Women in the Legal Academy. It was at this conference that the proposal for this work was first presented at an "incubator" presentation and given comments and support by faculty.

Contents

Land and Labor Acknowledgment

It is only fitting that this book begin with an acknowledgement of all of those people who go unnamed whose property has been taken. The same history that has dispossessed them of their rights has allowed the author the privilege of completing this work.

The land: As the author writes this, she sits on land that belonged to the Pawtucket, Wampanoag, and Massachusett people before they were dispossessed of it. The trauma of colonialism did not end when ownership of land was transferred; rather, indigenous groups, upon losing access to the land and resources of their ancestors, were robbed not only of their property but also of their culture, identity, and history. Though there is no way to correct this, the collective and reasonable grief that is associated with this wrongdoing deserves to be acknowledged (especially at the outset of a book about property). In acknowledging this wrongdoing and pain, let us consider our responsibilities, particularly as we take up the mantel as stewards of the rule of law and of justice, and continually assess how we can address it in ways big and small.

The labor: The author recognizes and acknowledges the labor upon which the country, state, institutions, and actual buildings are built. The United States is built by people who were kidnapped and brought to these shores as though they were property. I recognize the suffering, grief, and contributions of those people who were enslaved as well as the continuing contributions of their descendants. In addition, colonial forces around the world have resulted in immigrant labor, both voluntary and involuntary, documented and undocumented, trafficked and forced. All of these individuals have contributed and continue to contribute to the labor force in the United States, each having a unique and human story. A willful disregard for the humanity of some is a moral failure that sits at the foundation of our country, culture, and institutions, and it must be acknowledged before the work of beginning to correct it may begin.

In acknowledging these wrongdoings, let each of us consider our responsibilities to the people and to the property that has been impacted and stand in solidarity and actively support the Native, Indigenous, First Nations People, and people who were bought, sold, and born into slavery and servitude. Though their names and humanity may feel lost to history, doing our part to acknowledge and honor their struggles and sacrifices is essential.

Disclosure and Warning to the Reader

Dear Reader,

The material contained herein is not for the faint of heart. Even writing parts of it has made me deeply uncomfortable, and I wonder whether talking about race in this way is the right thing to do. Some of you may come to law school and to this book with a set of experiences that will fill you with rage, sadness, or discomfort, or make your heartbeat quicken for reasons you cannot quite explain. Here's my advice: sit with those feelings. If you need to, close the book for a few minutes (maybe your eyes, too) and try to inspect what is making you feel that way, and then decide what you are going to do about it.

The metaphor of tea is one that has always resonated with me. I share it with you now in the hope that you may find some comfort in your heart and mind in a warm cup of tea the way that I have. I am South Asian by heritage—impacted by colonialism as so many people are. For me, though the lines between India and Pakistan have made things complicated, my parents came to this country bursting with dreams and a new baby (me!) so that I might be born a citizen, and I was. I am, and have always been, American. Still, the routine and memory of making tea for my parents—the mixture, the smell, the ritual—is among my happiest memories. The smell of a good chai transports me back to that ritual that I looked forward to every day, not just for a break in my homework, but because it was time with the people who made me. We hardly discussed ground-breaking topics; in fact, I barely remember anything but the smell of the tea, the stress of dipping the cookies (hoping they would not disintegrate), and the sweetness and relief that continues to be one of my pure joys.

But those days ended, and I moved to Boston where I became a tax lawyer. Boston: where a different set of colonists expressed their rage at the British by throwing tea into the harbor. The protest was about tax. For me, tax has always been about property. The central and existential question has been how much of what someone earns is owned to someone else. For the daughter of immigrants, that question may have landed differently, but even as I represented corporate taxpayers, it never left me.

Perhaps the reason that the appeal of tea has persisted since ancient times is because of the indelible mark that it makes. As I sometimes drop my tea in hot water and watch the stain swirl, I always find a metaphor. When I start each academic year, particularly when I teach courses on critical race theory, I hope a new way of thinking will seep into my students like the tea. Stain them a little, change the flavor of everything they do. For all of the rich and beautiful flavor of the tea leaves that has evolved from generations of plants fed from soil, appropriated by colonists, and tended with care, there can be a bitter edge. That bitterness eventually becomes part of the beauty. Once it seeps in, it cannot be undone. For me, seeing and understanding issues related to systemic racism is a lot like that.

Ignoring these issues has never been the answer for me. Though I am generally someone who strives to bring joy to those around me, I write this book knowing that it will be very uncomfortable. The alternative is to not talk about race—to leave our history and our discomfort unexplored. This is a strategy inconsistent with our professional practice as lawyers. The legal profession is one that addresses problems: whether to address or avoid them for our clients, an effective advocate cannot ignore difficult problems. Like so many other essential skills, resilience and grace can be fortified with practice.

For those who read on, I am grateful for your bravery. Your courage, strength, and willingness to engage in understanding at a granular level what we mean when we use the words "systemic racism" will help to dismantle the structures that keep so many people from accessing justice. Remember that this work is difficult, sometimes in ways that you do not expect. Give yourself grace, and if things become unbearable, I find the ritual of a break with a warm cup of tea to be soothing.

With gratitude,
Natasha N. Varyani · MARCH 2024

Preface

Systemic racism is not new. Treating groups of people differently based on their race has been a part of the social, cultural, and legal history of this country from before the time that independence was established. In addition to being woven into our social fabric, treating classes of people differently based on their race has been a part of our legal systems and structures in ways that are inextricably linked with our national identity. This is not a critical way of thinking—it is our history.

What has changed in recent years is the discourse around systemic racism. The tone of that discourse varies by time, place, and context. It is undeniable, however, that understanding "systemic racism" has become a fascination in our social and political landscape. So many times has the phrase "systemic racism" been used that, for some, it has lost its meaning. Meanwhile, the changing and ongoing national discourse around systemic racism has inspired others to come to law school to clarify and do their part to correct its effects. This book is for those students and teachers—the ones who hope to integrate and highlight issues of systemic racism that have long been neglected by our system of legal education.

This book is intended to support both professors and students who are engaged in social justice and believe in the power of a legal education. Written with an awareness of the pressures coming from all sides of a first-year classroom, the text provides brief explanations of doctrine accompanied by detailed examples of how that doctrine connects to the systems that have served to discriminate or to those structures created to perpetuate already-established discriminatory practices. The purpose of this structure is to highlight areas in the first-year property law curriculum (with a focus on heavily (next-generation) bar-tested areas of law) that help to give meaning to the phrase "systemic racism," and to support the development of students' legal skills in a culturally responsive way.

Two mantras that recur throughout this work (as well as in my classrooms, office hours, and many of my professional and personal interactions) are these: (1) Words Matter, and (2) Relationships Are Everything. While both will be helpful as you read this book, engage with its exercises, and learn the law in all classrooms and forms, it is good practice to keep both in mind even in non-legal practice. Although these two maxims will be used separately on a number of occasions, they are nevertheless connected because our words and our relationships are inextricably intertwined.

Why Property Law?

Though most every first-year professor will tell you that their course is *the most* fundamental and important to the study and practice of law, only professors of property law are correct.

Many students enter law school expecting their property law course to exclusively cover real estate transactions and are surprised to find that its coverage is much more expansive. The law of property is concerned not only with land but also with *ownership*. Property Law is not a course that inspects the rights that people have over their owned property but rather is a study of our collective relationships with one another with regard to those things and places that are valuable to us.[1] At the beginning of the course, it is a useful exercise to consider those items of "personal property" that are most cherished and encourage students to write about them. Regardless of whether students decide to share their thoughts on this type of personal property, the exercise helps to underscore the ways in which the property that is most precious to individuals and worthy of protection sometimes has more to do with our personal experiences and relationships than its market value.

---

1. *See* Jennifer Nedelsky, *Law, Boundaries, and the Bounded Self*, 30 Representations 162 (1990); Jennifer Nedelsky, *Reconceiving Rights as Relationships*, 1 Rev. Const. Studies/Revue d'Etudes Constitutionelles 1 (1993). In these works, Professor Nedelsky suggests that instead of centering the idea of the *boundary* in property law, we should instead center the idea of *relationships*.

Writing Prompt: Personal Property	Reflection & Feedback
Consider what property is most valuable to you, and describe why. This may be land (real property) or an object (personal property). To what lengths have you gone to safeguard this property? What is the relationship between the fair market value of this property and its value to you?	In sharing stories about our most precious property, it quickly becomes clear that a great deal of our identity may be wrapped up in our property. As we explore different facets of identity and study the way that groups have been treated, this is an important concept to keep in mind.

Protection of rights in property is central to the story of the history and culture of the United States.[2] In addition to having a connection to our individual identities, the law of property and the ability to protect what we own is a fiercely protected tenet in the U.S. system of laws.[3] It is the denial of this central and protected right that is the basis of the systemic inequities that are explored in this book. There are classes of people, grouped by some facet of their identity, that have historically, intentionally, and systematically been denied rights in property that were granted to and protected by others. Too long has the canon of property law been silent about these groups. This book focuses on those marginalized groups which were denied rights based on their race, but people with intersecting marginalized identities have suffered particularly under these systems of law as well, and this book explores that issue when possible.

2. Thomas Jefferson, when drafting the Declaration of Independence and listing the inalienable rights of "Life, liberty, and the pursuit of happiness," borrowed ideas from John Locke, who, in his Second Treatise on Government (published in 1689), described three "inalienable" rights as life, liberty, and the pursuit of property. Locke describes the right to one's property as a right based in natural law, granted by God and designed to protect mankind.

3. Both the Fifth and Fourteenth Amendments to the U.S. Constitution use the same words to describe the concepts contained in each. Citizens may not be "deprived of life, liberty, or property without due process of law."

Lawyering Skills: Empathy

An important skill for any person practicing law, whether an advisor, advocate, or judge, is empathy. Understanding the position of a client, an adversary, or a third party is essential to the development of any legal argument, yet empathy is often considered a "soft" skill that is not given much (if any) attention in many legal education settings. As with any skill, those who are in the habit of practicing empathy will sharpen it. We will begin here by considering various perspectives.

Professor's Perspective

While insulated, law professors are not immune or blind to social change. There are many who have watched with interest or even participated in social movements addressing systemic racism in the United States. But even those who are marching and protesting in their free time may be reluctant to bring their social-justice views into a classroom. Consider the many good reasons for that reluctance and what supports may assist them:

First: it can be scary. Academia is a place with a strong sense of hierarchy and where pedigree matters. As a group, professors are likely to be acutely aware of a number of unwritten rules that surround them and also wary of navigating in an environment filled with hidden obstacles. For a predominantly white and privileged set,[4] speaking openly and vulnerably about race is simply something they are conditioned not to do. Though the lecture setting and grading structure may give rise to certain power dynamics between professors and students, it is nevertheless important for the latter to remind themselves of the professor's humanity, including the existence of hidden vulnerabilities and fears—and particularly so with regard to the untenured.

Second: course coverage must be considered. In addition to personal feelings of fear and vulnerability that may cause a professor to avoid talking about race and identity in their classroom, professors often cite the amount of material they already have to cover as a reason not to add more to their syllabus. While it is true that every subject area has far

4. Meera Deo, Unequal Profession: Race and Gender in Legal Academia (2019).

more than can be covered in any course (no matter the number of credits), it is still possible to continue to teach these areas of law while inspecting how they have been used to perpetuate systemic racism. Indeed, this book is designed to provide resources to conduct that inspection in heavily bar-tested areas while also assisting in the development of legal analysis skills. Institutionalized racism is so prevalent in our system of laws that it is nearly impossible to find an area of law unburdened by it. Accordingly, professors reluctant to change their course coverage can take heart: all the same bar-tested areas can be examined, and with some slight changes, students who relate to the material on a more personal or visceral level may even retain more of the information.

Third: property law is already too messy. Property Law is most often one of the first courses students take in law school, which means that professors have the combined challenge of teaching the doctrine and helping students develop legal-analysis skills. Unlike some other first-year courses, like Torts, Civil Procedure, or Criminal Law, Property Law courses do not have a natural structure; there are no elements or federal rules to follow. Property law has evolved organically and messily, and accordingly, it is difficult to arrange topics in any particular order. More than with other courses, it is up to each professor to weave the thread of their thoughts through topics that might, to the untrained eye, appear disconnected. Because of the particular challenges that come with teaching the law of property, this book seeks to provide a structure that is not tied to any particular casebook and may be used in any order.

Fourth: students do not yet have the skills to conduct this type of analysis. Licensing requirements and the legal profession have been placing an ever-increasing emphasis on legal-analysis skills. This book provides professors with the opportunity to engage with students in modeling these skills with the actual doctrine. Demonstrating how to effectively hone different parts of a legal analysis may come naturally to professors who have been in practice. This book seeks to help professors draw these skills out in digestible components while also providing examples of some common mistakes students may make as well as typical steps to correct these missteps that students may take early in their legal careers.

Professors are interested in partnering with and supporting students on their path to the legal profession. This book is designed to assist those professors in that goal.

Learner's Perspective

Students are coming to property law, and indeed law school, with fresh eyes. Eager to learn, it is often the case that the actual experience of the first year of law school subverts expectations. Even students who are prepared to be challenged find themselves challenged in different ways than expected. Confusion is a normal part of the law school learning experience. But, especially for those students whose racial identities are not well represented in the profession, many classroom discussions can also feel isolating. Particularly when the standard of "reasonableness" is invoked in a court's ruling or legal reasoning, the homogeneity of the bench, the bar, and even the parties that come before the court (let alone the appeals that find themselves in casebooks) leave very little chance for a culturally responsive rule or analysis. For this reason, students from different backgrounds and cultures from the normative ones presented in the cases may be left wondering whether their own sense of reasonableness has any place in the law. Let's be clear: EVERY SINGLE PERSPECTIVE has a place in the law.

Beginning a legal education is a unique experience. Most people entering law school have enjoyed academic success before arriving, only to find that, as a discipline, learning the law is unlike anything they have done before. Tried and true methods for study, including close reading, information retention, and strong organizational skills are all helpful, but by no means do they guarantee success. Learning the law is something like learning a new language, and with that language comes a culture and customs. Those rigid students who resist may experience frustration and difficulty and be flummoxed by disappointing GPAs for the first time in their academic careers. As with learning a language, however, those who immerse themselves in their studies and engage with as many native speakers as possible will soon develop their own fluency and style. Students should look to professors as guides and embrace the varied styles of each as opportunities to add to a totality of experiences that will determine the type of lawyer they will be. The people with whom you choose to associate yourself throughout your career will shape your identity as a professional and individual. So choose wisely: relationships are everything.

It is important for all law students to know when to speak and when to listen, regardless of whether or not they belong to a marginalized group. Dynamics in law school sections quickly emerge both inside and outside the classroom, and practicing humility, grace, patience, and bravery are all essential. There are as many approaches to the law classroom as there are individuals sitting in them, each with their own set of experiences and history. Each student should prioritize finding their trusted advisors, both inside and outside of the profession, and seek their counsel regularly. For so many students, the challenge of law school is not the amount of reading or any other academic burden but rather the lack of clear expectations, and this fuels self-doubt. For a profession that spends a great deal of time wrapping up our identities with our work, that self-doubt can be crippling[5]—especially for those students who find the meaning of a seemingly simple and clearly important word like "reasonable" to be elusive.

This book is for those students who are sitting in class and wondering whether what they are thinking has any place in the legal analysis. Whether or not a student sees their particular thoughts reflected or echoed in this book, I hope that engaging with this material gives each and every one confidence that they may find a place for their perspective. The beauty of the common law system is that it is alive and reflects the individuals that it serves. And lawyers have a particular duty and responsibility to shape it into a likeness fitting of the age. So, be empowered. Learn this language and find your voice—remember, *words matter*.

Considering questions related to race and identity while studying doctrine can be draining. Years of working in a doctrinal classroom and in academia suggests that developing a practice of spending time with the material before, during, and after class will help to process and retain information. Reading, rereading, and even transcribing can feel like a diligent and thorough exercise, but given the amount of reading required across doctrinal classes, it can be an impracticable and inefficient solution. Students should try instead an exercise in "active recall," which will take less time and yield better results, even if it feels more difficult.

5. Studies suggest that students from underrepresented communities, particularly Black and brown students in law school, have an increased cognitive load. Cognitive load theory suggests that our cognitive load is broken down into distinct types: intrinsic, extrinsic, and germane. Natasha N. Varyani, *Cognitive Load Theory and Learning the Law: How and Why Minority Students Struggle in Law School*, The Learning Curve (AALS Academic Support Publication), Winter/Spring 2018, at 13.

Active Recall Exercise	
Step 1:	Read an increment of your selection (casebook, class notes, or outline)
Step 2:	Close and remove from sight the selection. Take a short (1–2 minute) break.
Step 3:	On a blank page, recreate the highlights of the selection, filling in as much relevant/salient detail as possible.
Step 4:	Return to selection to check your work. Fill in any information that was missing from your memory.

Engaging in this active-recall activity gives your brain something to do beyond simply reviewing information. Actively engaging your brain by asking it to access information results in better retention. In addition, any relevant pieces that were forgotten on the first pass and added upon review have been flagged for your memory and will also stand out. Finally, getting in the habit of performing this mental exercise will change the way that you begin to read and assess your material the first time through because your brain will begin to put new flags near information that feels salient and relevant, which in turn, will make you a more efficient reader of details. In learning the law, having a command of the details will always be advantageous.

Author's Perspective

As connection and trust are central to my teaching style, it seems only fair that in introducing my work I share a bit about myself. I distinctly remember sitting in my first-year law school classrooms and feeling generally fine but also bewildered. I was able to achieve my goal of passing through law school basically unnoticed. After law school, I spent about a decade in private practice in the area of tax. Apart from a short time spent at an accounting firm, I worked mostly at medium to large law firms; and while I enjoyed the work, it never ignited my passion. While in practice, I felt personally driven to work tirelessly for affinity bar groups, to find and connect with others who, like me, felt like they didn't quite belong. Though we may not have had the language for it at the time, seeking out people who made me feel less alone was what I was passionate about, and mentoring was always a two-way street. I never dreamed that I would be a law professor. Even after a decade, it still sometimes feels incredible that teaching the law is a path available to me.

I am South Asian American, and my existence outside the Black/white racial binary that sometimes exists in policy discussions has required some intentional navigation. I have taught core courses in property, contracts, wills, and tax, and also seminars on tax and critical race theory and the law.

By nature, I am a person who prefers to make people feel good and comfortable. Teaching and writing in the area of critical race theory has changed that a bit. I have found that practice in having difficult conversations, while uncomfortable, can lead to a great deal of growth. I have been so honored and proud to watch many of my students conduct themselves with grace, bravery, and pride while initiating honest, personal, and important conversations about race and the law.

I have three children who inspire almost everything that I do. I try to see the world as I hope it will exist for them and make decisions accordingly. My children are mixed race and have their own paths to navigate with regard to belonging, and I hope that our legal system is one that they can look to and trust for justice when they come of age.

Classroom Management

Classroom dynamics require intentional and careful management when discussing systemic racism. As these issues relate to identity and can, depending on the individual and their lived experiences, be tense or painful to discuss, it may be tempting to avoid unpleasantness by avoiding discussion of these issues at all. But that would be a grave mistake. The price for avoiding a small daily discomfort is having students, especially those from racial minorities, who feel invisible and excluded from a law school curriculum. Presenting a complete picture of the legal history of this country is essential. Whether students come from marginalized groups or not, their knowledge of the law must be complete and they must be shown good models for putting their legal analysis skills to use in a cultural context. Engaging in informed civil discourse in matters that may be emotionally charged is difficult and potentially scary, but that is exactly the job of a lawyer. As with any skill, it is one that is developed and honed and becomes more familiar (if not easier) with practice. Before embarking on the substance of the chapters, I would like to discuss a few lessons I have learned while managing large classrooms in changing times with an increased focus on systemic racism.

Managing Identities

A course in property law is likely to be in a large lecture hall with very little opportunity for personal interaction. Still, particularly as students are beginning their law school journey, many are hyper-focused on presenting their own identities and gleaning what they can about those around them. A professor sets the tone for the classroom in so many ways, including what to share and how.

Speaking openly about my own racial identity in a classroom with more than 100 new and captivated students is consistently one of the most unnatural and uncomfortable experiences that I have each year, but I continue to provide details, and it continues to pay off. Having spent most of my life trying to erase all traces of my cultural heritage in order to "fit in" with various groups, it has become second nature for me to adapt. Working in the tax field in big law firms has meant operating in an environment with virtually no racial, gender, or cultural diversity; accordingly, my habits had evolved to scrub any traces of the parts of my identity that diverged from the norms of my peers. Increasingly, I have begun to share my discomfort with my students, as the reasons for why my habits around speaking about my racial identity have evolved in the way they have is an important part of my story. I understand (truly) how difficult it is for professors to speak about their own lived experiences, but I believe that it helps to engage students for the remainder of the term and sets the tone for the type of earnest efforts that are required for successful discussion.

When managing conversations about identity, it is important to acknowledge privilege when you have it. Many professors may be reluctant to speak about their racial identity because they "don't have one," but that is a way of thinking that may be reframed as a privilege. When speaking about one's own racial identity, it is most important to be honest, even if your personal story is that you never seriously considered race until the moment you opened this book (or more likely, until the #BlackLivesMatter movement shined a light on the significance of race). Owning that part of your story and understanding what that means in the current circumstance is important. Resist the temptation to discuss only the marginalized parts of your identity.[6] Being thoughtful and mindful of

---

6. Avoid the "Oppression Olympics." *See* Amen Gashaw, *In the Oppression Olympics, Don't Go for the Gold*, HARV. POL. REV. (Feb. 1, 2024), https://harvardpolitics.com/in-the-oppression-olympics-dont-go-for-the-gold/.

what privilege and advantages you have had[7] before speaking about your identity with your class will demonstrate the respect you have for and the importance you give to the issues and people before you.

People-First Language and Naming Groups by Race

When communicating about the interests and rights of people under the law and underscoring their humanity, using people-first language[8] can be a helpful tool. Once again, this may be a concept that is more familiar and natural to students than to professors, and some thoughtful research and discussion at the outset of class will go a long way in setting the tone for the semester. People-first language centers on the humanity of individuals instead of on the particular attribute that is the subject of discussion, for example, "person struggling with addiction" instead of "addict." People-first language originated in self-advocacy for disability groups in the 1970s but recently has been used more prevalently to help destigmatize mental-health and substance-abuse disorders. Destigmatization can be especially important when dealing with certain issues in property law—when speaking about the concept of nuisance, for example, the phrase "people who are unhoused" can be used instead of "the homeless." This small change will signal to students the importance of humanity and help them to keep a visceral connection to the application and analysis of the law.

Referring to racial groups can be a particularly thorny subject, and I have found it helpful to have a discussion with the class early on so that

---

7. For a starting point, see Peggy McIntosh, *White Privilege: Unpacking the Invisible Knapsack*, *in* RE-VISIONING FAMILY THERAPY: RACE, CULTURE, AND GENDER IN CLINICAL PRACTICE 147–52 (M. McGoldrick, ed. 1998), reprinted from PEACE AND FREEDOM 10–12 (July/Aug. 1989), also reprinted in modified form from "White Privilege and Male Privilege: A Personal Account of Coming to See Correspondences through Work in Women's Studies" (1988).

8. For more information and to learn a bit of the history of people-first language, see Shannon Wooldridge, *Writing Respectfully: Person-First and Identity-First Language*, NAT'L INST. OF HEALTH (Apr. 12, 2023), https://www.nih.gov/about-nih/what-we-do/science-health-public-trust/perspectives/writing-respectfully-person-first-identity-first-language. N.B. Many state and local jurisdictions have made it a priority to update their modus operandi to include people-first language throughout.

they understand we are collaborators. This requires that the professor actually be open to collaboration on this point, which may feel like a risk and requires a great deal of trust (perhaps a leap of faith early on in the semester). It can be particularly challenging to discuss older cases that were written using racial language that is now considered hate speech. There has been some discussion among law professors about how to navigate this issue,[9] and excellent professors have taken different approaches. Each professor each year must rise to the challenge of navigating what will work best with a new group of students in a constantly changing world. Below is an example of a prompt I have sometimes shared with a class to initiate discussion:

> As we begin, let us carefully consider together what words we will choose, because for everyone, ESPECIALLY lawyers, *words matter.* There are times that the words that we omit speak volumes: when we do not specify the race or gender or ability of a person, we demonstrate the assumptions we have about the race, gender, and ability that we have collectively centered: white, male, and able.
>
> Throughout the course of the semester, we will be speaking about the way that our laws, particularly our property laws, have treated a particular race, and since words are important, I want to agree, together, on how to refer to this race. In some cases in our text you will find the term "African American," and in other places you will find much more harsh language. While I recognize the context was different and understand that history is important, I see no reason to repeat it in this classroom and feel uncomfortable doing so. One modern trend is to use the term Black (with a capital B) because Black culture is now distinct from African culture. I would like to start the discussion by proposing that we use the word "Black" throughout the semester and want to invite a discussion on this topic. Agree? Do not agree? Why or why not? Without placing an additional burden on anyone, I want to say that I am particularly interested in those people with relevant experience.

---

9. Jeannie Suk Gersen, *The Importance of Teaching* Dred Scott, THE NEW YORKER (June 8, 2021), https://www.newyorker.com/news/our-columnists/the-importance-of-teaching-dred-scott.

Depending on the semester, there may be a lively and robust discussion that takes the remainder of the class and spills out into hallways and office hours. In other semesters, this may be met with radio silence. Regardless, encouraging students to think about this quietly while reading as well as throughout their career is advisable. Even in those semesters where little feedback is offered in class, this is a frequent topic of discussion among students from various races and communities in the safety of private discussions. Working collaboratively helps to build trust and develop skills that can be honed throughout the semester. Practicing civil discourse in law school classrooms is essential, and, though difficult, is increasingly a part of the profession that students will enter.

Technology

Though the sudden jolt to legal education caused by the COVID-19 pandemic is behind us, its effects continue to reverberate. While professors were required to distill their classroom goals and adapt their methods to teach traditional standards while imagining a new professional practice, student expectations were rapidly shifting. Even though the constraints of quarantine have lifted, some of the lessons learned and creative ideas that sprung up during that time may continue to be used to support teaching and learning goals and be particularly helpful in finding ways to increase law students' engagement.

Tools that were used extensively when classes were remote, such as polling questions, word clouds, and other types of micro-assessments periodically issued during the lecture, can continue to be utilized in in-person classes to help assess students' comprehension and legal-skills development and to maintain focus. Some question this latter objective, arguing that practicing lawyers have no one looking over them to ensure that they maintain their focus. While this may be true, law school may nevertheless serve as a bridge to the real world by providing students with the tools they need to begin to self-direct and become healthy, self-regulated learners. Accordingly, suggestions for such micro-assessments appear periodically through this work. Most effective, however, are those exercises that ask students to find a way to relate the material back to their own personal experiences, which helps to build particularly strong cognitive links to the substantive material.

Legal Skills in Cultural Context

As the practice of law evolves to fit the rapidly changing world, so does the barrier to entry. The NextGen bar exam will be administered for the first time in 2026, and the changes reflect the trends in legal practice and education. Designed to better assess candidates in those areas that are necessary to become an effective member of a modern bar, the NextGen bar exam takes into consideration the resources available to modern lawyers and emphasizes lawyering skills. This book attends to those skills, particularly with regard to the concept of practicing a culturally responsive legal analysis. Just as conducting a civil discourse in a classroom that deals with race and identity may seem difficult, so too may a written analysis dealing with cultural norms feel unnatural. Modern trends, however, demand that lawyers sharpen their skills in culturally responsive advocacy. For that reason, the second half of each chapter is dedicated to finding ways to do that in the most heavily tested areas in the NextGen bar exam.

Know Your Limits (and What to Do with Them)

It is essential to acknowledge that engaging in difficult discussions and learning the law in this way is hard work. Being mindful of one's limits is an incredibly helpful guiding principle. Each of us has two unique sets of limits: one internal and one external.

Awareness of our internal limits helps us to be the best possible version of ourselves we can be. Being able to honestly assess what comes naturally to us and what does not can help to steer us in the right direction, that is, where we can be most efficient and most useful in advancing the causes that mean the most to us. Knowing who you are and what you can make it easier to navigate the most direct path to success.

External limits are a different story. Unlike our internal limits, these constraints are placed on us by others—they are expectations from the outside world. Some of these limits are valid support structures set by experienced individuals which are meant to buttress your own work and assist you in building your own structure. Other limits, however, are nothing more than constraints disguised as supports, and knowing the difference is important, because these are the barriers and limits that must be broken through. It is my deepest hope that this work will help you, everyone engaged in learning the law to dismantle systemic racism, to know the difference and to act accordingly.

OWNING OUR VALUES

ONE

Incidents of Ownership

The slave narratives reveal a bitter understanding of the injustice of people as property and knowledge that the category "property" in the slave states was both stable and unstable. It was stable in the sense that treating human beings as chattel was seen as necessary to the economy and was firmly entrenched in the legal codes. It was unstable in that human beings are not suitable for the status of property. They think and feel and rebel and cause empathy in others. Reading both the slave codes and slave narratives shows that this instability was recognized all around. The legal system of slavery was under constant threat of disintegration, an example of the law of ownership as historically contingent and the concept of property as mutable.

—Mari Matsuda[1]

1. Remarks at the American Association of Law Schools Property Section Meeting (1990). *See* Mari Matsuta, Where Is Your Body?: And Other Essays on Race, Gender, and the Law 32 (1996).

Fruits of Labor: The "Fox Case" (Power Dynamics in Property)

The "fox case"[2] is canon in property law. Though many have distilled the holding into "possession is nine-tenths of the law," this case serves as a gateway to many issues that set the foundation for the study of property law. Despite being written in what may seem like a foreign language to modern students, various concepts explored by the court remain relevant, including the attributes that make for an effective law: fairness, predictability, and ease of administration. Though the opinion deals with the question of whether or not foxes are "noxious beasts," it is also a model for how a policy argument may be used in a decision. An important element of the fox case is the relationship between the customs that exist within a community and the laws that are created as that community grows and matures. Finding a balance between protecting and respecting the way things have always been done while allowing room for evolution and thoughtful planning is a continual challenge for anyone engaged in making or interpreting the law.[3] If several appeals and philosophical musings on a matter involving one fox seems odd, that's because, like many cases before and after it, the fox case was about more than the property at issue—it was about the *power dynamics* between the parties and the groups to which they belonged.[4] A struggle over a tired fox was a proxy for the type of discussion we continue to have today about who has control over our common spaces and why.[5]

---

2. *Pierson v. Post*, 2 Am. Dec. 264 (N.Y. 1805).

3. See also *Ghen v. Rich*, 8 F. 159 (D. Mass. 1881), a case involving the whaling industry's customs surrounding killing whales with a bomb lance. This frequent companion case to *Pierson v. Post* is a good opportunity to apply the rule on *ferae naturae* and capture and to engage in a robust discussion about how the details of a custom and circumstances may distinguish the weight that a custom is given in a legal analysis.

4. *See* Bethany Berger, *It's Not about the Fox: The Untold History of* Pierson v. Post, 55 Duke L.J. 1089 (2006).

5. *Id.*

Discussion Question

Why do these elements (fairness, predictability, and ease of administration) make for good law? For whom are these attributes "good"?

The matter of pursuit was central to the fox case because it raised an important threshold question in property law: What do we have the right to own? When we work for something, does it belong to us? In other words, this case sought to determine whether one has ownership rights in the fruits of one's labor. Some of these questions are dealt with during the discussion of intangible property rights,[6] a concept that predates the development of a formal system for protection of intellectual property.[7] However, some more basic and existential questions must be addressed first. Approaching this line of questioning from a modern viewpoint raises uncomfortable issues regarding the property rights we may have in the labors of others and the property rights that this country has granted over human beings.

As we begin to uncover the roots of systemic racism in U.S. legal history, it is impossible to ignore the dehumanization of the Black race through the institution of slavery. In a course about exploring the boundaries of ownership, it is important to discuss the history of laws that codified the right to treat humans as property. Note that this discussion does *not* require critical thinking but rather only requires an examination of history; this course is taken at the beginning of law school, and critical race theory requires a command of the foundational doctrines of law.[8] Instead, this examination of the history of the law of property helps us to see the way in which ownership rights have evolved over time. Finding and drawing a throughline in our legal history is worthy work in a classroom and an important skill for new lawyers to develop.

6. See landmark cases in copyright law (*Feist Publ'ns, Inc. v. Rural Tel. Serv. Co.*, 499 U.S. 340 (1991)) and trademark (*Qualitex Co. v. Jacobson Prods. Co.*, 514 U.S. 159 (1995)) that seek to offer protection for the fruits of labor. The theory underlying these protections is to provide incentive to for creativity and ensure that the profits of creators will be protected for a reasonable amount of time. This, too, is complicated by race and power dynamics. *See* Ch. 9, *infra*.

7. The Lanham Act, 15 U.S.C. §§ 1051 *et seq.*

8. See the conclusion in Chapter 9 for a primer on the tenets of critical race theory.

Lawyers who understand the granular details of the circumstances that came before them as well as the larger contexts which surround them will be among the most effective advocates.

Incidents of Ownership (A Bundle of Sticks)

Early in a course, especially a course in property, it can be a challenge to take concepts that have been known and viscerally understood since childhood, such as ownership, and suddenly have to articulate them in new legal language. But it is a good opportunity to connect these concepts to our own experiences and interests. So, before examining what may be owned, let's make sure we understand what is meant by "ownership":

Challenge: What are the incidents of ownership? (Please provide personal examples.)	
Possession	Possession is sometimes broken down further into two elements: (1) actual possession and (2) intent to possess.[9] Are there examples of property that a person may possess but not own? Or may someone have possession but lack dominion and control? (Example: a coat check) How might you describe a landlord and tenant's relationship using this language?
Dominion & Control	Consider countless examples from the world of sports. In the National Football League there are replays seeking to determine whether a receiver had control of a football while in the endzone.
Alienability/ Transferability	Owners of property have the right to transfer that property, either by gift or sale, or to give it away in their will (bequeath), or to receive it from someone else's will (inherit). Not all of these rights are absolute. How and when should they be limited?

9. *See* Popov v. Hayashi, No. 400545, 2002 WL 31833731 (Cal. Super. Ct. Dec. 18, 2002).

Right to Use & Enjoy	Property rights are protected because owners value the right to use their property as they please, but owners must co-exist,[10] and in a multicultural society, this can become a challenge. Consider the grinding of chili peppers to make family-recipe hot sauce that has a special place in Chinese culture and causes eye and throat irritation in the United States.[11]
Right to Exclude	Consider what factors or attributes of property may impact the limitations on the right to exclude.[12]
Other	Articulate your own

Completing this challenge may at first seem deceptively simple. Now that you have considered the incidents of ownership and found examples in the world around you, return to some of the basic language of the law you have picked up and begin to build a summary of the concepts with their elements. Reading and understanding the words may make you feel as if you have a command over the material, but it is not enough—it is vital to practice generating the words from scratch. Doing so is *much* more difficult than it seems, even (especially) after having reviewed material that appears to be simple and make sense. Working to find the words to articulate foundational concepts like ownership that are viscerally understood but must be expressed in legal language is the sometimes frustrating but essential work of a first-year law student.

What Can (Not) Be Owned?

What *is* property, anyway? What is it that is subject to the rule of law that will be developed in this course, and more importantly, why? The first and easiest distinction to draw is that between real property (land fixtures attached to land) and personal property. The law may treat real and personal property distinctly. Further, personal property may be divided into tangible and intangible property based on whether it has a physical form—a deceptively simple concept that may be easy to under-

10. *Sic utere tuo alienum non laedas*: use your property in such a way that it does not damage others.

11. *See* Ch. 3, *infra*.

12. *See* Ch. 2, *infra*.

stand but difficult to articulate. Intangible property may be connected to the "fruits of labor" discussed in the fox case; sometimes the work we do gives us the right to the property resulting from that work. The metaphor is drawn from gardening: when we take the time to plant the seeds and tend to our plants, they will one day bear fruits which will be ours to possess, have for ourselves, trade, sell, or do with what we please. There are some types of intangible property that have been afforded protection by federal statute, and we refer to them and that area of law as "intellectual property." Intellectual property is a subset of intangible property and may be understood as a part of the schema of property seen below:

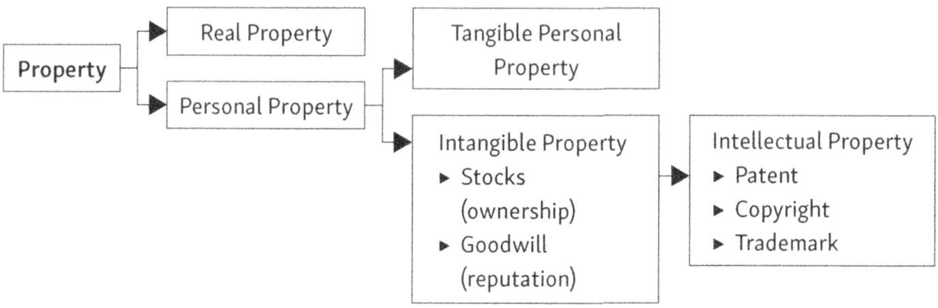

Making a mental map, or "cognitive schema," to illustrate how these big concepts fit with one another is a very effective tool for intellectually organizing the information. Doing this will help to keep you oriented when you are studying, and that feeling of orientation will provide comfort and predictability can help to lessen the uncertainty that increases cognitive load.

Discussion Question

Are there some things that should *never* be subject to ownership? Why? Use elements and language from incidents of ownership to explain.

Another way to approach understanding what is included in the universe of "property" is to define what is beyond the reach of this area of the law. Thoughts, feelings, and emotions are common responses to this prompt. These types of intangibles, until they are affixed to some type of property that can be exchanged or sold, present a logistical challenge when administering right in property. This sort of pragmatism is not determinative but is instead a helpful way to start practicing how to apply the tools and logic used by courts to discussion questions. Additionally, thoughts, feelings, and emotions are private, and some may argue that their intensely personal nature may preclude them from being owned—in other words, they are uniquely human and defy ownership.

Human beings are an example of something that should not be subject to the laws of property or "owned." To say the least, it is an example that is complicated by our legal past and present. As you start to unravel definitional and existential issues in property, take time to explore the history of property laws as they relate to human beings and human bodies. As you do so, recognize it as important opportunity to practice navigating a discussion that may be emotionally charged for some students and nuanced and scary for others. Finding a way to have an informed discourse that respectfully accounts for a variety of perspectives is a high order skill in and of itself.

Slavery, Abolition, and Aftermath (Throughline)

The plain fact is that an important part of U.S history revolved around the question of whether human beings can be owned. This question is inextricably linked with classifying people by their race and treating groups differently under the law based on their race. Before the United States was established, white colonists were engaging in the slave trade and treating Black people as though they were property. These white colonists justified their actions with concerns about property: in order to protect and serve economic interests, the labor of people who were enslaved was needed. Once economic habits in the colonies and eventually the United States were established, the reliance on the labor of the people who were enslaved, coupled with the magnitude of the economic change that would take place if the practice of slavery were abolished, perpetuated a system that disregarded the humanity of people who were forcibly taken from their homes and their descendants. The acceptance of the system of slavery and racism into U.S. cultural and colonial norms is an example of the way in which racial classification and differentiation under the law has been woven into the fabric of this country's history.

Throughout American history, however, there have always been those who recognized the negative cultural effects that could result from the dehumanization of an entire race. The American Civil War—fought over the issue of slavery and whether states had the right to make their own laws[13]—nearly divided the new nation. But with the passage of the 13th Amendment formally abolishing slavery, those who were enslaved as well as those who advocated for recognition of their humanity prevailed. This amendment rejects the notion that people may be treated as property and represents a victory in this country's history. But taking a step back and drawing a throughline in our history may reveal a different perspective from that of moral congratulations sometimes presented in American history books.

Attending closely to the language of the 13th Amendment, it is clear that the prohibition on slavery and indentured servitude is not absolute (indeed, there are few things that are absolute in the law). The language of the amendment provides "... except as a punishment for crime whereof the party shall have been duly convicted ..." as the circumstance under which people may be forced into labor, or treated as property, as they were before its ratification. Taking a broad view of history reveals that, particularly in those states that resisted the prohibition on treating people as property, the passage of the 13th Amendment was followed by changes in the criminal code that had the effect of criminalizing Blackness. Many of these statutes criminalized the violation of race-based segregation rules, and they also resulted in a large number of Black people being "duly convicted" of crimes and subsequently forced into labor or servitude. Depending on the jurisdiction, on both private and public property, the law required Black people to eat, travel, be educated, and be entertained separately from the rest of the population—in short, to exist separately. Combined with the withholding of public funding from Black institutions, particularly public education institutions, this segregation on public and private property[14] and the criminalization of at-

13. *See* Dred Scott v. Sandford, 60 U.S. (19 How.) 393 (1857).

14. The law of public accommodation is another area of property law that is essential to an understanding of systemic racism. The ways in which the U.S. system of laws allows

tempted racial integration resulted in a perpetuation the ills of slavery and indentured servitude, despite the Union victory and passage of the 13th Amendment. In short, the practical impact of new state laws was to ensure that Black people continued to be treated as property.

Close Reading & Reflection

What specific text of the 13th Amendment has been used to perpetuate slavery and indentured servitude? How?

Having legal rights and rights as citizens allowed for some progress, even though obstacles and barriers built into power-granting institutions persisted. Leading up to and including the civil rights movement, a movement which sought access to those spaces and institutions from which Black people had been excluded following ratification of the 13th Amendment, those who sought racial justice and equity in our legal system were able to make some incremental progress. Their efforts led to the passage of federal legislation in the 1960s that addressed equal access to spaces for people living outside the criminal justice system. Drawing a throughline helps to illustrate the series of steps which were taken in the pursuit of equality for Black people in the United States.

Modern Application and Incidents of Ownership

The criminalization of Blackness can feel like a difficult topic to discuss, particularly in modern and refined law school classrooms. But avoiding this difficult topic is a pedagogical choice that not only fails to acknowledge history but is also a lost opportunity to refine students' understanding of a legal concept.

---

owners to determine how and when to grant access to or to exclude or discriminate on their property is an example of how the tensions in our system of property laws uphold and perpetuate systemic racism.

When considering the incidents of ownership and defining the sticks on the bundle of rights, there is an opportunity to find nuanced ways to pull apart what each of these incidents means in varying contexts. This is an essential legal skill. Some students may be familiar with the history of police brutality in the Black community. Though a great deal can be said about this topic in a course on, for example, criminal law or criminal procedure, *this* is a course on property—accordingly, it is important to find ways to use the language of property law to describe legal circumstances and facts.

Whether discussing a fox,[15] a baseball,[16] a whale,[17] or any number of other items, a gateway topic to property law is the consideration and definition of the relationship between possession and ownership. How the concept of dominion and control, that is, a person's ability to determine the use or disposition of property, may relate to ownership rights is a fundamental question; and, as many of the cases demonstrate, whether a person has dominion and control of property is a heavily fact-based analysis.

HISTORY "THROUGH-LINE":
INCIDENTS OF OWNERSHIP & BLACK BODIES

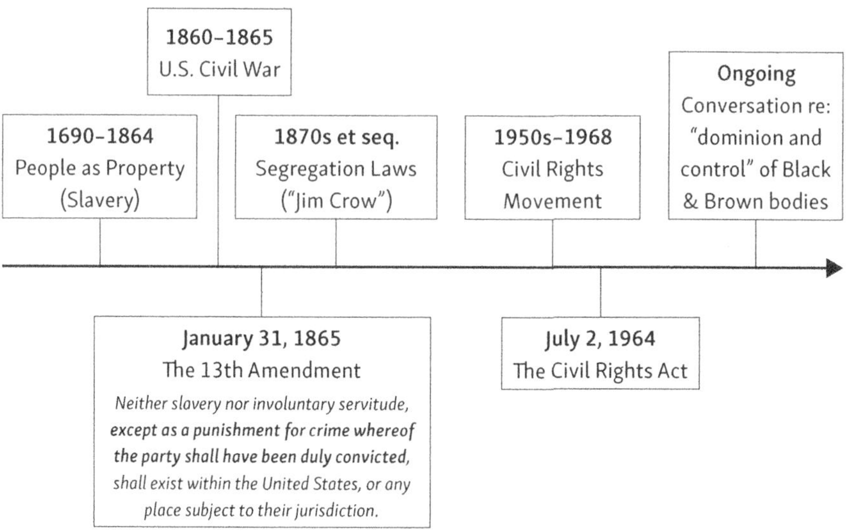

15. *Pierson*, 2 Am. Dec. 264.

16. *Popov*, No. 400545, 2002 WL 31833731.

17. *Ghen*, 8 F. 159.

> Happily for the whole human family, their rights have been defined, declared, and decided in a court higher than the Supreme Court. 'There is a law,' says (Henry Lord) Brougham, "above all the enactments of human codes, and by that law, unchangeable and eternal, *man cannot hold property in man.*"
>
> —Frederick Douglas, May 1857 (in a speech reacting to the U.S. Supreme Court's decision in the *Dred Scott* case)

Many may have already determined that human bodies are not property and not subject to ownership or the laws of property on moral grounds, and there is plenty of psychology and philosophy to justify that position. But in the United States, we have a history of treating human beings as property—and we should consider how the incidents of ownership, combined with the context of our laws and cultural norms, may be applied in a modern context. During the period in which slavery was legal, it is clear that humans were treated as property: They were bought, sold, and commodified. And the owners of people who were enslaved imposed dominion over them by dictating where and with whom they lived, what they did, what they ate—all aspects of life. While slavery and indentured servitude are no longer permitted, "except as a punishment for a crime for which an individual has been duly convicted," the modern #BlackLivesMatter movement may be framed in a similar context—in terms of incidents of ownership and whether people have appropriate dominion and control over their bodies.

Inspecting the historical throughline in more detail reveals that a major moment in U.S. history took place in 1991, one that involved policing and Black bodies and which occurred in the wake of highly publicized acts of police brutality against Rodney King. Whether it was the cultural response to the police's treatment of Rodney King as an individual or how Black people felt about how they could be treated by the police in general, the public's reaction may be seen a precursor to the #BlackLivesMatter movement. In response to increased racial tensions stemming from the criminal acquittals of the officers who beat Rodney King, the U.S. Department of Justice filed a civil lawsuit against the Los Angeles Police Department, which resulted in a jury's awarding Rodney King $3.8 million for the injuries he had sustained. So it was not criminal accountability but rather an *award of property* that our system of laws deemed as the appropriate resolution in this circumstance and which came to mean a great deal in the ongoing national conversation about race and the rights of Black bodies relative to police officers.

The Civil Rights Division of the U.S. Department of Justice was created by the Civil Rights Act of 1957 and "works to uphold the civil and constitutional rights of all Americans, particularly some of those most vulnerable members of society."[18] In doing that work, the division studies the patterns and practices of police departments around the United States and will, from time to time, investigate particular circumstances or police departments as the federal administration directs. This work has moved to the center of a national conversation about policing and race relations, owing to a renewed focus on the way that Black people are treated by law enforcement in the wake of several high-profile deaths—George Floyd, Eric Garner, Michael Brown, Tamir Rice, Philando Castile, and Breonna Taylor—and numerous lesser-known ones.

Being able to personalize incidents of ownership and combine that understanding with the weight of history can help us to see that having dominion and control over one's own body, particularly when the police are involved, may vary by race and identity. This is not a choice or something based only on personal experience, but on the weight of history and law. Taking time to consider the ways in which property concepts, such as incidents of ownership, including dominion and control over one's own body, may be connected to the facets of one's identity is high order work in the area of property law and an important aspect of developing skills as a culturally responsive lawyer. For some, this type of analysis is second nature, happening in a matter of seconds on a regular basis in the course of daily life.

Addressing policy questions related to criminal law and criminal justice reform are indeed important. The way we frame the fundamental values underlying our nation and its property laws can affect how we view such issues. For example, in the past, a careful student may have applied reason to determine whether dominion and control had been exerted in a given situation. However, a modern approach may begin by asking whether, in the current climate, it is *reasonable* to craft an argument about dominion and control of Black bodies. Who has the right to exclude? What does that mean in the context of a human body?

---

18. Civil Rights Division Homepage, U.S. Dep't of Justice, https://www.justice.gov/crt (last visited Feb. 5, 2024).

Considering the application of all the incidents of ownership within this context, at the end of the throughline in our history, is important for understanding why protection of property rights is so fundamental and central to our country's history, its legal system, and law school's first-year curriculum.

Skills Practice: Reading and Briefing Cases: What Is Important?

Whether it's law school in general or your property law course in particular, it is wise to focus on establishing good habits at the outset. In doing so, understanding what concepts and skills will help you do well on actual assessments is important. In other words: keep your eye on the prize. Many students spend a great deal of time writing very detailed case briefs only to find that those briefs do not serve them well when it comes time to prepare for the final exam. Students should think of each class as an incremental preparation for the final exam. Regardless of the form (usually either a written fact pattern or multiple-choice questions), a law school assessment demands that a student demonstrate understanding of the law by applying it to a novel fact pattern that slightly but materially differs from facts encountered in cases covered in class. Accordingly, the ability to recall, deconstruct, and reconstruct a case is the goal of the case brief. Below you will find some general advice based on the author's many years of experience in teaching students in their first year of law school.

Own Your Briefs

There are many resources available to 1L students, and it can sometimes be tempting to use them as shortcuts, especially when faced with many pages of required reading. For instance, instead of preparing your own briefs, you may consider whether to use commercially available briefs or videos or materials prepared by upper-class students or friends to save some time. Resist the temptation. The value of case briefs lies not in having them but in preparing them. So own the process and prepare the briefs. As you do so, take the time to think carefully about the concepts presented in the case and how each part of the analysis may relate to the larger concept you are discussing. For example: How did possession relate to ownership when it came to catching a fox? What about a baseball? Attending to these concepts will help you be prepared for a final assessment.

Less Is More (Facts)

They are called "briefs" for a reason. Particularly in the fact section of your case brief, include only those facts which are salient. If the holding of the case turns on the existence of that fact, then it is salient. Ideally, this section of a case brief should be two to four sentences long. In the beginning, you may find it easier to transcribe the facts from the case; however, using the active-recall method will not only be more efficient but will also result in better retention of the case and concepts contained therein.

Be Sparing with Procedure

When you are new to the study of law, the procedural history can feel like an essential part of a case brief. However, the procedural disposition of a case will very rarely be relevant, so be sparing in your brief. Remember that your ultimate goal is to be able to apply the case concepts to a novel fact pattern on an exam. Cases included in law school textbooks are in the minority of cases that are granted multiple appeals and overturned upon review. This is notable in practice but rarely relevant for succeeding on law school exams. In some limited circumstances, the *reason* for the case's being reviewed or overturned is important for understanding the holding, but that should be included in the analysis section of a case brief.

Issue: Embrace the "Whether"

Articulating the issue in the case is an opportunity to practice a skill that will be used during final exams and in legal practice. A simple, well-honed issue statement is the foundation for a strong and robust legal analysis. Articulating the issue with precision and brevity may seem like a simple endeavor when it is, in fact, a skill that requires a great deal of practice. Later chapters will focus more on the skill of articulating issues in a legal analysis, but for the purposes of case briefs, it is helpful to get in the practice of beginning with the word "whether." Doing this will help to avoid a binary answer and allow for an analysis that explores the factors on which the issue depends. Beginning your issue statement with the word "does" or "will" automatically tempts the reader to respond with a "yes" or a "no," which may prematurely cut off opportunities for a detailed analysis that explores nuanced areas of fact and law.

Distinguish "Rule" from "Holding"

The rule section of a case brief should identify the rule that the court is seeking to apply. Whether a statute, a common law rule, or a rule from any other source, it is the starting point for the court's analysis. This rule should be clearly identified by the court at the beginning of the case and accordingly should also be clearly identified in the case brief. The holding, on the other hand, is where the court lands after completing its analysis. After considering how the facts before the court have stretched the understanding or application of the initial rule in a novel way, the court then articulates a holding that demonstrates a novel application of the applied rule.

Break Up the Analysis

Pay close attention to the way a court conducts its analysis of the case at hand. Each opinion is an opportunity to see how accomplished lawyers and writers organize a legal analysis. Most often there are multiple components to the issues before the court, and sometimes the issues are intertwined and depend on one another in complex and messy ways. In writing their opinions, judges demonstrate their skill in breaking down each issue into digestible increments and dealing with each according to its relevance to the case. Let the writing in the cases serve as a model, and use your case briefs as opportunities to practice the skill of breaking up intertwined issues into their component parts and dealing with them accordingly. The analysis is the heart of what lawyers do, and the mark of a skilled lawyer is to take complex issues and distill them into manageable, comprehensible, and accessible components.

Take a Breath

Learning the law can be demanding. Cases may begin to run together, and the sheer amount of reading assigned can sometimes be overwhelming. It is important to have a purpose and remember why you are engaged in learning the law. It is also important to remember that case briefs will never be submitted for a grade: they will be used only to support learning throughout the semester. Those briefs that make references to personal experiences or to concepts that attach to your identity will be the most likely to "stick."

	Common Diligent 1L Brief	Improved 1L Brief
Facts	Post had dogs and hounds under his command and was on land that was wild and uninhabited while hunting a fox.	Post hunting a fox. Pierson captures the same fox while witnessing Post's pursuit.
Issue	Does the plaintiff's pursuit of ferae naturae in this manner result in the acquisition of a right in property to the fox such that he may sustain an action in trespass against another for killing the beast and taking him away.	Whether Post's chasing the fox amounted to "occupancy" and applied to the right of wild animals.
Procedural History	Action of trespass commenced and a verdict rendered for plaintiff. Defendant filed for certiorari, seeking that the matters contained were not sufficient to maintain an action.	(Really, it's unnecessary)
Rule	Justinian Institutes: Puffendorf & Barbeyrac on occupancy, mortal wounding, bodily seizure intent and ferae naturae.	Ownership established when a wild animal is in actual physical possession.

Analysis	Barbeyrac and Grotius have a theory of occupancy regarding the natural liberty of wild animals and the efforts that hunters put forth in pursuit of those animals that may or may not result in property rights in those animals. Limiting occupancy to ferae naturae (as distinguished from privately owned and tended animals) to circumstances in which they are mortally wounded or ensnared will avoid many quarrels and much litigation.	The rule has evolved from requiring the manifestation of intent for individual use to possession. Consider (1) the nature of wild animals; (2) the policy of controlling foxes; (3) the custom of sportspeople; (4) administrability of rules. Distinguish from duck decoy pond case.
Holding	Lower court reversed.	Possession → Ownership
Dicta	Livingston Dissenting opinion.	Consider fairness & justice. Relationship between customs and rules.

Cases and Concepts

Students learning the law should know early on that they are in charge of their own learning. No matter how many innovative teaching strategies a professor may have, there is nothing more important than a student's willingness to engage with the cases and concepts. Keeping in mind that the job of a lawyer (and law student) will always be to apply existing rules to novel facts, a high-order skill that students can begin to practice early on is coming up with new fact patterns to test their comprehension of the cases and concepts.

Which is most similar?	*Pierson v. Post*	*Popov v. Hayashi*	*Wilcox v. Stroup*
Indoor cat			
Dropped lottery ticket (winner!)			
Fancy gloves left in coat room			

Comparing cases can be helpful, but so can comping concepts. Consider a very similar exercise:

How may each incident of ownership be applied?	Possession	Dominion & Control	Use & Enjoyment	Alienability/ Transferability
Indoor cat				
Dropped lottery ticket (winner!)				
Fancy gloves left in coat room				

SUGGESTIONS FOR FURTHER READING

Ta-Nehisi Coates, *The Case for Reparations*, THE ATLANTIC (June 15, 2014), https://www.theatlantic.com/magazine/archive/2014/06/the-case-for-reparations/361631/.

Frederick Douglass, The *Dred Scott* Decision, Address Before the American Anti-Slavery Society (May 14, 1857).

Jeannie Suk Gersen, *The Importance of Teaching* Dred Scott, THE NEW YORKER (June 8, 2021), https://www.newyorker.com/news/our-columnists/the-importance-of-teaching-dred-scott.

Bryan Stevenson, The 1619 Project: *Slavery Gave America a Fear of Black People and a Taste for Violent Punishment. Both Still Define Our Criminal-Justice System*, N.Y. TIMES MAG. (Aug. 14, 2019), https://www.nytimes.com/interactive/2019/08/14/magazine/prison-industrial-complex-slavery-racism.html.

TWO

The Right to Exclude/Trespass and Adverse Possession

(Get Off My Land!)

The land knows you, even when you are lost.

—Robin Wall Kimmerer[1]

The right to exclude is one of the most basic and protected rights related to ownership of real property. The ability to decide who is able to enter property creates power to control what happens on land. This is a fundamental right of ownership and, in many cases, one that grants individuals the power to exercise personal liberties and create spaces where they can be the most authentic version of themselves. The right to exclude is a neutral rule that can and has been used in different contexts by different groups in ways that are so common that we have come to take them for granted. A violation of the right to exclude is a trespass. Because of the strength of the protection of an owner's right to exclude others from their property, the consequences of trespass can be grave. The way the word "trespass" has entered into our social and religious vocabulary reveals something about the gravity with which we view this violation.[2] Given that the right to exclude is such a centrally protected part of the bundle of rights that make up property ownership, under-

1. Braiding Sweetgrass: Indigenous Wisdom, Scientific Knowledge and the Teachings of Plants (2015).

2. "Forgive us our trespasses, as we forgive those who trespass against us" is a line in the Lord's Prayer. It is an example of a non-literal use of the term, one that has the more general meaning of committing an offense against another. These different meanings—a

standing the limits of this right can help to uncover some of the cultural priorities and inequities that have been codified into the system of law.

This chapter uncovers the ways in which the right to exclude depends on the "who" and the "where," while subsequent chapters uncover the different ways in which property laws have been used to exclude, that is, the "how." An analysis of the who requires asking about parties on both sides: (1) how do policy considerations and demographics impact the question of which party has the right to exert control over the property, and (2) what is the history of the identities of those who have been excluded from property? As we explore the history of these questions, we will consider how our system of property laws has served to uphold racial segregation. An analysis of the where requires following the through-line of history. Paying particular attention to the impact of civil rights legislation as you do so will help to inform your understanding of the spectrum of protections afforded to private residential property on the one hand and publicly held and used property on the other. From lunch counters, inn-keepers, and common carriers, to private homes and farms that hire migrant workers, understanding the relationship between the nature of the property and the right to exclude will help you to see how legal arguments about exclusion have evolved over time. Each of these questions will be addressed in turn, with particular attention paid to how racial identity relates to the right to exclude or the exclusion.

Finally, with the understanding that trespass is the failure to exclude, the chapter explores the concept of adverse possession, sometimes described as "trespass that ripens to ownership." This element-based area of law provides an opportunity to practice honing a very specific issue statement that will lead to a targeted legal analysis. The specific element requiring that a party seeking to acquire title to land be "adverse" or "hostile" is but one example of an area in our system of property laws where cultural responsiveness has been lacking. This chapter explores how some cultures, particularly Indigenous ones, relate to land as stewards rather than owners, and how the theory of adverse possession does not account for this cultural difference but rather serves to uphold a systemic preference for the white Anglo-Saxon view of ownership to the detriment of Indigenous peoples.

---

general offense and unpermitted entry onto the land of another—suggest the fierceness with which rights in property are protected.

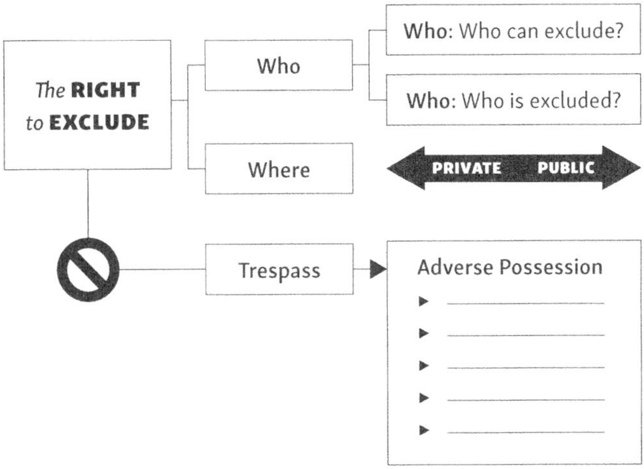

The Right to Exclude: Who Has It?

The right to exclude is one of most important incidents of ownership, or stick in the bundle of property rights. It is clear that this right is reserved for owners with a full interest in property and also for those who are in possession of an interest that is less than a full ownership. For example, if residential property is rented by an owner to a tenant, that tenant, who now has the right to possess the property, will also take the right to exclude others from that property, with some narrow exceptions drawn for the owner of the property.[3] When beginning to consider the right to exclude, it is common for property students to consider landowners that are engaged in the business of agriculture and require the assistance of migrant workers to ensure that the profits from their farms are efficiently gained. Though cases are read in different areas and contexts, the set of facts is common: landowners must hire migrant farm workers, thus setting up a power dynamic that, when overlaid with demographic information about these groups, reveals a great deal about racial dynamics.[4]

3. For further discussion of leaseholds and the dynamics contained therein, see Chapter 8, *infra*.

4. *See* State v. Shack, 277 A.2d 369 (N.J. 1971) (a case commonly read as relating to a landowner's right to exclude from his property the guests of a migrant worker); Vasquez

Land-owning farmers, because of their superior rights to the underlying property, have the strongest right to exclude and the stronger position in the power dynamic that is established in this common fact pattern. A land-owning farmer is able to use methods in our system of property law, such as eminent domain,[5] eviction,[6] or the right to exclude itself,[7] to assert his will over the will of the migrant worker in the name of land rights. As Chief Justice Joseph Weintraub noted in *State v. Shack*, "Property rights serve human values. They are recognized to that end, and are limited by it. Title to real property cannot include dominion over the destiny of persons the owner permits to come on the premises."[8] Exclusion is the purest attempt by owners of property to accomplish just that: to exert dominion over others. Whether by excluding a fired farm worker from his home away from home or excluding those who seek to help and advise migrant workers, attempting to exclude others from their owned property is the first line of defense for land-owning farmers. The right to exclude is the bluntest tool a landowner seeking to keep control over his land and maintain the established power dynamics has.

The exploitive nature of this power dynamic is noteworthy. Income from a farm depends on the ability to tend to the land. In order to maximize profits, farmers must rely on a large number of laborers who will not need to be paid for those parts of the year during which there is no labor to be done. Without migrant workers, farmers would be unable to enjoy the income from their land; exploitation of farm workers, or keeping wages as low as possible, serves to allow landowners to maximize their profits.[9] When considering *who* has the right to exclude others

---

v. Glassboro Servs. Assn., Inc., 415 A.2d 1156 (N.J. 1980) (migrant farm worker dismissed from his position and excluded from barracks) (while *Vasquez* is commonly read in relation to leaseholds and what rights a tenant might have with regard to eviction notice as well as whether a migrant worker is a tenant or not, the *Shack* and *Vasquez* opinions are nevertheless connected in consideration and policy). *See also* Cedar Point Nursery v. Hassid, , 594 U.S. ___, 141 S. Ct. 2063 (2021) (a labor regulation allowing a union representative to visit a migrant farm worker violated the Takings Clause of the Fifth Amendment).

5. *Cedar Point Nursery*, 141 S. Ct. 2063.

6. *Vasquez*, 415 A.2d 1156.

7. *Shack*, 277 A.2d 369.

8. *Id.* at 372.

9. Organizers like Dolores Huerta were aware of this dynamic and helped to create the Farmworkers Union.

from a piece of property, keep in mind that the migrant workers who are housed on these farms are rarely given property rights that are sufficiently strong to be tested. It is also notable that, despite having made their homes (even if temporarily) on the premises and having the most intimate connection with the property, migrant workers are rarely the individuals who can exercise the right to exclude others from the property or who have the affirmative right to receive personal visitors to their place of residence. Our system has established that residential property is the most protected type of property, so a holding that focuses on how the rights of a landowner may be limited not only removes the migrant worker from the center of the analysis but ignores the migrant worker entirely. Continuing this practice of ignoring the rights of migrant workers in a first-year property classroom is a mistake. Encouraging a healthy discussion about the relativity of property rights is a way to begin to correct this problem and introduce humanity into the analysis. Understanding who is absent from the common law as it relates to the right to exclude speaks volumes about the power dynamics underlying these cases. But these power dynamics do not exist in cases alone—legislatures have taken actions to protect these workers not because of philosophical or theoretical beliefs about collective human values, but because they recognize the importance of migrant workers to the national economy. The discourse around such rights is fluid; sometimes, the rights of migrant workers are only recognized as part of a general trend toward stripping away some of the significance of *State v. Shack*.[10] It is worth noting that a very similar set of facts in the *Cedar Point Nursery* case had a different outcome when the owner of property advanced a theory of takings (see Chapter 7). Though the doctrine advanced in these two cases is distinct and often is covered in different phases of a first-year course in Property, it is worth highlighting the alternate ways in which similar facts are addressed by courts. In flagging the similarities in these fact patterns, students can glean as much about priorities of courts from those priorities that are not underscored, including the rights and humanity of migrant workers, as from the priorities that are.

10. 277 A.2d 369. *See Cedar Point Nursery*, 141 S. Ct. 2063.

The Right to Exclude: Who Is Excluded? Exclusion Based on Race

Throughout U.S. history, certain individuals and groups have, more often than not, been excluded from property for various reasons, but this text focuses on those who were excluded based on the immutable characteristic of race. Since the emancipation of people who were enslaved, Black people have been systematically denied ownership of property in the United States[11] and regularly excluded from property, both public and private. Post-Reconstruction, race-based segregation laws that separated non-white people from white people in schools, restaurants, and other spaces, or which entirely excluded non-white people from certain spaces, became the norm in various parts of the country. This system was constructed and perpetuated by the incidents of ownership and the fierce protection of the rights of property owners.

Exclusion on the basis of race is a part of the history of the United States. Long before migrant farm workers entered into litigation in the courts of New Jersey in the early 1970s,[12] at a time when white Americans were inspired by the idea of Manifest Destiny to claim and settle land across North America, an unofficial competition was established to see which of two railroad companies could lay down the most track as quickly as possible, and those two rail lines would eventually be joined together to form the country's first transcontinental railroad.[13] This important work was incredibly lucrative and meaningful not only to the individuals in charge of the two rail companies but also to the country as a whole—but the work was temporary. In order to complete the project and maximize profit margins, workers from China were recruited to perform the most high-risk jobs. Aware that the number of foreign workers required to fill these jobs would be sufficient to change the demographics and dynamics of the quickly growing country, Congress passed new laws excluding women and children from coming to the

11. *See* Chapter 5 on mortgages and redlining.

12. *Shack*, 277 A.2d 369.

13. Leland Stanford, owner of the Central Pacific Railroad and founder of Stanford University, first hired Chinese workers after white workers did not respond to an advertisement for labor that was dangerous and difficult. Mr. Stanford continued to hire more and more Chinese workers despite strong anti-Chinese sentiment at the time.

United States to ensure that the men who came here to work did not establish communities. Despite widespread anti-Chinese sentiment in the United States at the time, an estimated 15,000 to 20,000 Chinese workers contributed to the completion of the transcontinental railroad, only to be excluded from entry to the United States by the Chinese Exclusion Act of 1882.

This explicit exclusion based on race was followed by the creation of specific rules concerning who may immigrate and become a naturalized citizen of the United States. These rules would have systemic consequences for land ownership and all of its attendant benefits. The Naturalization Act of 1906[14] allowed only "free white persons" and "persons of African nativity or persons of African descent" to naturalize. Two important cases focus on what qualifies as "whiteness" for purposes of applying this statute. *Ozawa v. United States*[15] is the first of these cases. In *Ozawa*, a Japanese American argued that he qualified as a "free white person" and therefore qualified for citizenship. In the opinion, Justice Sutherland contemplated the arguments about skin color, writing,

> Manifestly the test afforded by the mere color of the skin of each individual is impracticable, as that differs greatly among persons of the same race, even among Anglo-Saxons, ranging by imperceptible gradations from the fair blond to the swarthy brunette, the latter being darker than many of the lighter hued persons of the brown or yellow races. Hence, to adopt the color test alone would result in a confused overlapping of races and a gradual merging of one into the other, without any practical line of separation.... [T]he federal and state courts, in an almost unbroken line, have held that the words "white person" were meant to indicate only a person of what is popularly known as the Caucasian race. With the conclusion reached in these several decisions we see no reason to differ.[16]

Later, in *United States v. Bhagat Singh Thind*,[17] Justice Sutherland revisited and refined his thinking about the standard for determining who

14. P.L. 59-338.
15. 260 U.S. 178 (1922).
16. *Id.* at 197.
17. 261 U.S. 204 (1922).

belongs in this country. *Thind* involved a man who was from the Caucasus region of Asia and therefore fit the very definition of "Caucasian." Just three months after publishing his decision in the *Ozawa* case, Justice Sutherland, faced with Mr. Thind, a man who was ancestrally, scientifically, and geographically Caucasian, revisited the intent of the framers and sought to understand the "common parlance" of the word "Caucasian" rather than the literal meaning suggested by Mr. Thind. Justice Sutherland opined that "the words of the statute are to be interpreted in accordance with the understanding of the common man from whose vocabulary they were taken."[18] Mr. Thind was Punjabi, a South Asian. Justice Sutherland reasoned that, although Mr. Thind was technically Caucasian, he was not white according to the common understanding, which is how the statute should be interpreted.

Everybody knew what a white person was, and neither Mr. Thind nor Mr. Ozawa were it. With this pair of decisions, Justice Sutherland enshrined the social construction of race in our Supreme Court jurisprudence. Having conceded in *Thind* that there may have been a common ancestor between the "blond Scandinavian and the brown Hindu," Justice Sutherland changed the focus of his reasoning from the scientific meaning of the "racial test" to the cultural understanding:

> It may be true that the blond Scandinavian and the brown Hindu have a common ancestor in the dim reaches of antiquity, but the average man knows perfectly well that there are unmistakable and profound differences between them today. . . .
>
> It does not seem necessary to pursue the matter of scientific classification further. We are unable to agree with the District Court, or with other lower federal courts, in the conclusion that a native Hindu is eligible for naturalization under § 2169. The words of familiar speech, which were used by the original framers of the law, were intended to include only the type of man whom they knew as white. . . .[19]

More than half a century after the end of slavery, in the middle of the U.S. racial segregation era and at the very beginning of the civil rights movement, Justice Sutherland gave voice to an uncomfortable truth

---

18. *Id.* at 209.
19. *Id.* at 209, 213.

that has long been at the heart of race relations in the United States: defining race is difficult, yet we collectively manage to do it. Race is tied to social and cultural dynamics which are constantly shifting. An examination of the people and groups being excluded from public and private property is an effective way to shed some light on collective racial hierarchies and dynamics.

Continuing with a theme introduced in the first chapter, identity may impact the way that rights in property are exercised. We have already considered the impact of the construct of race on the incident of ownership over one's own body, particularly with regard to dominion and control. As we move on and consider the right to exclude, a review of early 20th-century Supreme Court jurisprudence on the topic of immigration and naturalization may strike some familiar chords. The psychological impact of being categorically excluded takes its toll on multiple generations and can never be fully undone. It is woven into the fabric of our national character. We are best served by acknowledging and identifying the echoes of exclusion in our common law and their continuing harmful effects.

Discussion Question

The *Ozawa* and *Thind* cases, despite being over a century old, have language that resonates loudly in modern race relations, yet they are rarely discussed in contemporary curricula. Why?

UNITED STATES V. BHAGAT SINGH THIND

261 U.S. 204 (1923)

MR. JUSTICE SUTHERLAND, GEORGE, delivered the opinion of the Court.

This cause is here upon a certificate from the Circuit Court of appeals requesting the instruction of this Court in respect of the following questions:

> 1. Is a high-caste Hindu, of full Indian blood, born at Amritsar, Punjab, India, a white person within the meaning of § 2169, Revised Statutes?

> 2. Does the Act of February 5, 1917 disqualify from naturalization as citizens those Hindus now barred by that act who had lawfully entered the United States prior to the passage of said act?

The appellee was granted a certificate of citizenship by the District Court of the United States for the District of Oregon, over the objection of the Naturalization Examiner for the United States. A bill in equity was then filed by the United States seeking a cancellation of the certificate on the ground that the appellee was not a white person, and therefore not lawfully entitled to naturalization. The district court, on motion, dismissed the bill and an appeal was taken to the circuit court of appeals. The sole question is whether he falls within the class designated by Congress as eligible.

Section 2169, Revised Statutes, provides that the provisions of the Naturalization Act "shall apply to aliens being free white persons and to aliens of African nativity and to persons of African descent."

If the applicant is a white person within the meaning of this section, he is entitled to naturalization; otherwise not. In *Ozawa v. United States*, 260 U.S. 178, we had occasion to consider the application of these words to the case of a cultivated Japanese, and were constrained to hold that he was not within their meaning. As there pointed out, the provision is not that any particular class of persons shall be excluded, but it is, in effect, that only white persons shall be included within the privilege of the statute. "The intention was to confer the privilege of citizenship upon that class of persons whom the fathers knew as white, and to deny it to all who could not be so classified. It is not enough to say that the framers did not have in mind the brown or yellow races of Asia. It is necessary to go farther and be able to say that, had these particular races been suggested, the language of the act would have been so varied as to include them within its privileges," citing *Dartmouth College v. Woodward,* 4 Wheat. 518, 644. Following a long line of decisions of the lower federal courts, we held that the words imported a racial, and not an individual, test, and were meant to indicate only persons of what is popularly known as the Caucasian race. But, as there pointed out, the conclusion that the phrase "white persons" and the word "Caucasian" are synonymous does not end the matter. It enabled us to dispose of the problem as it was there presented, since the applicant for citizenship clearly fell outside the zone of debatable ground on the negative side; but the decision still left the question to be dealt with, in doubtful and different cases, by the "process of judicial inclusion and exclusion." Mere ability on the part of an applicant for naturalization to establish a line of descent from a Caucasian ancestor will not *ipso facto* and necessarily conclude the inquiry. "Caucasian" is a conventional word of much flexibility, as a study of the literature dealing with racial questions will disclose, and, while it and the words "white persons" are treated as synonymous for the purposes of that case, they are not of identical meaning—*idem per idem.*

In the endeavor to ascertain the meaning of the statute, we must not fail to keep in mind that it does not employ the word "Caucasian," but the words "white persons," and these are words of common speech, and not of scientific origin. The word "Caucasian" not only was not employed in the law, but was probably wholly unfamiliar to the original framers of the statute in 1790. When we employ it, we do so as an aid to the ascertainment of the legislative intent, and not as an invariable substitute for the statutory words. Indeed, as used in the science of ethnology, the connotation of the word is by no means clear, and the use of it in its scientific sense as an equivalent for the words of the statute, other considerations aside, would simply mean the substitution of one perplexity for another. But, in this country, during the last half century especially, the word, by common usage, has acquired a popular meaning, not clearly defined to be sure, but sufficiently so to enable us to say that its popular, as distinguished from its scientific, application is of appreciably narrower scope. It is in the popular sense of the word, therefore, that we employ is as an aid to the construction of the statute, for it would be obviously illogical to convert words of common speech used in a statute into words of scientific terminology when neither the latter nor the science for whose purposes they were coined was within the contemplation of the framers of the statute or of the people for whom it was framed. The words of the statute are to be interpreted in accordance with the understanding of the common man from whose vocabulary they were taken. *See Maillard v. Lawrence,* 16 How. 251, 261.

They imply, as we have said, a racial test; but the term "race" is one which, for the practical purposes of the statute, must be applied to a group of living persons now possessing in common the requisite characteristics, not to groups of persons who are supposed to be or really are descended from some remote common ancestor, but who, whether they both resemble him to a greater or less extent, have at any rate ceased altogether to resemble one another. It may be true that the blond Scandinavian and the brown Hindu have a common ancestor in the dim reaches of antiquity, but the average man knows perfectly well that there are unmistakable and profound differences between them today, and it is not impossible, if that common ancestor could be materialized in the flesh, we should discover that he was himself sufficiently differentiated from both of his descendants to preclude his racial classification with either. The question for determination is not, therefore, whether, by the speculative processes of ethnological reasoning, we may present a probability to the scientific mind that they have the same origin, but whether we can satisfy the common understanding that they are now the same or sufficiently the same to justify the interpreters of a statute—written in the words of common speech, for common understanding, by unscientific men—in classifying them together in the statutory category as white persons. In 1790, the Adamite theory of creation—which gave a common ancestor to all mankind—was generally accepted, and it is not at all probable that it was intended by the legislators of that day to submit the question of the application of the words "white persons" to the mere test of an indefinitely remote common ancestry, without regard to the extent of the subsequent divergence of the various branches from such common ancestry or from one another.

The eligibility of this applicant for citizenship is based on the sole fact that he is of high-caste Hindu stock, born in Punjab, one of the extreme northwestern districts of India, and classified by certain scientific authorities as of the Caucasian or Aryan race. The Aryan theory, as a racial basis, seems to be discredited by most, if not all, modern writers on the subject of ethnology. A review of their contentions would serve no useful purpose....

The term "Aryan" has to do with linguistic, and not at all with physical, characteristics, and it would seem reasonably clear that mere resemblance in language, indicating a common linguistic root buried in remotely ancient soil, is altogether inadequate to prove common racial origin. There is, and can be, no assurance that the so-called Aryan language was not spoken by a variety of races living in proximity to one another. Our own history has witnessed the adoption of the English tongue by millions of negroes, whose descendants can never be classified racially with the descendants of white persons, notwithstanding both may speak a common root language.

The word "Caucasian" is in scarcely better repute. It is, at best, a conventional term, with an altogether fortuitous origin, which, under scientific manipulation, has come to include far more than the unscientific mind suspects. According to Keane, for example, (The World's Peoples, 24, 28, 307, *et seq.*) it includes not only the Hindu, but some of the Polynesians (that is, the Māori, Tahitians, Samoans, Hawaiians, and others), the Hamites of Africa, upon the ground of the Caucasic cast of their features, though in color they range from brown to black. We venture to think that the average well informed white American would learn with some degree of astonishment that the race to which he belongs is made up of such heterogeneous elements.

The various authorities are in irreconcilable disagreement as to what constitutes a proper racial division. For instance, Blumenbach has five races; Keane, following Linnaeus, four; Deniker, twenty-nine. The explanation probably is that "the innumerable varieties of mankind run into one another by insensible degrees," and to arrange them in sharply bounded divisions is an undertaking of such uncertainty that common agreement is practically impossible.

It may be, therefore, that a given group cannot be properly assigned to any of the enumerated grand racial divisions. The type may have been so changed by intermixture of blood as to justify an intermediate classification. Something very like this has actually taken place in India. Thus, in Hindustan and Berar, there was such an intermixture of the "Aryan" invader with the dark-skinned Dravidian.

In the Punjab and Rajputana, while the invaders seem to have met with more success in the effort to preserve their racial purity, intermarriages did occur producing an intermingling of the two and destroying to a greater or less degree the purity of the "Aryan" blood. The rules of caste, while calculated to prevent this intermixture, seem not to have been entirely successful.

It does not seem necessary to pursue the matter of scientific classification further. We are unable to agree with the district court, or with other lower federal courts, in the conclusion that a native Hindu is eligible for naturalization under § 2169. The words of familiar speech, which were used by the original framers of the law, were intended to include only the type of man whom they knew as white. The immigration of that day was almost exclusively from the British Isles and Northwestern Europe, whence they and their forebears had come. When they extended the privilege of American citizenship to "any alien being a free white person," it was these immigrants—bone of their bone and flesh of their flesh—and their kind whom they must have had affirmatively in mind. The succeeding years brought immigrants from Eastern, Southern and Middle Europe, among them the Slavs and the dark-eyed, swarthy people of Alpine and Mediterranean stock, and these were received as unquestionably akin to those already here and readily amalgamated with them. It was the descendants of these, and other immigrants of like origin, who constituted the white population of the country when § 2169, reenacting the naturalization test of 1790, was adopted, and, there is no reason to doubt, with like intent and meaning.

What, if any, people of primarily Asiatic stock come within the words of the section we do not deem it necessary now to decide. There is much in the origin and historic development of the statute to suggest that no Asiatic whatever was included. The debates in Congress during the consideration of the subject in 1870 and 1875 are persuasively of this character. In 1873, for example, the words "free white persons" were unintentionally omitted from the compilation of the Revised Statutes. This omission was supplied in 1875 by the act to correct errors and supply omissions. C. 80, 18 Stat. 318. When this act was under consideration by Congress, efforts were made to strike out the words quoted, and it was insisted, upon the one hand, and conceded upon the other, that the effect of their retention was to exclude Asiatics generally from citizenship. While what was said upon that occasion, to be sure, furnishes no basis for judicial construction of the statute, it is nevertheless an important historic incident which may not be altogether ignored in the search for the true meaning of words which are themselves historic. That question, however, may well be left for final determination until the details have been more completely disclosed by the consideration of particular cases as they from time to time arise. The words of the statute, it must be conceded, do not readily yield to exact interpretation, and it is probably better to leave them as they are than to risk undue extension or undue limitation of their meaning by any general paraphrase at this time.

What we now hold is that the words "free white persons" are words of common speech, to be interpreted in accordance with the understanding of the common man, synonymous with the word "Caucasian" only as that word is popularly understood. As so understood and used, whatever may be the speculations of the ethnologist, it does not include the body of people to whom the appellee belongs. It is a matter of familiar observation and knowledge that the physical group characteristics of the Hindus render them readily distinguishable from the various groups of persons in this country commonly recognized as white. The children of English, French, German, Italian, Scandinavian, and other European parentage quickly merge into the mass of our population and lose the distinctive hallmarks of their European origin. On the other hand, it cannot be doubted that the children born in this country of Hindu parents would retain indefinitely the clear evidence of their ancestry. It is very far from our thought to suggest the slightest question of racial superiority or inferiority. What we suggest is merely racial difference, and it is of such character and extent that the great body of our people instinctively recognize it and reject the thought of assimilation.

It is not without significance in this connection that Congress, by the Act of February 5, 1917, c. 29, § 3, 39 Stat. 874, has now excluded from admission into this country all natives of Asia within designated limits of latitude and longitude, including the whole of India. This not only constitutes conclusive evidence of the congressional attitude of opposition to Asiatic immigration generally, but is persuasive of a similar attitude toward Asiatic naturalization as well, since it is not likely that Congress would be willing to accept as citizens a class of persons whom it rejects as immigrants.

It follows that a negative answer must be given to the first question, which disposes of the case and renders an answer to the second question unnecessary, and it will be so certified.

Answer to question No. 1, No.

NOTES ON *BHAGAT SINGH THIND*

1. Supreme Court Jurisprudence Defining Race. Though the *Thind* case was decided more than a century ago, the way it speaks about and defines race continues to resonate, even if not in the way Justice Sutherland intended. Justice Sutherland's opinion enshrines, in our Supreme Court jurisprudence, the concept that race is a social construct. After considering biological categories, common ancestry, scientific classifications, and common languages, he establishes in our law the idea that there is a common understanding of what a "white person" is and that legal weight should be given to that understanding. Despite the relevance of that framework to many legal, political, and policy-related discussions that have occurred since the decision, *Thind* is not frequently read, taught, or discussed in classrooms. Why? Legal professor and critical race theorist Cheryl Harris has explored the emergence and characteristics of "whiteness" as property, something that will be discussed in more detail in later chapters. But for now, can you think of any attributes of property that whiteness has?

2. Citizenship Status and Property Rights (Alien Land Laws). Status as a U.S. citizen is about far more than belonging. Certain rights are conferred only on citizens of the United States, including the right to vote and, at the time *Thind* was decided, the right to own property. And, as we have been discussing, property is one of the most protected and fundamental rights in the system of U.S. laws. Denying non-citizens access to ownership while also denying citizenship based on race is not consistent with the race-neutral story of "opportunity for all" that is sometimes presented by history books. Additionally, at the time *Thind* was decided, there were some jurisdictions, particularly in the western United States, that explicitly enacted what came to be known as "alien land laws." These laws restricted land ownership by race and ethnicity and often targeted Asian individuals specifically. Alien land laws were often enacted in response to heightened public anxiety surrounding global politics and war:

> California enacted its first alien land law in 1913 and then in 1920 added further limitations on lease-holding. Similar laws were passed in Washington, Oregon, Idaho, Montana, Arizona, New Mexico, Texas, Kansas, Louisiana, Missouri, Minnesota, Wyoming and Florida. The rationale for these laws, in addition to suppressing economic competition, was, according to [Professor Keith] Aoki, the perceived threat of Japan's growing industrial strength, its imperial military aspirations, and the projection on to Japanese immigrants an image of disloyalty as a "fifth column waiting to be activated by the emperor's command."[20]

20. Edgar Chen, *With New "Alien Land Laws" Asian Immigrants Are Once Again Targeted by Real Estate Bans*, JUSTSECURITY.ORG (May 26, 2023), https://www.justsecurity

State and federal courts overturned these laws in the mid-20th century, holding that they violated the 14th Amendment because they discriminated on the basis of race without a sufficiently compelling state interest.[21] In 2023, alien land laws resurfaced in Florida, which passed legislation preventing "foreign principals" and anyone domiciled in certain countries from purchasing agricultural property or any land within 10 miles of military or other defined secure infrastructure.[22] Similar legislation has been proposed by sponsors from both political parties in California, New York, Texas, Louisiana, South Carolina, and Alabama.[23]

The Right to Exclude: Where Does It Apply?

The Civil Rights Act of 1866 addresses directly the rights of citizens with respect to race and property rights: "All citizens of the United States shall have the same right, in every State and Territory, as enjoyed by white citizens thereof to inherit, purchase, lease, sell, hold and convey real and personal property."[24] Though this law had been in place since shortly after the end of the Civil War, it had been interpreted to regulate only state conduct and was not widely enforced.

But even after its passage, individuals and activists seeking to live with dignity continued to advocate for equal housing rights, and their efforts ultimately contributed to some of the legislation passed during the civil rights era. The Civil Rights Act of 1964 further clarified the rights of access to places of public accommodation: "All persons shall be entitled to the full and equal enjoyment of the goods, services, facilities, privileges, advantages, and accommodations of any place of public accommodation, as defined in this section, without discrimination or segregation on the ground of race, color, religion or national origin."[25] This section of the statute describes what qualifies as places of "public accommodation" and includes hotels, common carriers, restaurants, and places

---

.org/86722/with-new-alien-land-laws-asian-immigrants-are-once-again-targeted-by-real-estate-bans/.

21. *See* Oyama v. California, 332 U.S. 663 (1948); Sei Fujii v. State of California, 242 P.2d 617 (1952).

22. Fla. S.B. 264.

23. *See* Chen, *supra* note 20.

24. 42 U.S.C. § 1982.

25. 42 U.S.C. § 2000a(a).

of entertainment. Tellingly, the section ends with a protection for private property: "The provisions of this subchapter shall not apply to a private club or other establishment not in fact open to the public."[26]

In this way, even though the Civil Rights Act of 1964 expanded the rights of people to access property regardless of their race, it continues to allow property owners to choose whom to exclude from their private property and dictate how they should act while on it. Accordingly, it is an example that demonstrates how a civil rights victory may still serve to highlight persistent and unequal racial and power dynamics. As with most things in the law, rights in property and rights to be free from racial discrimination are not absolute; they instead fall on a spectrum and depend on the type and nature of the property in question.

This spectrum provides room for boundaries to be pushed, both by those who seek to exclude based on race and those who seek to break down racial barriers. An understanding of the workings of the common law, some ways in which property may be characterized as either available for public use or not, and whether there may be affirmative defenses for trespass (necessity, for example) are issues that will change over time as social and cultural values change. It is not sufficient to change the letter of the law; in this system, hearts, minds, and practices must evolve, too.

An intersection with tort law reveals that some property owners have used concerns about unsubstantiated assault to exclude on the basis of race, even on premises that are held open to the public. Reading the footnotes in *Utson v. Resorts International Hotel*,[27] a case involving an individual who was excluded from a casino because of his suspected card counting, one wonders whether excluding someone who appears to be Italian American (implying a connection to the Mafia) would violate a civil rights statute or be an appropriate use of the property holder's discretion under the court's holding. The fundamental skill in property

26. *Id.* § 2000a(e).

27. 445 A.2d 370 (N.J. 1982).

law is to balance the interests of the parties seeking access or rights in property. Understanding how to effectively use a public policy argument about race to buttress an argument supported by a statute or the common law is a skill that lawyers continually develop.

Applying policy arguments to support legal analysis when dealing with race in the law is particularly challenging because of the subject's emotionally charged nature and the weight of history. In the introduction to her groundbreaking article *Spirit Murdering the Messenger: The Discourse of Fingerpointing as the Law's Response to Racism,*[28] Professor Patricia Williams describes the experience of being excluded from a "buzzer store" in New York City while doing her holiday shopping. She masterfully describes the way in which exclusion on the basis of race carries a psychological violence. Given the many ways in which the application of property law is connected to individual and collective identities, the psychological weight of exclusion should not be understated when working to understand and contribute to the common law in this area. One big problem with the law as a profession, however, is that people who have a history of being excluded based on their race are wildly underrepresented. It is therefore incumbent on all practitioners to try to make informed and practical contributions that take into account what real exclusion feels like.

Reflection

Social exclusion has impacted almost everyone in some way. Our psychological and criminal systems ostracize or remove people from larger groups as a response to errant or undesirable behavior. This exclusion, separation and sometimes isolation has an emotional impact on individuals and groups. How can and should law and policy account for that?

28. Patricia Williams, *Spirit Murdering the Messenger: The Discourse of Fingerpointing as the Law's Response to Racism*, 42 U. Miami L. Rev. 127 (1987).

Consequences: Trespass

A trespass is an unprivileged entry onto to the property of another—in other words, a failure to exclude. Even when there is no damage, the law takes this violation of property rights so seriously that it awards punitive damages in some cases. "The law recognizes that actual harm occurs in every trespass. [...] Society has an interest in punishing and deterring intentional trespassers beyond that of protecting the interests of the individual landowner. Society has an interest in preserving the integrity of the legal system."[29] The common law system has drawn strong borders around each parcel of land and allows the owner to protect it against trespassers at the surface, above the ground, and below the ground.[30] The ability to draw strong borders around owned property and to control what happens on that property is one of the most fiercely protected tenets of our system of laws in the United States. Private property owners may choose to discriminate or exclude from their property or use the resources contained on their property however they see fit. As these interests in property pass from generation to generation, they become more than just what individuals own—they become connected with the property owners' identities. The norms and values of communities and the ways in which nearby property owners act can also significantly influence both property rights and identities. So engrained in the national identity is the strength of property rights that it is easy to forget that there are different ways of doing things.

An alternative to the theory of control and ownership of property that is contained in our common law system is one of stewardship that is held by some non-European cultures. Many of the communities and cultures indigenous to the land that is now the United States espouse this alternative view of property rights. The English language is sometimes ill-equipped to capture the nuances of the relationship dynamics between humans and the natural world in these cultures.[31] Often the common law

---

29. Jacque v. Steenberg Homes, 563 N.W.2d 154 (1997).

30. The common law maxim about property ownership's dimensions has been "cujus est solum ejus est usque ad coelum et ad infernos," or "whoever owns the soil also owns up to the heavens and down to hell."

31. "Objectification of the natural world reinforces the notion that our species is more deserving of the gifts of the world than the other 8.7 million species with whom we share the planet. Using 'it' absolves us of moral responsibility and opens the door to ex-

concept of ownership vastly differs from these cultures' long-held beliefs and traditions: for example, instead of having absolute rights to defined parcels, some people may share rights to fish, gather, hunt, or reside on property. Using and caring for property together and resolving disputes as they arise in a system that respects shared rights is something that existed long before the common law system arrived in the United States. In fact, the dispossession of land from Indigenous peoples likely occurred, at least in part, because the concept of "owning" land, espoused by the colonists, was completely foreign to them.

A common law system is constantly, if slowly, adjusting and adapting to shifting values to meet the new needs of the individuals and groups it serves. Even in an adaptive and flexible common law system, there will be embedded, rigid structures around which institutions and systems are built—for instance, the concept of ownership. How does a system respond when faced with something that challenges the foundations on which its built? Undoing the racism and inequity built into our systems and structures begins with developing the ability to conduct a culturally responsive legal analysis. In the context of trespass, this may require attorneys to look beyond the binary created by the borders of fee simple ownership and consider cultural contexts, such as how different groups may act differently toward the land, or toward one another with regard to the land, and how these different ways of viewing things may impact their rights and liabilities under the law.

---

ploitation. When Sugar Maple is an 'it' we give ourselves permission to pick up the saw. 'It' means it doesn't matter. But in Anishinaabee and many other indigenous languages, it's impossible to speak of Sugar Maple as 'it.' We use the same words to address all living beings as we do our family. Because they are our family." Robin Wall Kimmerer, *Nature Needs a New Pronoun: To Stop the Age of Extinction, Let's Start by Ditching "It,"* YES! MAG. (Mar. 30, 2015), https://www.yesmagazine.org/issue/together-earth/2015/03/30/alternative-grammar-a-new-language-of-kinship.

Adverse Possession

Sometimes described as "trespass that ripens to ownership," the concept of adverse possession comes as a surprise to many first-year law students. Broadly speaking, adverse possession is a doctrine under which a party who uses and treats property as if they are the owner for a long enough time (the statutory period) may gain title to that property, thereby becoming the actual legal owner. In short: pretend it is yours for long enough, and it becomes yours. This concept completely flummoxes some law students because of the way it seems to reward those who break the rules. But one of the underlying policy reasons for transferring title by adverse possession is to ensure the best and highest use of the land. A careful and critical thinker may wonder who decides what the "best and highest use" means.

Each jurisdiction has its own language, but each generally requires that during the statutorily defined period, an adverse possessor meet the following elements:

Element	Description
Adverse/Hostile	There is no permission to be on the property.
Actual	There is a sufficiently substantial presence on the property.
Open & Notorious	The use of the property is obvious and noticeable upon reasonable inspection of the land.
Exclusive	Dominion and control over the property in question has been established by the adverse possessor.
Continuous	There has been no interruption in the use of the property.

Disputes over whether a party has gained title by adverse possession are fact-intensive and rely heavily not only on the way in which the parties have been using the property but also on what the custom of the locality is. Built into the standard for acquiring title by adverse possession is that a party must act the way a true owner of property in that locality would act for the prescribed amount of time. The local jurisdiction matters a great deal because the standards for how property is used vary greatly. In some "resort towns," it may be commonplace for a true owner to leave the property for a substantial part of the year, and so an adverse possessor may do so and still meet the continuous requirement. Urban areas have different needs from rural ones, and natural forces, like weather, may impact the actions and outcomes of cases as well. In some cases, such as where a fence required for establishing "exclusivity" has been ruined by weather, a court may be required to parse the parties' ability to meet the elements from other surrounding facts and circumstances.

Though applying the standard for how a true owner in the locality would act requires a fact-intensive analysis, there are some cases and opportunities to unpack the policy foundations upon which the common law is built. The requirement that a party seeking title establish the element of "adverse" or "hostile" is the one that relates to the right of a title owner of property to exclude: the adverse possessor must begin as a trespasser. To determine whether this element has been met, many jurisdictions apply the "objective test" because it is the simplest for courts to apply and the most predictable, making for most efficient jurisprudence.[32] As applied to the adverse possessor, the objective test requires nothing about their state of mind; it only requires that they lacked permission to enter the property.[33] Though this is the rule in the majority of jurisdictions, it is built around a fundamental concept of ownership and permissive entry that is inconsistent with many Indigenous cultures' relationships to the land. In *Nome 2000 v. Fagerstrom*,[34] a case often discussed in first-year property classrooms, a party was seeking to gain title by adverse possession to two parcels of land in Alaska. One of the spouses in the marriage had Indigenous heritage and was granted an adjacent parcel in accordance with a land grant. The title owner of the property argued that the adverse or hostile element "was lacking as the Fagerstroms thought of themselves not as owners but as stewards pursu-

32. Note that there are also three subjective tests, including (1) claim of right, (2) intentional dispossession, and (3) good faith. Each requires some examination of the state of mind of the party seeking to acquire title by adverse possession and is therefore subjective. It is for this reason that only a minority of jurisdictions look to these tests. In addition, there is disagreement among jurisdictions about the state of mind that should be rewarded.

33. *See* Yourik v. Mallonee, 921 A.2d 869, 878 (Md. 2007).

34. 799 P.2d 304 (Alaska 1990).

ant to the traditional system of Native Alaskan Land usage." The court rejected this argument. It held that all elements of adverse possession were met for a small portion of the land. However, the court also held that the Fagerstrom's activities on the larger (southerly) portion of the land, which included using existing trails and picking up litter, "[did] not evince an exercise of dominion and control over the entire parcel" and remanded to a lower court with instructions to split the parcel and grant title to the portion of the land over which the adverse possessors did exert noticeable dominion and control.

An expert witness was called in this case: Dr. Steven McNabb, an anthropologist who testified about the traditional Native Alaskan system of land use. He testified that "the traditional Native system does not recognize exclusive ownership of land.... The claim is not exclusive and is not a matter of ownership, but is more in the nature of a stewardship. That is, other members of the claimant's social group may share in the resources of the land without obtaining permission, so long as the resources are not abused or destroyed." As to the larger parcel of land, it was the nature of this relationship—where stewards of the land have priority to use its resources but may not exclude others—that kept the claimants from obtaining the entire parcel by adverse possession. The use was not sufficiently "hostile" to satisfy the element.

To consider the nature of the land in Alaska, or even the rate of depletion of natural resources in the United States, from the perspective of a system of stewardship that predates the common law in United States is not an approach that comports with the ideas of ownership and exclusion to which the law is accustomed. But a policy argument may be made that prioritizing the best and highest use of the land may require looking to theories outside of our canon of law. Reconceiving the common law theory of ownership and keeping an open mind about cultures that were originally viewed as "savage" can lead to a more culturally inclusive and responsive legal analysis. But doing so may also address some pressing environmental and shared-resource issues; as population density increases and cultural values trend toward stewardship and sharing, a return to Indigenous concepts, theories, and rituals may be helpful.

▲ ▼ ▲

Skills: Articulation of Issues in Element-Based Law

Being able to read and understand case law is a skill that all lawyers must possess. They must glean from every case the issues dealt with by the court and the ways that a rule may be nuanced by each novel set of facts. Though the skill of briefing cases is an important one, the remainder of this book will focus on the application. In some formal settings, such as in a legal writing class, using a structure that includes a conclusion, rule, explanation, analysis, and conclusion (CREAC) is the appropriate form. During timed exams that test law students' skills and doctrinal knowledge, such as first-year exams and the bar exam, the shorter issue, rule, analysis, and conclusion (IRAC) structure is more appropriate.

Using a short fact pattern based on adverse possession, this chapter provides an overview of the process of crafting a strong legal analysis and includes common errors made by students who are new to it. Providing samples of common mistakes alongside models demonstrating how to correct those mistakes will help students get into the habit of self-assessing their work, leading to a strong and robust legal analysis. As with every skill, there is no substitute for practice and experience.

It is worth noting that there are several substantive and pedagogical critiques of the IRAC structure. First and foremost, this structure insists on the application of existing rules; there is no room for debate about whether the rule should exist or how the rule might be changed. Critics say that this method may constrict our vision and force our thinking into a shape that makes it more difficult to think creatively about rules and reforms. This is a sound criticism, and it is a helpful one to keep in mind when thinking critically about the system of laws as a whole or when seeking to review and reform how justice is administered. We persist with IRAC here, nevertheless. We will stick to the IRAC structure as it provides the foundation for developing more complex critical thinking skills later on.

Yet another criticism of the IRAC form relates to a more pragmatic lawyering skill. Some professors argue that in practice, clients and judges will rarely seek an opinion from a lawyer that does not first articulate the ultimate legal conclusion. While this may be true, using the IRAC framework allows first-year students to find ways to expand their thinking about the analysis section without being constricted by the conclusion. Once again, practicing IRAC is but an early step on the path toward honing a set of sharp legal skills.

Step one of the IRAC method is to identify the issue presented. In a complex fact pattern, there may be multiple issues at hand, with some being more obvious than others. The first task is to spot the issues, but the more difficult task is to articulate them in a way that will prompt a focused, robust, and thorough legal analysis. Common mistakes include stating an issue too broadly and forming binary questions. When the response to an issue is "yes" or "no," it can be difficult to write an effective legal analysis. In contrast, stating the issue in an open-ended way demands an explanation in response. Beginning with the word "whether" helps to set up a balancing test and allows for the consideration of factors that could tip the scales in either direction. Though these tactics may not be the most effective ones in every circumstance, it is nonetheless helpful to get in the habit of practicing them early on.

An additional consideration to keep in mind as you practice how to effectively articulate an issue is whether you are being as specific as possible about what the legal issue at stake is. Stating an issue too broadly will demand a response that is too broad, and a broad explanation of a rule does not make for an effective legal analysis. Consider the examples raised by the following fact pattern:

> In the northern part of Westeros, Jon Snow lived at Castle Blackacre. Mel owned and formerly resided on the adjacent property, Redacre. Jon had been trying to keep wild animals off his property, so he decided to build a giant wall around Castle Blackacre. Jon had a survey done to establish the boundaries of his parcel because his intent was to enclose only his property and no more.
>
> Due to a storm during construction, the wall foundations were set on his neighbor's property, Redacre. As a result, a 10′ strip of Mel's land was enclosed by the wall built by Jon to protect Castle Blackacre. Once the wall was built, Jon cared for everything enclosed by it, even digging a latrine at the end of the strip. When the summer came and the snows melted, it became clear that the wall enclosed part of Redacre as the garden Mel maintained at the edge of her property was revealed.

Because she was busy establishing her new business, Mel did not return to Redacre for 12 years. In her absence, Jon tended the garden, and when he had an excess of peppers from the plants, he sold them at the local farmer's market. When Mel returned to Redacre, she was pleased at the progress of her pepper plants, and gave Jon gardening tips and asked that he share some peppers in exchange.

First, you must find a way to effectively state the issue. First-year law students tend to identify the issue but articulate it much too broadly. Consider this issue statement: ***(1) Was title gained by adverse possession?*** This construction demands a "yes" or "no" response, which, as we've already discussed, does not prompt the best possible legal analysis. The logical rule (the "R") that follows the issue statement will be a statement of the elements necessary to prove adverse possession. The subsequent analysis (the "A") will provide a necessarily brief description of how the given facts address each of the elements. While this may all seem perfectly logical, it does not provide much specificity or clarity about the facts at hand with regard to the dispute being addressed.

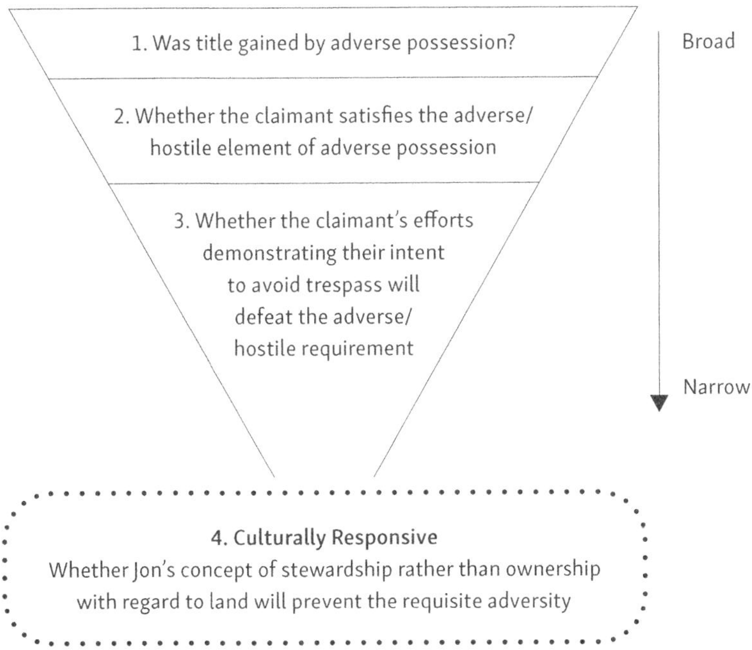

Accordingly, the next example of an issue statement is: ***(2) Whether the claimant satisfies the adverse/hostile element of adverse possession.*** This version begins with the word "whether," which allows for a response that explains rather than answers. Additionally, this articulation isolates one element of the issue that must be analyzed, thus allowing for a more in-depth examination. Students who feel compelled to demonstrate that they have memorized all the elements of adverse possession should note that this is *not* an exercise in memorization. Understanding which of the elements require careful thought and detailed analysis and which are clear is a lawyering skill, not the ability to memorize elements of a statute that can be referenced. Some students wonder whether they are required to do an IRAC for each and every element: the answer is that an analysis should only be completed for those elements that actually present an issue. A preliminary statement demonstrating knowledge of the elements of adverse possession may be made at the threshold of the analysis. But a writer who can identify the elements that are at issue with the particular facts at hand will be understood by the reader (whether a professor or judge) to be familiar with all the elements.

But there is an even more effective way to articulate the issue than focusing on the element of adverse possession at hand: ask "Why?" For instance, understanding that the adverse/hostile element may require discussion, you may ask, "Why? What facts would render the use of the land adverse or hostile, and what argument may be made that the use is permissive?" Understanding the standard to apply[35] will help you to articulate an effective issue statement. The third version of the issue statement makes an open-ended inquiry about *why* the claimant's use of the land may or may not meet the requirement: ***(3) Whether the claimant's efforts demonstrating their intent to avoid trespass will defeat the adverse/hostile requirement.*** Continuing to refine and rearticulate the issue will help you to realize that there is no single "correct" way to frame or state an issue. There are as many effective ways to state an issue as there are creative people. The important thing is to continue to practice.

---

35. See the rule synthesis exercise in Chapter 3.

After the Issue

An effectively stated issue sets the tone and foundation for a well-reasoned and robust legal analysis, but it is only the first component of an IRAC response. Subsequent chapters will provide more details on how to complete an effective rule and analysis (with an emphasis on the different tools and methods available for a strong analysis). Below is the type of response that a diligent law student may submit to the prompt above early in their legal career:

> *Whether an AP'ers efforts demonstrating their intent to avoid trespass will defeat the "adverse" or "hostile" requirement. Under the objective standard, the intent of the adverse possessor is irrelevant, so long as they lacked permission to enter the property. Jon lacked Mel's permission to be on Redacre when he entered, and therefore, under the objective test, satisfies the element of adversity.*

This IRAC begins with the narrow and specifically stated issue from above and goes on to articulate a rule responsive to the issue. It is clear, concise, well written, and seemingly logical to so many law students. There is one major problem with it, though: it does *not* contain a legal analysis. Breaking the IRAC into its components helps to demonstrate that a strong issue statement and responsive rule followed by a conclusion can seem like a complete answer; however, a trained legal eye will notice immediately that the entire analysis is missing.

	Likely Student Answer
Issue	Whether the efforts of an AP'er to avoid trespass will defeat the hostile requirement.
Rule	Under the objective standard, the intent of the AP'er is irrelevant so long as they lacked permission to enter the property.
Analysis	
Conclusion	Jon lacked Mel's permission to be on Redacre when he entered, and ***therefore***, under the objective test, satisfies the element of adversity.

It is helpful for students who are beginning to develop their habits to err on the side of rigidity with regard to the IRAC structure. For many, visually or physically separating each component—the issue, rule, analysis, and conclusion—ensures that distinctions are made between each to achieve clarity in writing. After doing so, an answer that seemed clear, cogent, logical, and strong, like the one in our example, can seem frighteningly inadequate.

But take heart. The mistake made by so many is *not* not knowing the law but instead being unsure of how to articulate or draw out an analysis about what is known. A legal analysis is made up of a synthesized rule[36] applied to the facts of the novel fact pattern that is given. **Rule + Facts.** The common law system requires a comparison of similar cases, and that is the most effective tool in a legal analysis. Similar cases are compared in an analysis that identifies the *salient* facts, that is, the facts on which the holding of a case might turn. Comparing those salient facts and weighing them in each case is the work of a legal analysis.

Students and lawyers sometimes fail to conduct the most thorough legal analysis possible, not because they are unable to but because they are unsure of themselves. Due to the nature of the common law, it reflects the people only to the extent that lawyers are able to incorporate their experiences and expectations into a legal argument. Doing this in a culturally responsive way will only help to broaden the law's reach and application in a way that feels like justice to more people.

Subsequent chapters will expand on the skills necessary for drafting strong rule and analysis sections. Knowing when an analysis is missing is an important skill, but knowing how to craft an effective analysis simply requires being shown. A very good source containing many models for strong analysis is the casebook: read closely the opinions contained therein and seek out a structure to emulate. Judges are human, too, and so these opinions provide a good opportunity to take note of good, best, and poor practices, especially for students seeking to establish their own style.

Consider the following rigidly structured responses to the short fact pattern above.

---

36. *Id.*

	Draft #2	Draft #3 (Culturally Responsive)
Issue	Whether the efforts of an AP'er to avoid trespass will defeat the hostile requirement.	Whether Jon's concept of stewardship rather than ownership with regard to land will prevent the requisite adversity/hostility element from being met.
Rule	Under the objective standard, the intent of the AP'er is irrelevant so long as they lacked permission to enter the property.	Adversity / hostility rests on the premise that real property can be owned by individuals and does not account for variations in cultures or ideas about the relationship between people and property.
Analysis	Like in *Brown v. Gobble*, Jon never intended to trespass, but tended the land as a true owner would. The building of a treehouse and a latrine are similar levels of permanence and impact the outward appearance of ownership and expectations of the community regarding ownership. The fence and wall around tended property demonstrate an effort to exclude the way a true owner would.	Similar to the *Nome* case, the party seeking to quiet title by adverse possession does not believe that land can be owned. A difference in the fundamental concept of ownership will impact the way parties act to assert dominion and control or try to exclude others from their property. Stewardship of land is a different relationship as it is premised on a duty to care for property that is for public use. Similar to the indigenous party in the *Nome* case, Jon's actions are consistent with her default beliefs, which the elements of adverse position are not equipped to consider.
Conclusion	Element met.	

When an issue is worthy of a protracted analysis, it is likely because reasonable minds can disagree. A strong analysis is one that does not ignore those facts inconsistent with their conclusion; it acknowledges them and weighs them against the facts that *do* support the ultimate conclusion. The work of a strong legal analysis is not to answer a question—instead, once an issue is identified, it is to look through the lens of the facts at hand, trying to understand the types of questions that may arise in the course of resolving the issue based on the precedent. It is for this reason that the final IRAC component, the conclusion, is the least important—a notion that may require some "unlearning" for those law students who hail from certain academic disciplines where it is sufficient to know the material taught throughout the semester and draw conclusions. The law is the opposite. Knowing the cases that make up the common law is only a starting point. Being able to use the cases and apply them to a new set of facts is the skill that professors (and, ultimately, clients and judges) are interested in testing. Take the opportunity before exams to practice this skill—it is, after all, the real subject of the test.

SUGGESTIONS FOR FURTHER READING

Bell Hooks, Belonging: A Culture of Place (2009).

Robin Wall Kimmer, Braiding Sweetgrass: Indigenous Wisdom, Scientific Knowledge and the Teachings of Plants (2015).

Patty Krawec, Becoming Kin: An Indigenous Call to Unforgetting the Past and Reimagining Our Future (2022).

Christopher Stone, Should Trees Have Standing?: Law, Morality and the Environment (1972).

Patricia Williams, *Spirit Murdering the Messenger: The Discourse of Fingerpointing as the Law's Response to Racism*, 42 U. Miami L. Rev. 127 (1987).

THREE

Nuisance, Purchased Injunctions & Environmental Justice

Whether by conscious design or institutional neglect, communities of color in urban ghettos, in rural "poverty pockets," or on economically impoverished Native-American reservations face some of the worst environmental devastation in the nation.

—Dr. Robert Bullard[1]

The EPA (Environmental Protection Agency) does not place a dollar value on individual lives. Rather, when conducting a benefit-cost analysis of new environmental policies, the Agency uses estimates of how much people are willing to pay for small reductions in their risks of dying from adverse health conditions that may be caused by environmental pollution. In the scientific literature, these estimates of willingness to pay for small reductions in mortality risks are often referred to as the "value of a statistical life."

—U.S. Environmental Protection Agency website[2]

Sic utere tuo ut alienum non laedas.
(Use your own property in such a way that you do not injure others.)

—Legal Maxim

---

1. Dumping in Dixie: Race, Class and Environmental Quality (3d. ed. 2000).

2. *Mortality Risk Valuation*, U.S. Envt'l Protection Agency (last updated Mar. 14, 2023), https://www.epa.gov/environmental-economics/mortality-risk-valuation.

Frustration with a neighbor is one of the most common and accessible areas of property law. Though the concept of nuisance is familiar and understandable, articulating it in legal language and fitting it into a legal framework can be challenging, and doing so with cultural sensitivity is rare in our common law. While adverse possession is determined by applying an element-based rule to the facts at hand, nuisance is determined by performing a balancing test, one in which the rights of property owners are weighted against each other. Courts and legislatures have rightly tried to formalize an approach to this process to provide for a predictable system of laws, but in doing so, they have sometimes formalized some of the power dynamics and features of dominant cultures. Providing access to justice for people from different ethnic backgrounds or races could help to inform and expand the current common law understanding of what may be considered "reasonable use" of property.

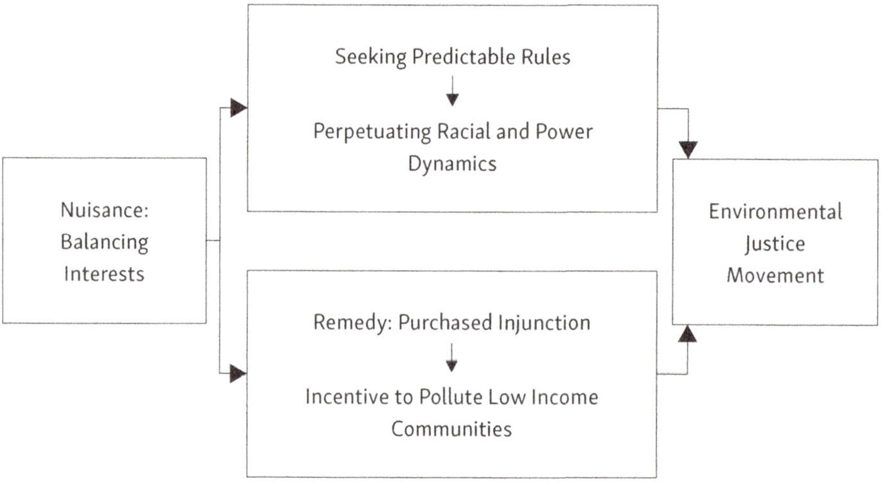

In a fact-intensive analysis utilizing a balancing test, one property owner must prevail in an action for nuisance. Courts aim to create solutions that maximize fairness and justice in the administration of property rights, and these solutions are based in a system of entitlements and equitable remedies. This chapter explores the remedy of the purchased injunction and its impact on shaping communities. It also explores the environmental justice movement that has sprung up in response to this and other features of our property law system that continue to perpetrate inequitable racial, economic, and power dynamics.

Nuisance: Balancing Interests

We have by now established that rights in property are afforded particular attention and protection under our system of laws.[3] Nuisance is a challenging subject because it requires courts to decide on how to balance the rights of one property holder against the rights of another. In doing so, courts inspect the features not only of the property but also of the owners and all the facts and circumstances surrounding the dispute. Each time a court is required to determine what is "reasonable" under the circumstances, a great deal is revealed about collective values. The incident of ownership, or the stick in the bundle of rights of ownership, at issue when determining nuisance is the *right of use and enjoyment*. Each owner of property has the right to use and enjoy their property. The doctrine of nuisance considers what happens when one landowner's use and enjoyment of their property causes an *unreasonable harm* to another landowner's use and enjoyment of their property. Note that damage to the land is not necessary—nuisance requires only that the right to use and enjoy one's own land be diminished unreasonably. Inherent in this standard is a set of value judgements and a measuring of the property rights of parties against one another.

This balancing-test type of rule requires a different kind of administration from other types. Although the standard's flexibility helps to promote justice in very specific circumstances, it also makes it difficult to predict outcomes. One feature of an effective law in a well working system is that it is clear and predictable, so that individuals who are subject to it understand how their behavior will be interpreted not just by the legal system but also by the social and cultural structures that support the legal system.[4] For instance, if one is able to glean from the surrounding standards, including the law, that burning a bonfire on a back patio will create an actionable nuisance for one's neighbors, then that knowledge will serve as a deterrent. This is a positive outcome in the eyes of the law (and the neighbors). Courts have provided this clarity by devel-

3. An entire required law-school course devoted to these rights plus the attention it receives on the bar exam should emphasize that.

4. For a very interesting work about the relationship between jurisprudence (particularly U.S. Supreme Court jurisprudence) and popular opinion, see Barry Friedman, *The Will of the People: How Public Opinion Has Influenced the Supreme Court and Shaped the Meaning of the Constitution* (2009).

oping factors that must be considered when reviewing claims between owners of property. Factors generally considered include the extent and character of the harm done to the rights of the complaining property owner (the plaintiff of or complainant); the value of the activity that is causing the harm, both social and economic (which can sometimes be more difficult to distinguish than you might hope); the suitability of that activity for that particular locality; and the cost to each property owner to avoid the nuisance causing harm, including how practical or fair it may be.[5] And, though it may appear in different ways and with different words, courts will also consider fault or accountability in these cases. Whether by way of a question about notice and which party "came to the nuisance" or a categorization of the necessity or character of the activity, for example, value judgments will be made throughout the application of the balancing test.

Discussion Question

What are the features of an effective law? Predictability? Fairness? Broad applicability? Ease of administration? *Are any of the features in conflict?*

But having a predictable set of rules and standards in law also has its downsides. Standardizing factors and considerations may have the effect of making more rigid some of the existing racial and cultural hierarchies. It is good to have structure because it makes laws easy to know and administer. This clarity is beneficial to our system because it strengthens our social fabric. Sometimes, though, that structure has the unintended consequence of weaving our biases and power dynamics into the social fabric, and removing them can be difficult, though not impossible, to undo. Particularly when value judgments about what constitutes "reasonable" behavior are inherent in a court's analysis, the lack of diversity of the bench and bar will result in a white-centric view of property. As nuisance is related to use and enjoyment of property, it is an incredibly personal area of the law. Given the personal nature of many of these value judgments, nuisance offers students an excellent opportunity to practice how to bring their own personal set of experiences to an already

5. *See* Joseph Singer, Property Law 349 (8th ed. 2021).

existing structure of standards and considerations. Even though a nuisance analysis should focus on whether the nature and scope of *harm* is unreasonable, many times courts (and students) spend time considering whether the behavior causing the nuisance is unreasonable. When this behavior is attached to a culture or practice that is not in the mainstream, it should be viewed carefully and with respect, and with an awareness of how that culture has been historically treated. Consider the following example:

> Sriracha hot sauce factory and residents of Irwindale California began warring when residents began to complain of a spicy odor that caused headaches, heartburn, and watering eyes. Huy Fong Foods, the manufacturer of Sriracha, was encouraged to come to many cities in the United States to manufacture their popular hot sauce and chose Irwindale. In doing so, Huy Fong Foods guaranteed thousands of jobs and contributed to the city budget significantly, by way of their tax increment financing agreement and their making the town something of a tourist destination.
>
> During the pepper-grinding process that usually occurs each fall, residents complain of a harmful odor. The Air Quality Management District did not find enough evidence of a harmful smell to justify issuing a violation, but a "smell study" conducted by a private firm hired by the city did find harmful odor levels in multiple areas of the city. The first complaint came from a city councilperson whose child experienced symptoms that were particularly damaging to his health.

This fact pattern[6] requires a more complex balancing of interests than one involving two neighbors who want to enjoy a party and sleep (respectively). Judgments must be made about the value of the nuisance-causing use and the gravity of the harm it causes to human health. When reading opinions, students should note whether racial dynamics are left unaddressed by the court or whether they are articulated. Regardless, racial dynamics are always present.

This particular hot sauce is famous for being culturally *un*-American, but it is interesting that nowhere in the case is that fact described in this

6. *See generally* Ernesto Hernandez-Lopez, *Sriracha Shutdown: Hot Sauce Lessons on Local Privilege and Race*, 46 SETON HALL L. REV. 189 (2015).

manner. The common law is supposed to reflect society, and society is made up of individuals and the sum of their individual experiences. Law students and lawyers should therefore feel empowered to consider how existing as an "other" may impact the balancing test. Whether or not this will always be sufficient to tip the scales is not as important as making a racially sensitive and culturally responsive legal argument that is informed both by history and common sense.

Remedies for Nuisance and the Rise of the Environmental Justice Movement

In initial filings, the city suggested that Huy Fong Foods purchase an air filter to eliminate the harmful odor at a cost of approximately $600,000. Though ultimately this dispute was resolved and the nuisance lawsuit was dropped, the question of how property owners can co-exist is an issue as old as neighbors. The way in which race-neutral nuisance laws were used in this highly contentious local dispute demonstrates how the application of laws, and not necessarily the laws themselves, can reflect cultural biases. As the population continues to increase, and racial and other types of diversity increase along with it, our system of laws would be well served to evolve to better manage these disputes. In nuisance cases, one of the property holders will have to bear a burden, and it is the work of courts to determine which party should bear the cost. The court has established a framework of "purchased injunctions" for doing this, discussed in the next section.

Entitlements, Remedies, and Purchased Injunctions

Each owner of property has certain entitlements, in the case of nuisance, to use and enjoy their property how they please. Following the language of the courts can sometimes be difficult in this area, but understanding a few basics will help. The plaintiff in nuisance cases is the property owner who is suffering the harm (and bringing an action for nuisance). The defendant is the property owner who is engaged in the activity causing the harm. Courts have available a menu of remedies and may choose to do nothing, to award money damages, or to impose a remedy based in powers of equity, including an injunction. Each of these, or a combination, will result in a resolution between the parties and, at the very least, set expectations regarding how the property in that area, in those particular parcels, may relate to one another.

An interaction between an award of damages and an order of injunction began occurring when high-value properties were at stake. Often the services required to support large numbers of people can be environmentally hazardous or result in a lot of pollution that becomes a nuisance. Whether it is the dumping of waste, manufacture of cement[7] (or hot sauce), or production of energy, many services that are necessary to support comfortable lifestyles are unpleasant to be near and create, for some, a nuisance. As demographics shifted and populations moved from urban areas to suburbs,[8] those nuisance-causing services had to be established somewhere.

	Property owner who is suffering the harm from the nuisance: Plaintiff	Property owner who is engaged in the activity causing the nuisance: Defendant
Dismissal (no action)		Defendant prevails: entitled to continue using their property engaged in activity causing nuisance.
Damages	Plaintiff is compensated for the harm caused by the nuisance.	Defendant may continue to cause harm if willing to pay damages for harm (absent injunction)
Injunction	Plaintiff prevails and has the right to enjoin or stop the defendant from engaging in the activity that is causing the harm.	
Purchased Injunction	Plaintiff can enjoin or stop the nuisance causing conduct of the defendant ONLY if willing to pay damages to defendant for loss.	Defendant may continue the nuisance causing activity unless they are compensated by the plaintiff in the amount that stopping the nuisance causing activity would cost.

7. Boomer v. Atlantic Cement Co., 257 N.E.2d 870 (1970).

8. See Chapters 4 and 5, *infra*.

In the landmark case *Boomer v. Atlantic Cement*,[9] a cement plant that was built at a great expense near Albany, New York, was producing a great deal of "dirt, smoke and vibration." A private nuisance was found and initially an injunction was denied. On appeal, the court considered the interaction between private disputes and public policy and expressed its reluctance to do anything to resolve the dispute between the parties before it, given the resources devoted by the state and federal government to air quality. Despite this reluctance to weigh in on larger policy, the court did just that when it weighed the relative cost of the defendants' homes against the investment made by the cement company. The court's holding granted an injunction that would be vacated once the cement company compensated the homeowners for the "permanent damage"[10] to their respective properties. This sent a message to other industrial operators looking to establish themselves in a new location: go where the cost will be the least: poor communities.

The predictability of the courts' handling of nuisance cases, combined with a system that denied Black and immigrant families the opportunity to purchase property and build wealth by prohibiting their access to desirable neighborhoods where property values were likely to increase (i.e., "redlining," discussed in later chapters), led many industrial operators to make the strategic decision to locate harmful functions/services in low-income communities—a practice that continues to the present day. Although the *Boomer* holding was racially neutral on its face, we can see that in practice, it gave rise to a system of purchased injunctions that incentivizes industries to carry out their most harmful activities in a way that disproportionally affects Black and brown people living in low-income neighborhoods. It is but one example of how a rational rule, whose original purpose was to promote justice between individuals can, when formalized, framed, and scaled up, result in a system that promotes injustice—in this particular example, by making the environment disproportionally less healthy and clean for people of color.

9. 257 N.E.2d 870 (N.Y. 1970).

10. The court makes a distinction between temporary and permanent damages. In short, temporary damages mitigate the effects of the nuisance, while permanent damages reflect the change in value of the property because of its proximity to the nuisance. The effect is that the plaintiff may sell their property and be compensated for the value (taking into account the permanent damages) and the new owner will be on notice of the nuisance and have paid a fair price for the property.

The Rise of Environmental Justice

The impact of poor air quality or other hazardous environmental factors goes beyond the remedies for nuisance. The individuals living in such communities have likely been subject to discrimination for generations, and they continue to access the institutions of and resources offered by the United States differently from their white counterparts. Even if property was acquired at a discounted rate, proximity to vibrations or to poor air quality can impact, among other things, sleep and health, which, in turn, can impact school or work performance during the day, thereby perpetuating the cycle of poverty. It can be difficult to go to school with or work alongside those who do not suffer from the same health challenges, and narratives about "hard work" and "pulling oneself up by the bootstraps" do not account for the systemic barriers that Black and immigrant communities face.

Reflection

There are (too) many nuisance cases about hazardous sites and housing projects and Black communities, many of which deal with the framework of damages and injunctions. Why do so few of these cases appear in first-year law casebooks?

The environmental justice movement evolved alongside the civil rights movement. Many believe this movement began with the filing of a class action lawsuit by attorney Linda McKeever Bullard to enjoin the Whispering Pines Sanitary Landfill from being built near an enclave of Black-owned homes and very near public schools.[11] Though the court admitted that it would have denied the permit in the first place to protect the safety of the children and the homeowners, it ultimately denied an injunction, which resulted in the landfill's being built. Nevertheless, this case is credited with giving rise to a new branch of the social justice movement. Importantly, Bullard's husband, Dr. Robert Bullard, continued the research he began for the lawsuit and eventually published his findings in

11. Bean v. Sw. Waste Mgmt. Corp., 482 F. Supp. 673 (S.D. Tex. 1979).

the landmark study *Solid Waste Sites and the Black Houston Community*.[12] While he was working on his study, over 500 environmentalists and civil rights activists from around the United States came together in North Carolina for a non-violent protest against a landfill in Warren, North Carolina. Though this effort was also unsuccessful, it turned out to be an inflection point for the movement.[13] Dr. Bullard's study plus the new attention being paid to civil rights and the environment led the U.S. General Accounting Office (GAO) to commission its own study.[14] The GAO study attracted attention to and provided empirical support for claims of environmental racism that had been raised by activists.

BEAN V. SOUTHWESTERN WASTE MGMT. CORP.

482 F. Supp. 673 (1979)

McDONALD, District Judge.

Between November 7 and 28, 1979, the Court conducted an eleven day hearing on the plaintiffs' Motion for Preliminary Injunction. The Court has carefully considered the post-hearing briefs and the arguments of counsel and examined in detail the exhibits offered, many of which contain considerable statistical data. For the reasons stated herein, the plaintiffs' Motion for Preliminary Injunction is denied.

On October 26, 1979, plaintiffs filed their complaint and Motion for Temporary Restraining Order and Preliminary Injunction contesting the decision by the Texas Department of Health ("TDH") to grant Permit No. 1193 to defendant Southwestern Waste Management to operate a Type I solid waste facility in the East Houston-Dyersdale Road area in Harris County. They contend that the decision was, at least in part, motivated by racial discrimination in violation of 42 U.S.C. § 1983 and seek an order revoking the permit.

---

12. Robert Bullard, *Solid Waste Sites and the Black Houston Community*, 53 Sociological Inquiry 273 (1983).

13. *We Birthed the Movement: The Warren County PCB Landfill Protests, 1978–1982*, UNC Univ. Libr. (Aug. 18, 2022), https://library.unc.edu/2022/08/we-birthed-the-movement/.

14. U.S. Gen. Acct. Off., Report: Siting of Hazardous Waste Landfills and Their Correlation with Racial and Economic Status of Surrounding Communities, June 1, 1983, http://archive.gao.gov/d48t13/121648.pdf.

THE PRELIMINARY INJUNCTION

There are four prerequisites to the granting of a preliminary injunction. The plaintiffs must establish: (1) a substantial likelihood of success on the merits, (2) a substantial threat of irreparable injury, (3) that the threatened injury to the plaintiff[s] outweighs the threatened harm the injunction may do to defendant[s], and (4) that granting the preliminary injunction will not disserve the public interest. *Canal Authority of State of Florida v. Callaway*, 489 F.2d 567, 572 (5th Cir. 1974).

The plaintiffs have adequately established that there is a substantial threat of irreparable injury. They complain that they are being deprived of their constitutional rights. That, in itself, may constitute irreparable injury, *Henry v. Greenville Airport Commission*, 284 F.2d 631, 633 (4th Cir. 1960); see *Ethridge v. Rhodes*, 268 F. Supp. 83, 88–89 (S.D. Ohio, E.D.1967), but more is present here. The opening of the facility will affect the entire nature of the community; its land values, its tax base, its aesthetics, the health and safety of its inhabitants, and the operation of Smiley High School, located only 1700 feet from the site. Damages cannot adequately compensate for these types of injuries. Similarly, if a substantial likelihood of success on the merits were shown, there is no doubt that the threatened injury to the plaintiffs would outweigh that to the defendants and that the public interest would not be disserved by granting the plaintiffs an injunction.

The problem is that the plaintiffs have not established a substantial likelihood of success on the merits. The burden on them is to prove discriminatory purpose. *Washington v. Davis*, 426 U.S. 229, 96 S. Ct. 2040, 48 L. Ed. 2d 597 (1976); *Village of Arlington Heights v. Metropolitan Housing Development Corp.*, 429 U.S. 252, 97 S. Ct. 555, 50 L. Ed. 2d 450 (1977). That is, the plaintiffs must show not just that the decision to grant the permit is objectionable or even wrong, but that it is attributable to an intent to discriminate on the basis of race. Statistical proof can rise to the level that it, alone, proves discriminatory intent, as in *Yick Wo v. Hopkins*, 118 U.S. 356, 6 S. Ct. 1064, 30 L. Ed. 220 (1886), and *Gomillion v. Lightfoot*, 364 U.S. 339, 81 S. Ct. 125, 5 L. Ed. 2d 110 (1960), or, this Court would conclude, even in situations less extreme than in those two cases, but the data shown here does not rise to that level. Similarly, statistical proof can be sufficiently supplemented by the types of proof outlined in *Arlington Heights, supra*, to establish purposeful discrimination, but the supplemental proof offered here is not sufficient to do that.

Two different theories of liability have been advanced in this case. The first is that TDH's approval of the permit was part of a pattern or practice by it of discriminating in the placement of solid waste sites. In order to test that theory, one must focus on the sites which TDH has approved and determine the minority population of the areas in which the sites were located on the day that the sites opened. The available statistical data, both city-wide and in the target area, fails to establish a pattern or practice of discrimination by TDH. City-wide, data was produced for the seventeen sites operating with TDH permits as of July 1, 1978. Defendants' Exhibit 21. That data shows that 58.8% of the sites granted permits by TDH were located in census tracts with 25% or less minority population at the time of their opening and that 82.4% of the sites granted permits by TDH were located in census tracts with 50% or less minority population at the time of their opening. In the target area, an area which roughly conforms to the North Forest Independent School District and the newly-created City Council District B and is 70% minority in population, Plaintiffs' Exhibit 2, two (2) sites were approved by TDH. One, the McCarty Road site, was in a census tract with less than 10% minority population at the time of its opening. The other, the site being challenged here, is in a census tract with close to 60% minority population. Defendants' Exhibit 20. Even if we also consider the sites approved by TDWR in the target area, which, as discussed earlier, are not really relevant to TDH's intent to discriminate, no pattern or practice of discrimination is revealed. Of all the solid waste sites opened in the target area, 46.2 to 50% were located in census tracts with less than 25% minority population at the time they opened. Defendants' Exhibit 20 and Plaintiffs' Exhibit 48. It may be that more particularized data would show that even those sites approved in predominantly Anglo census tracts were actually located in minority neighborhoods, but the data available here does not show that. In addition, there was no supplemental evidence, such as that suggested by *Arlington Heights, supra*, which established a pattern or practice of discrimination on the part of TDH.

The plaintiffs' second theory of liability is that TDH's approval of the permit, in the context of the historical placement of solid waste sites and the events surrounding the application, constituted discrimination. Three sets of data were offered to support this theory. Each set, at first blush, looks compelling. On further analysis, however, each set breaks down. Each fails to approach the standard established by *Yick Wo, supra*, and *Gomillion, supra*, and, even when considered with supplementary proof, *Arlington Heights, supra*, fails to establish a likelihood of success in proving discriminatory intent.

The supplementary non-statistical evidence provided by the plaintiffs in the present case raises a number of questions as to why this permit was granted. To begin with, a site proposed for the almost identical location was denied a permit in 1971 by the County Commissioners, who were then responsible for the issuance of such permits. One wonders what happened since that time. The plaintiffs argue that Smiley High School has changed from an Anglo school to one whose student body is predominantly minority. Furthermore, the site is being placed within 1700 feet of Smiley High School, a predominantly black school with no air conditioning, and only somewhat farther from a residential neighborhood. Land use considerations alone would seem to militate against granting this permit. Such evidence seemingly did not dissuade TDH.

If this Court were TDH, it might very well have denied this permit. It simply does not make sense to put a solid waste site so close to a high school, particularly one with no air conditioning. Nor does it make sense to put the land site so close to a residential neighborhood. But I am not TDH and for all I know, TDH may regularly approve of solid waste sites located near schools and residential areas, as illogical as that may seem.

It is not my responsibility to decide whether to grant this site a permit. It is my responsibility to decide whether to grant the plaintiffs a preliminary injunction. From the evidence before me, I can say that the plaintiffs have established that the decision to grant the permit was both unfortunate and insensitive. I cannot say that the plaintiffs have established a substantial likelihood of proving that the decision to grant the permit was motivated by purposeful racial discrimination in violation of 42 U.S.C. § 1983. This Court is obligated, as all Courts are, to follow the precedent of the United States Supreme Court and the evidence adduced thus far does not meet the magnitude required by *Arlington Heights, supra*.

PERMANENT RELIEF

The failure of the plaintiffs to obtain a preliminary injunction does not, of course, mean that they are foreclosed from obtaining permanent relief. Because of the time pressures involved, extensive pre-trial discovery was impossible in this case. Assuming the case goes forward, discovery could lead to much more solid and persuasive evidence for either side. Ideally, it would resolve a number of the questions which the Court considers unanswered.

Where, for instance, are the solid waste sites located in each census tract? The plaintiffs produced evidence that in census tract 434, a predominantly Anglo tract, the site was located next to a black community named Riceville. If that was true of most sites in predominantly Anglo census tracts, the outcome of this case would be quite different.

How large an area does a solid waste site affect? If it affects an area a great deal smaller than that of a census tract, it becomes particularly important to know where in each census tract the site is located. If it affects an area larger than that of a census tract, then a target area analysis becomes much more persuasive.

How are solid waste site locations selected? It may be that private contractors consider a number of alternative locations and then select one in consultation with city or county officials. If that is so, it has tremendous implications for the search for discriminatory intent. It may be that a relatively limited number of areas can adequately serve as a Type I solid waste site. If that is so, the placement of sites in those areas becomes a lot less suspicious, even if large numbers of minorities live there. Either way, this is information which should be adduced. At this point, the Court still does not know how, why, and by whom the East Houston-Dyersdale Road location was selected.

What factors entered into TDH's decision to grant the permit? The proximity of the site to Smiley High School and a residential neighborhood and the lack of air conditioning facilities at the former were emphasized to the Court. It is still unknown how much, if any, consideration TDH gave to these factors. The racial composition of the neighborhood and the racial distribution of solid waste sites in Houston were primary concerns of the plaintiffs. It remains unclear to what degree TDH was informed of these concerns.

CONCLUSION

At this juncture, the decision of TDH seems to have been insensitive and illogical. Sitting as the hearing examiner for TDH, based upon the evidence adduced, this Court would have denied the permit. But this Court has a different role to play, and that is to determine whether the plaintiffs have established a substantial likelihood of proving that TDH's decision to issue the permit was motivated by purposeful discrimination in violation of 42 U.S.C. § 1983 as construed by superior courts. That being so, it is hereby ORDERED, ADJUDGED, and DECREED that the plaintiffs' Motion for a Preliminary Injunction be, and the same is, DENIED. For the reasons stated above, the defendants' Motions to Dismiss are also DENIED.

NOTES ON *BEAN V. SOUTHWESTERN WASTE MGMT. CORP.*

1. **A Flummoxed Court.** This court says clearly that it would not have granted the permit itself, but it nevertheless denies the injunction. Consider the way the legal argument is related to the way the plaintiffs present the statistics and how that may be different from the way the court interprets those same statistics. Recall that the collection and organization of those statistics is what set attorney Linda McKeever Bullard's husband, Dr. Robert Bullard, on his career path for environmental justice.

2. **Permanent Damages.** How do the district court's unanswered questions (left for another court to consider if the case moves forward) related to the potential award of permanent damages relate to its view of the circumstances at hand?

Grassroots Campaigns Grow Together

Elsewhere in the country, a focused and informed "next chapter" of the civil rights movement was also taking shape. Hazel Johnson was born in Louisiana in 1935 in an area now known to have been hazardous. She was the only one of four children to survive past her first birthday, and both of her parents were deceased by the time she was 12 years old. Years later, when she met her husband and moved to the Chicago area, she found a new home in the neighborhood of Altgeld Gardens. Though she had been an activist who worked on housing segregation issues, Ms. Johnson's focus shifted when her husband died of lung cancer at the age of 41, despite his having very few risk factors. At that time, Ms.

Johnson began speaking to others in her community and discovered that many had similar illnesses, breathing problems, high rates of miscarriages, and birth defects. After conducting some research, Ms. Johnson found that her beloved neighborhood, Altgeld Gardens, a public housing project built for Black World War II veterans and their families, was built amid the highest concentration of hazardous waste sites in the nation. She subsequently founded the organization People for Community Recovery and worked tirelessly to mitigate the hazards in her home and to call attention to and bring justice to her community, which had been egregiously mistreated by the government planners of the public housing project.[15] Her activism included mentoring and working with young activists and community organizers in Chicago, including future president Barack Obama. Hazel Johnson had also traveled to Washington, D.C., to be featured at the first National People of Color Environmental Leadership Summit in 1991. Shortly thereafter, in 1992, the U.S. Environmental Protection Agency (EPA) established the Office of Environmental Equity.[16] Now named the Office of Environmental Justice, it devotes resources to issues stemming from the building of public housing projects on top of toxic sites decades ago.

Reflection

Given the attention given to both racial justice and environmental issues in the media, why is there less attention given to environmental racism/justice?

As the law of property is administered at the state level, it is notable that some states have, by statute, become involved in the environmental justice movement. In California it is required that cities and towns adopt policies in their General Plan to address environmental justice,[17] and

---

15. *See generally* Hazel M. Johnson's Legacy, PEOPLE FOR COMMUNITY RECOVERY, https://www.peopleforcommunityrecovery.org/our-story/legacy (last visited Feb. 16, 2024).

16. This was changed to the Office of Environmental Justice in 1994, which is the name under which it operates today.

17. Calif. S.B. 100 (Planning for Healthy Communities Act).

jurisdictions in California have done so.[18] Other states, including Minnesota, have articulated an environmental justice framework.[19] The forward progress is heartening, and the urgency of climate change is only increasing. Yet, despite this urgency, it may feel to some as though a national reckoning with and grieving for the needless loss of life has not occurred—and that one is needed before a real environmental justice effort may begin.

Skill: Rule Synthesis

Recall the basic IRAC structure for legal analysis: issue, rule, analysis, and conclusion. Understanding that the analysis is the most important component, the most time and attention should be spent on developing it. The last chapter described some best practices for articulating an issue statement that will prompt a robust analysis. But before turning to the analysis, we will first focus on the skill of rule synthesis. Though it may seem that the rule is the simplest part of the IRAC method because it is already articulated by a court or in a statute, certain skills and best practices can help ensure that the rule you articulate is synthesized from the most relevant cases and is tailored and responsive to the specifically stated, focused issue.

Law students are inundated with a great deal of reading and material each semester. Engaging with this practice of rule synthesis forces you to consider and work with the caselaw in a more active way, which helps with retention of the material. Educational psychologists have created a taxonomy, known as Bloom's Taxonomy, that describes different ways that brains may optimize learning:[20]

---

18. *See, e.g.*, *Environmental Justice Framework*, San Francisco Gen. Plan, https://generalplan.sfplanning.org/Environmental_Justice_Framework.htm (last visited Feb. 16, 2024).

19. Ned Brooks, Minnesota Pollution Control Agency, *Environmental Justice Framework: Our Vision, Strategies, and Implementation Actions for Integrating Environmental Justice Principles into Our Work*, Doc. No. p-gen5-05, May 2022, https://www.pca.state.mn.us/sites/default/files/p-gen5-05.pdf.

20. Copyright © Vanderbilt University Center for Teaching. Reprinted with permission.

BLOOM'S TAXONOMY

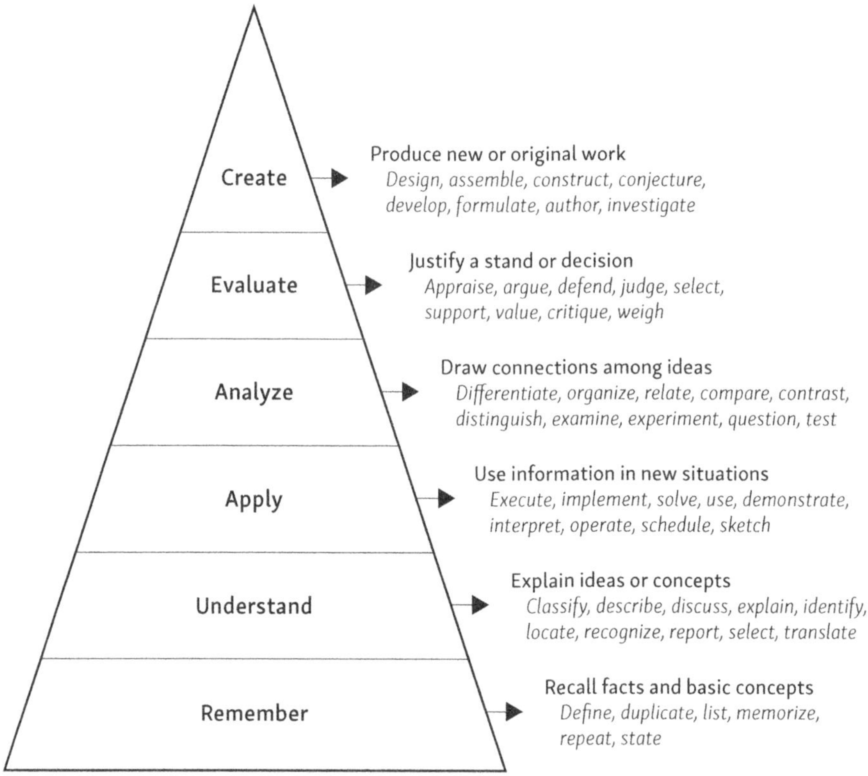

Most of the work of a law student—reading and briefing cases—is in the bottom two tiers of the pyramid. Though foundational, these tiers are not the most efficient for working with and retaining material. Engaging in a rule-synthesis exercise for every module or group of cases related to a particular topic will help students to apply and analyze the doctrine. Repeated practice will help to build this skill and make it second nature so that it can be employed automatically, even in high-stress or high-pressure situations.

The threshold task is to identify the *type* of rule at hand: is it a rigid rule or a flexible standard? An example of a rigid rule is that people must be a certain age (18 years old) to vote. This is an effective rule because we collectively agree that some people are too young to have the capacity to vote. The age of 18 is a bright-line criterion that the law has made and rigidly adheres to. The rule is predictable, easy to administer, and promotes fairness and justice in that it applies evenly to all people. However, some might argue that rigid rules can result in poor outcomes around the edges—for example, there may be people under the voting age who are very qualified to vote but are not yet allowed to, while there may be others over the voting age who are relatively less qualified. Still, for all the reasons stated above, we accept this rigid rule. Meanwhile, other areas of the law require flexible standards. Nuisance is an example of a flexible standard. Though these standards do promote justice between parties, they can take a great deal more time and energy to administer and may be a great deal less predictable for individuals who are seeking clear expectations in the law.

Rules also can also have different structures. Nuisance is a balancing test wherein the rights of property owners are balanced against one another under the specific facts and circumstances of the case. Adverse possession, which we dealt with in the previous chapter, is an element-based rule. There are various types of element-based rules, and some, like adverse possession, require that *all* elements must be proven by a certain standard. Others require consideration of all elements but only that most (a preponderance) or some of them are met. Each individual should find a way to define and categorize the type and structure of the rule in a way that makes sense for them. Different minds may work differently, and in many cases, a diversity of thought and presentation may help others to see things in new ways.

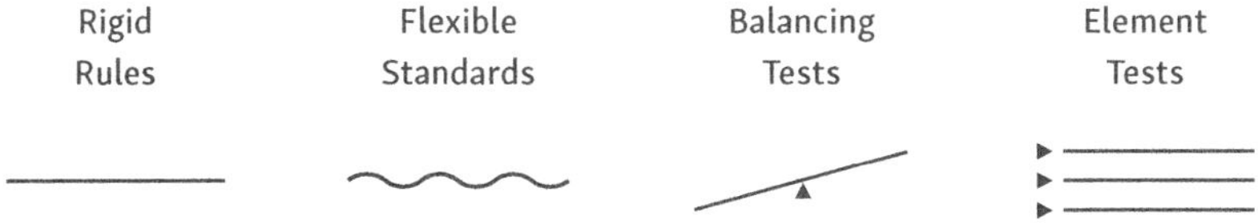

In a rule-synthesis exercise, you will look to already completed case briefs, identify the area in each brief that considers the rule that the court was dealing with, and identify the holding of the court. Understanding how these rules work together is the purpose of rule synthesis. Some think of synthesis as building rules from the component cases. It is the opposite of the work performed in the analysis section, where the rule is dismantled and the specific components are used to address only what is needed in the fact pattern. In this way, a strong rule synthesis is the foil for and companion to a strong legal analysis.

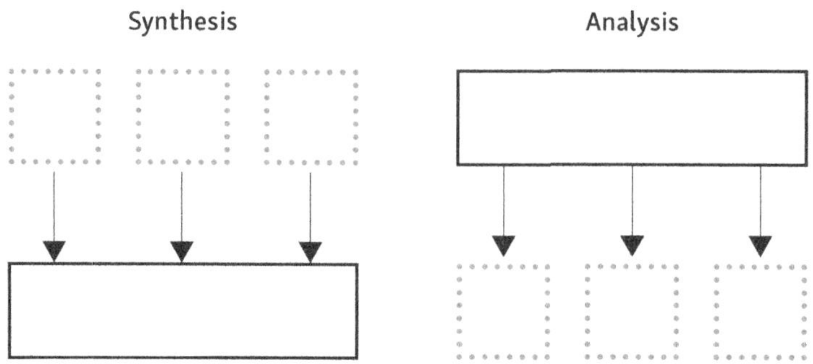

This is work that is particular to the discipline of the study of law. Accordingly, our initial example is simple and accessible and intended to illustrate the skill and its use without the weight of doctrine. We start with a rule that is both common and simply stated: "No throwing!" The protracted version of the rule is as follows: *The throwing of objects with intent to harm or injure is punishable by law where the party knew or reasonably should have known the likely result.* This rule is a good one to start with because many have likely heard it outside the law school classroom. This exercise is intended to encourage you to let go (for a few minutes) of the stresses of law school and reconnect with what you know about rules.

In considering the brief descriptions of the following short "cases," strive for this very basic level of detail of ***salient*** (facts on which the holding turns) facts in case briefs. There may be some dispute or discussion with regard to the holdings, but such is the case with many fine points of the law. Consider the actions of the three parties: Nanak, aged 6; Krish, age 4; and Kamal, age 2:[21]

21. If these seem strangely personal, it is because they are loosely based on real life. The author has three sons who were, at one time, these ages. And they knew better.

Case #	Salient Facts	Holding
1	Nanak (age 6) picks up a block that Krish (age 4) is playing with and throws it, hitting Krish in the head.	Timeout.
2	Nanak (age 6) accidentally drops his cheese on the sidewalk, then picks it up and throws it into a trash can that he is unable to reach.	No timeout.
2.5	Kamal (age 2) sees his brother throwing cheese, and in an attempt to mimic the gesture, picks up a rock and throws it.	No timeout.
3	In a game of catch, Nanak (age 6) throws a ball to Krish (age 4), hitting him on the head.	No timeout.
3.5	In retaliation, Krish (age 4) picks up a pinecone and tries to throw it at Nanak, but it slips from his hand before he is able.	Timeout.
4	Nanak (age 6), in an effort to help Krish eat, throws a fork across the room, poking Krish (age 4) in the head and resulting in a lot of crying.	Timeout.

Considering these "cases" leads to a better understanding. As you perform this exercise and think about how the rule may apply, nuances in the cases will become clearer, such as whether or not *actual* throwing was necessary, the context of the throwing, how the intent to injure related to damages, and also what the parties may have known or reasonably should have known. This will not happen if you are simply transcribing a rule from a book to an outline.

The most important skill is application. In order to complete this short exercise and bring together the importance and value of a protracted rule synthesis, consider the following short fact pattern:

While in basketball class, Nanak (age 6) passes the ball to Krish (age 4), who is unable to catch it. As a result, the ball hits Krish on the nose (which hurts—a lot.). Trying to hide his tears, Krish gets his water bottle, but instead of drinking, he decides to open it and throw the contents on Nanak.

Having already completed the exercise of crafting and articulating a synthesized rule will help you to identify the issues in this short fact pattern *and* to find ways to compare and distinguish the facts of the precedent cases and the facts at hand. This is an essential lawyering skill.

Let's return to the doctrine of nuisance. Though nuisance is heavily dependent on the parties, facts, and circumstances at hand, there are certain frameworks and factors that the common law has established to address the parties to a dispute. Accordingly, the synthesized rule for nuisance is that it is an area of law "that provides remedies for conduct that causes substantial and unreasonable harm to the use and enjoyment of land." Some additional factors that courts consider include who "came to the nuisance," which is a question of which party had notice about reasonable use and enjoyment of land, and the extent, gravity, and character of the harm, all of which may be distinct. In some cases, there may be what the common law refers to as an "unusually sensitive plaintiff"—which raises questions relating to how the harm is received by the plaintiff and whether it is unfair or unreasonable to ask the defendant to work around the plaintiff's special circumstances or sensitivities. With regard to the remedies available, courts seek to understand how easily each party could avoid the nuisance and the fairness of asking the parties to do so. There are as many ways of understanding and synthesizing these rules as there are cases. Practicing the level of detail of salient facts required for a rule synthesis by working with the rules that are the subject of class discussion is a wise choice.

SUGGESTIONS FOR FURTHER READING

ROBERT D. BULLARD, DUMPING IN DIXIE: RACE, CLASS, AND ENVIRONMENTAL QUALITY (3d ed. 2000).

BARRY FRIEDMAN, THE WILL OF THE PEOPLE: HOW PUBLIC OPINION HAS INFLUENCED THE SUPREME COURT AND SHAPED THE MEANING OF THE CONSTITUTION (2010).

KENT GREENFIELD, THE MYTH OF CHOICE: PERSONAL RESPONSIBILITY IN A WORLD OF LIMITS (2011).

Ernesto Hernandez-Lopez, *Sriracha Shutdown: Hot Sauce Lessons on Local Privilege and Race*, 46 SETON HALL L. REV. 189 (2015).

DORCETA F. TAYLOR, TOXIC COMMUNITIES: ENVIRONMENTAL RACISM, INDUSTRIAL POLLUTION, AND RESIDENTIAL MOBILITY (2014).

FOUR

Non-Possessory Rights in Land

Beyond *Shelley v. Kraemer*— Levittowns and Planned Communities

Quiet isn't always peace,
And the norms and notions of what "just is"
Isn't always justice.

—Amanda Gorman,
National Youth Poet Laureate 2017[1]

When we think of interests in property, we think of land and tangible property. It can be difficult to think of nonpossessory interests in property as important to our institutions and structures. Understanding and navigating the law around nonpossessory rights is vitally important for understanding how systems of segregation across the United States persisted even after segregation became unlawful. In the last chapter, we discussed the rules of nuisance and their basis in certain "entitlements" in property. In this chapter, we discuss the ways in which some groups may disproportionately (and understandably) fail to demand their entitlements and, in doing so, relinquish some interests in property.

1. Excerpted from Amanda Gorman, "The Hill We Climb: An Inaugural Poem for the Country" (2021). Gorman read this poem during the inauguration ceremony of President Joseph R. Biden Jr. on January 20, 2021.

This chapter begins with a high-level overview of the various types of nonpossessory rights in property, including easements, covenants, and equitable servitudes, followed by an inspection of how the requirements for "notice" may be more complicated for some parties who exist as "others" in communities and how that may result in a loss of rights in property. Many students will study the landmark case *Shelley v. Kraemer*,[2] either in a property law course or in a constitutional law course (or both), but this text seeks to look beyond *Shelley* to understand the way that racially restrictive covenants in deeds have impacted not only urban and suburban planning but also the shape of our nation. Finally, the chapter concludes with an introduction to the most important part of the IRAC method, the legal analysis, as well as a model for how to apply a rule to a novel set of facts and avoid a premature conclusion.

Distinguishing Nonpossessory Rights

There are many terms of art in this area of the law, and some of them have different meanings depending on the context in which they are used. Precision in language is always important for attorneys, but keeping focused on the underlying concepts can help maintain clarity. The word "servitude" is one such word. It is used to describe the umbrella of nonpossessory interests that run with the land, but it is distinct from an "equitable servitude," which is a particular type of nonpossessory interest that is sometimes created by a court when a covenant is not established. All of these interests are interests in real property, which means that they can be owned, transferred, sold, inherited, bequeathed, or gifted. In short, they are alienable.

2. 334 U.S. 1 (1948).

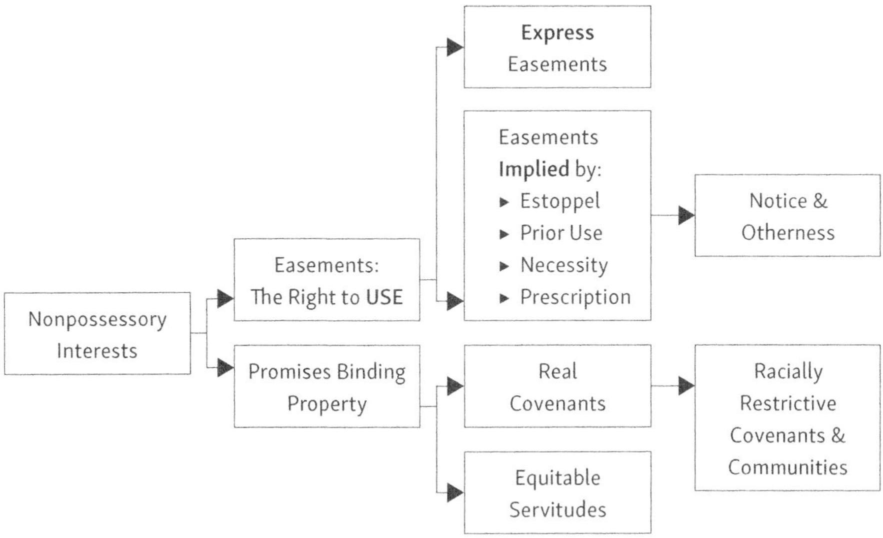

Easements: The Right to Use

An *easement* is the right to use the land of another. This is often an affirmative right to use land, for example, a right of way. The right to use a path across property that belongs to another is an example of an easement. The two parcels involved were traditionally referred to as the dominant estate and the servient estate, but these terms have been replaced by more modern and accurate language and are now referred to as the *benefitted estate* and the *burdened estate*. In the example illustrated below, Parcel A is the benefitted estate because it gets the benefit of using the path, or easement, across Parcel B. Parcel B is the burdened estate because it bears the burden of allowing Parcel A's use. Because easements are interests in property, they are subject to the statute of frauds; accordingly, their transfer should be in writing. All easements are classified as either *appurtenant*, or running with the land, meaning that the easement binds successive owners, or *in gross*, meaning that there is no benefitted estate but only a party that has the right to use a burdened estate. Easements in gross are frequently used by utility companies that want to maintain poles or power lines.

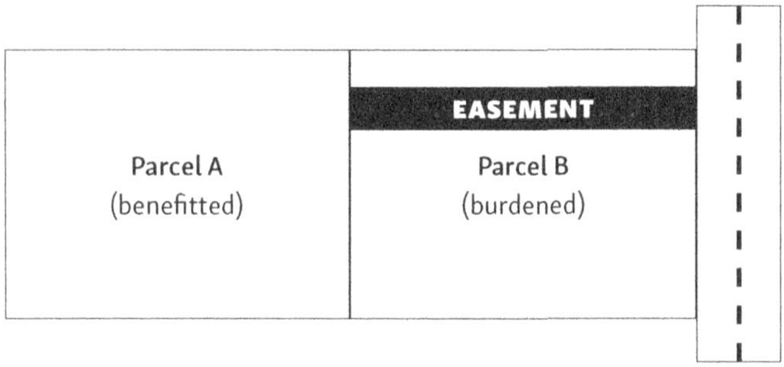

Frequently, adjacent property owners begin and continue use of neighboring property (that is, they establish easements) without putting anything in writing. In some cases, it would be unjust not to recognize these established easements despite their noncompliance with the statute of frauds, and for that reason, a number of types of implied easements have been created under the common law. The common law has provided some basic structure around each type of implied easement. Recall, however, that each implied easement arises from a dispute about property, unlike express easements, which are born from bargained-for exchanges between parties. The basics of easements implied by necessity are as follows:

Easement Implied by Estoppel (Irrevocable License)	This property interest has all the features of the equitable remedy of estoppel. Although courts will consider the totality of the circumstances, including the relationship between the parties, the following elements must be met: ✓ The burdened estate must have expressly permitted initial entry and use ✓ The user of the easement reasonably and justifiably relied on permission not being revoked ✓ Substantial change in position of the benefitted state ✓ Only finding an easement would prevent an injustice between the parties.

Easement Implied by Prior Use (Quasi Easement) **Previous common ownership and severance required.**	This type of easement permits a court to reach an agreement that the parties *would have* reached had they discussed an easement at severance. It requires ✓ Unity of ownership severed ✓ One parcel to benefit the other ✓ The use in question was in place prior to the severance ✓ The use was visible or apparent at the time of the severance ✓ The easement is reasonably necessary for the use and enjoyment of the benefitted estate
Easement Implied by Necessity (Right of Way) **Previous common ownership and severance required.**	This type of easement is most commonly used for landlocked parcels, that is, those properties that have no means of entry or exit (ingress and egress) without use of an easement. Cases related to easements implied by necessity often make inquiries not about the necessity of the easement but about the location and scope of the easement. In some cases, a previously available route becomes blocked and a new easement must be established, requiring a court to use its power of equity to determine the manner and extent to which the burdened estate must be burdened to accommodate the needs of the benefitted estate.
Easement Implied by Prescription	This type of easement is parallel to adverse possession except that a successful claim wins the right to *use* property instead of the right to *own* property. Elements will be interpreted accordingly and include ✓ Adversity/acquiescence ✓ Continuous ✓ Known, open, and notorious ✓ Exclusive ✓ Actual ✓ Statutory period

The Problem with Notice[3]

Implied easements, in order to be established and recognized by courts, require some notice to and acquiescence by burdened estate holders. The permissive nature of implied easements, particularly easements implied by estoppel and prescription, means that an owner of a burdened estate who does not speak up about the use of property may find that their property is bound by an easement for their lack of protest, therefore dispossessing them of an interest in property. This standard assumes that owners will speak up for their property rights without considering the circumstances and reasons why they might not.

> **Reflection**
>
> Consider a time when you felt like an outlier in a group. How might being the one distinct person among many similar people impact conduct?

Consider that through the history of the United States, neighborhoods have been segregated along racial and cultural lines for a variety of reasons having to do with institutions, systems, structures, and social values, both collective and individual. History, culture, and statistics reveal that upward social mobility requires that people of color move to predominantly white neighborhoods. Doing so can make that owner of property feel like an "other." Similarly, immigrants who are new to the country may feel a similar sense of being out of place and seek opportunities to quietly fit in. Feeling "othered" or like an outlier in a space has a particular psychological impact.[4] For many, it results in their quietly absorbing the traditions and norms of a space and learning the unwritten rules before speaking up. This can be particularly true when a history of tension or even violence underlies the dynamic; members of communities who have weathered violence are a great deal less likely to

3. Credit for this section goes to a former student, Agnes Kolbeck, who ruminated on the concept of notice in a most thoughtful and insightful way that has served as inspiration for this work.

4. For more on this phenomenon in the workplace, see generally Rosebeth Moss Kanter, *A Tale of "O": On Being Different in an Organization* (1980), and the related training video, Trainer's Toolchest, *A Tale of "O" Video on Diversity*, YouTube (May 21, 2010), https://www.youtube.com/watch?v=p56b6nzslaU.

speak up when they see a non-violent or "friendly" use of their owned property. This failure to speak up upon seeing a neighbor use their property may result in an easement implied by estoppel or prescription, a burden on their interest in property to the benefit of their neighbor.

Types of Notice

Actual Notice → There is evidence that a party is aware of the use. Example: a letter written by the holder of the burdened estate acknowledging the easement.

Constructive Notice → The legal fiction that a party has received notice; deemed notice. If the easement is recorded in a deed, it serves as constructive notice.

Inquiry Notice → Based on the facts, a reasonable person would inquire about the use of the property and seek further information that would allow them to decide how to proceed with regard to their property rights.

The concept of notice seems to the common law to be one that is objective and reasonable and that fits well in a set of elements giving structure to a rule. In practice, however, an impact of being an "other" might be a feeling of unawareness of unwritten rules. In a set of circumstances where almost everything seems foreign, or at least outside the cultural norms to which someone is accustomed, it can be difficult to determine when to speak up to grant or withhold permission in order to protect property rights. Consider the position of a Black family which has worked tirelessly and undertaken many risks to move from their neighborhood to an "upper-class" white neighborhood. They worked hard and saved to purchase the parcel adjacent to a neighborhood pond, and they feel fortunate and happy with their home. Having moved here from an urban neighborhood, they are acutely aware of the many forms racial discrimination can take and have seen it turn to violence. They are the only Black family in the neighborhood, and so they feel under a particular sort of scrutiny as well as a desire to fit in with their neighbors and make their new home work. When this family sees their white neighbors walking across their lawn to access the pond, they smile and wave, not wanting to make themselves stand out or upset anyone.

Though this is an entirely fabricated fact pattern, it is one that is likely common. In it, we can see how the weight of being different can affect one's actions (or inactions)—here, it resulted in a wave and a smile that could be reasonably read as a continuing permission or, if it continues, as an understanding or reliance that will become an easement. The standards for notice take into account how a reasonable and diligent owner would act, but they fail to consider the psychological impact of standing out.

Property Promises for Individuals: Covenants and Equitable Servitudes

Covenants are sometimes referred to as "negative servitudes" because, instead of giving the holder an affirmative right to use the property, a covenant often relates to a promise *not* to use the property in some way. For example, to preserve an area's residential quality, property owners in a residential neighborhood may create a covenant to never use property for commercial purposes. As the name suggests, a "real covenant" has many features of a contract that relates to real property. Like an easement, a real covenant is an interest in property, and accordingly, one element is that it must exist in writing to be in compliance with the statute of frauds. But there are additional elements that must be met for a real covenant to be valid.

To determine the validity of a real covenant, courts first look back to the time of the creation of the covenant and seek evidence that the original parties intended to bind successive owners of the property. This *intent to bind successive owners* is an important part of holding that the covenant is "appurtenant," or that it runs with the land.

Real covenants are also required to *touch and concern* the land. This means that the promise must somehow be related to the use of the property and is not something that can be fungible or traded. Real property/land is a unique asset; the law affords it special treatment in many cases because of the understanding that it is not fungible, particularly residential property. In some disputes, parties may be made whole with compensation in money damages; however, because of property's unique nature, the loss of property frequently requires the remedy of specific performance. Touch and concern uses this same logic: because property is unique, the promise related to the covenant must relate to use of the unique property.

Finally, courts require *privity or notice* of the covenant. Formerly, both horizontal and vertical privity were required of a real covenant; if one of those were to fail, then notice would suffice for the court to find and enforce an equitable servitude. The modern trend is a narrowing of the gap between them. Horizontal privity requires that the original owners of the property had an agreement regarding the covenant that would bind successors. Vertical privity requires that the entire interest in property was passed on to each successive owner. Both horizontal and vertical privity were required for privity of estate. But courts now tend to be less rigid about the requirements of privity, asking only that the owners of the property had adequate notice of the covenant that was intended to bind successors in interest in it.

Together, these features of real covenants distinguish the doctrine of property from that of contracts. A real covenant may bind parties to promises with respect to their property that they had no part in negotiating. Often, a real covenant is enforced long after the parties that established it have become unavailable, and in this way, those owners bind the property long after they are gone. In contrast, in interpreting and resolving a contract dispute, considerable weight is paid to the bargained-for exchange between and among the parties.

Understanding the constitutional limitations on public property[5] and state actions,[6] property owners used real covenants as a way to exercise control over their privately held residential property in a way that comported with the spirit and letter of the law in the early 20th century. In 1926, in *Corrigan v. Buckley*,[7] a case involving the validity of a racially restrictive covenant, the U.S. Supreme Court upheld the covenant over objections that it violated the 5th, 13th, and 14th Amendments and was counter to public policy. Writing for a unanimous Court, Justice Sanford stated,

> It is obvious that none of these amendments prohibited private individuals from entering into contracts respecting the control and disposition of their own property, and there is no

5. *See* Ch. 2, *supra*.
6. See Ch. 6, *infra*; Buchanan v. Warley, 245 U.S. 60 (1917).
7. 271 U.S. 323 (1926).

> color whatever to the contention that they rendered the indenture void. And plainly, the claim urged in this Court that they were to be looked to, in connection with the provisions of the Revised Statutes and the decisions of the courts, in determining the contention, earnestly pressed, that the indenture is void as being "against public policy" does not involve a constitutional question....[8]

Encouraged by this upholding of racially restrictive covenants, the National Association of Real Estate Boards created a model covenant which led to a sharp increase in the use of racially restrictive covenants in 1926 and 1927.[9] In this way, racially restrictive covenants became prevalent across the United States. During the Great Migration, to escape the oppression of Jim Crow laws, Black people moved out of the American South and into the northern and western states, only to find that these northern jurisdictions were using tools—condoned by the government—to effect racial segregation.

CORRIGAN V. BUCKLEY

271 U.S. 323 (1926)

APPEAL FROM THE COURT OF APPEALS OF THE DISTRICT OF COLUMBIA

Justice Sanford, Edward T., delivered the opinion of the Court.

This is a suit in equity brought by John J. Buckley in the Supreme Court of the District of Columbia against Irene H. Corrigan and Helen Curits to enjoin the conveyance of certain real estate from one to the other of the defendants.

The case made by the bill is this: the parties are citizens of the United States, residing in the District. The plaintiff and the defendant Corrigan are white persons, and the defendant Curtis is a person of the negro race. In 1921, thirty white persons, including the plaintiff and the defendant Corrigan, owning twenty-five parcels of land, improved by dwelling

8. *Id.* at 330.

9. Cheryl W. Thompson et al., *Racial Covenants, a Relic of the Past, Are Still on the Books Across the Country*, heard on MORNING EDITION, Nov. 17, 2021, https://www.npr.org/2021/11/17/1049052531/racial-covenants-housing-discrimination.

houses, situated on S Street, between 18th and New Hampshire Avenue, in the City of Washington, executed an indenture, duly recorded, in which they recited that, for their mutual benefit and the best interests of the neighborhood comprising these properties, they mutually covenanted and agreed that no part of these properties should ever be used or occupied by, or sold, leased or given to, any person of the negro race or blood, and that this covenant should run with the land and bind their respective heirs and assigns for twenty one years from and after its date.

In 1922, the defendants entered into a contract by which the defendant Corrigan, although knowing the defendant Curtis to be a person of the negro race, agreed to sell her a certain lot, with dwelling house, included within the terms of the indenture, and the defendant Curtis, although knowing of the existence and terms of the indenture, agreed to purchase it. The defendant Curtis demanded that this contract of sale be carried out, and, despite the protest of other parties to the indenture, the defendant Corrigan had stated that she would convey the lot to the defendant Curtis.

The bill alleged that this would cause irreparable injury to the plaintiff and the other parties to the indenture, and that the plaintiff, having no adequate remedy at law, was entitled to have the covenant of the defendant Corrigan specifically enforced in equity by an injunction preventing the defendants from carrying the contract of sale into effect, and prayed, in substance, that the defendant Corrigan be enjoined during twenty-one years from the date of the indenture, from conveying the lot to the defendant Curtis, and that the defendant Curtis be enjoined from taking title to the lot during such period, and from using or occupying it.

The defendant Corrigan moved to dismiss the bill on the grounds that the "indenture or covenant made the basis of said bill" is (1) "void in that the same is contrary to and in violation of the Constitution of the United States," and (2) "is void in that the same is contrary to public policy." And the defendant Curtis moved to dismiss the bill on the ground that it appears therein that the indenture or covenant "is void in that it attempts to deprive the defendant, the said Helen Curtis, and others of property, without due process of law; abridges the privilege and immunities of citizens of the United States, including the defendant Helen Curtis, and other persons within this jurisdiction [and denies them] the equal protection of the law, and therefore, is forbidden by the

Constitution of the United States, and especially by the Fifth, Thirteenth, and Fourteenth Amendments thereof, and the laws enacted is aid and under the sanction of the said Thirteenth and Fourteenth Amendments."

Both of these motions to dismiss were overruled, with leave to answer. And the defendants having elected to stand on their motions, a final decree was entered enjoining them as prayed in the bill. This was affirmed, on appeal, by the court of appeals of the District. The defendants then prayed an appeal to this Court on the ground that such review was authorized under the provisions of §250 of the Judicial Code—as it then stood, before the amendment made by the Jurisdictional Act of 1925—in that the case was one "involving the construction or application of the Constitution of the United States" and "in which the construction of" certain laws of the United States, namely, §§1977, 1978, 1979 of the Revised Statutes were "drawn in question" by them. This appeal was allowed in June, 1924.

Under the pleadings in the present case, the only constitutional question involved was that arising under the assertions in the motions to dismiss that the indenture or covenant which is the basis of the bill, is "void" in that it is contrary to and forbidden by the Fifth, Thirteenth and Fourteenth Amendments. This contention is entirely lacking in substance or color of merit. The Fifth Amendment "is a limitation only upon the powers of the General government," *Talton v. Mayes*, 163 U.S. 376, 382, and is not directed against the action of individuals. The Thirteenth Amendment denouncing slavery and involuntary servitude—that is, a condition of enforced compulsory service of one to another—does not in other matters protect the individual rights of persons of the negro race. *Hodges v. United States*, 203 U.S. 1, 16, 18. and the prohibitions of the Fourteenth Amendment "have reference to state action exclusively, and not to any action of private individuals." *Virginia v. Rives*, 100 U.S. 313, 318; *United States v. Harris*, 106 U.S. 629, 639. "It is state action of a particular character that is prohibited. Individual invasion of individual rights is not the subject matter of the Amendment." *Civil Rights Cases*, 109 U.S. 3, 11. It is obvious that none of these amendments prohibited private individuals from entering into contracts respecting the control and disposition of their own property, and there is no color whatever for the contention that they rendered the indenture void. And plainly, the claim urged in this Court that they were to be looked to, in connection with the provisions of the Revised Statutes and the decisions of the courts, in determining the contention, earnestly pressed, that the indenture is void as being "against public policy" does not involve a constitutional question within the meaning of the Code provision.

The claim that the defendants drew in question the "construction" of §§ 1977, 1978 and 1979 of the Revised Statutes, is equally unsubstantial. The only question raised as to these statutes under the pleadings was the assertion in the motion interposed by the defendant Curtis that the indenture is void in that it is forbidden by the laws enacted in aid and under the sanction of the Thirteenth and Fourteenth Amendments. Assuming that this contention drew in question the "construction" of these statutes, as distinguished from their "application," it is obvious, upon their face that, while they provide, *inter alia,* that all persons and citizens shall have equal right with white citizens to make contracts and acquire property, they, like the Constitutional Amendment under whose sanction they were enacted, do not in any manner prohibit or invalidate contracts entered into by private individuals in respect to the control and disposition of their own property. There is no color for the contention that they rendered the indenture void; nor was it claimed in this Court that they had, in and of themselves, any such effect.

We therefore conclude that neither the constitutional nor statutory questions relied on as grounds for the appeal to this Court have any substantial quality or color of merit, or afford any jurisdictional basis for the appeal.

And while it was further urged in this Court that the decrees of the courts below in themselves deprived the defendants of their liberty and property without due process of law, in violation of the Fifth and Fourteenth Amendments, this contention likewise cannot serve as a jurisdictional basis for the appeal. Assuming that such a contention, if of a substantial character, might have constituted ground for an appeal under paragraph 3 of the Code provision, it was not raised by the petition for the appeal or by any assignment of error, either in the court of appeals or in this Court, and it likewise is lacking is substance. The defendants were given a full hearing in both courts; they were not denied any constitutional or statutory right, and there is no semblance of ground for any contention that the decrees were so plainly arbitrary and contrary to law as to be acts of mere spoliation. *See Delmar Jockey Club v. Missouri,* [210 U.S. 324,] 335. Mere error of a court, if any there be, in a judgment entered after a full hearing does not constitute a denial of due process of law. *Central Land Co. v. Laidley*, 159 U.S. 103, 112; *Jones v. Buffalo Creek Coal Co.*, 245 U.S. 328, 329.

It results that, in the absence of any substantial constitutional or statutory question giving us jurisdiction of this appeal under the provisions of § 250 of the Judicial Code, we cannot determine upon the merits the contentions earnestly pressed by the defendants in this Court that the indenture is not only void because contrary to public policy, but is also of such a discriminatory character that a court of equity will not lend its aid by enforcing the specific performance of the covenant. These are questions involving a consideration of rules not expressed in any constitutional or statutory provision, but claimed to be a part of the common or general law in force in the District of Columbia; and, plainly, they may not be reviewed under this appeal unless jurisdiction of the case is otherwise acquired.

Hence, without a consideration of these questions, the appeal must be, and is

Dismissed for want of jurisdiction.

Real Covenants for Communities: Mutual Enforcement and Common Interest

Enforcement of real covenants between individual landowners gave rise to a new opportunity, one where groups of landowners could establish and enforce a set of mutual covenants, even when those landowners' properties were non-adjacent. These arrangements only amplified the effects of racially restrictive covenants. Commonly enforced covenants, or common schemes, are particularly useful in planned communities, where a group of property owners come together to create a desirable residential community. Many of the covenants in these shared communities are practical, raise the standard of living, and may include a sharing of burdens and resources in a way that benefits the group. Maintenance agreements, recreational resources, and aesthetic standards are all common examples of covenants relating to shared resources in a planned community. In the early mid-twentieth century, as many American soldiers were returning home following the end of World War II, the U.S. population continued to trend away from urban areas. Accordingly, the marketability of shared communities often depended on the nature of their mutual covenants, and the racial composition of a community had a profound impact on its desirability and market value.

Whether in the city or the suburbs, "condominiums, cooperatives, and planned-unit development with home-owners associations have become a widely accepted form of real property ownership."[10] Their popularity and prevalence has resulted in courts' recognizing a mutuality of obligations in "common interests" or "common schemes." Though the law of real covenants originated from agreements between two adjacent owners of property, it has evolved to allow a group of nonadjacent landowners to enforce agreements among themselves without ever having been in privity of contract. In the absence of privity between two property owners, notice takes a greater role in the enforcement of these servitudes. Creating communities that were enclaves segregated by race gave each community its own set of cultural rules. If a property owner of a different race were to acquire a parcel in that common scheme, the concept of notice, particularly inquiry notice, would be difficult to determine, given that the "other" owner may not yet have learned the many rules and norms.

Loren Miller in Sugar Hill, California: Setting the Foundations for *Shelley v. Kraemer*

In the neighborhood of West Adams Heights outside of Los Angeles, California, homeowners, who were mostly upper-class and white, were made to sign racially restrictive covenants of the type that were validated by the Supreme Court in *Corrigan v. Buckley*, discussed and excerpted above, in the early 20th century. During the Great Depression, however, many of these white homeowners sold their homes to any party willing to pay, without regard to the restrictions contained in their deeds. In this way, West Adams Heights became an enclave for affluent members of the Black community, becoming home to well-known figures including Norman Houston, the founder of the Golden State Mutual Life Insur-

10. Nahrstedt v. Lakeside Vill. Condo. Ass'n, Inc., 878 P.2d 1275 (Cal. 1994).

ance Company; Drs. John and Vada Somerville, who co-founded Hotel Somerville, later renamed the Dunbar Hotel; and a number of entertainment-industry elite, including singer and actress Ethel Waters and Oscar-award winning actor Hattie McDaniel. The homes in the West Adams Heights area were large and luxurious, and many of the white families who lived there were unwilling to accept the new character of the neighborhood, which had come to be known as "Sugar Hill," a tribute to the Harlem, New York, neighborhood where wealthy Black individuals settled. In 1945, some of the remaining white families in Sugar Hill filed suit to enforce the covenants, claiming that a failure to enforce them would cause their properties to lose value and that racial clashes would ensue.[11]

On December 5, 1945, the trial came to a Los Angeles Superior Court courtroom packed with observers. In opening arguments, as in their pleadings, attorneys for the plaintiffs argued that the Black residents were in violation of the law and that the racially restrictive covenants were enforceable and comported with the law. In addition, the attorneys prayed that the Black residents surrender their homes immediately. In response, attorney Loren Miller did not defend the actions of the Black residents but rather argued that the covenants were in violation of the 14th Amendment and the California State Constitution, which demanded equal protection under the law. Judge Thurmond Clark, seated in front of a portrait of President Lincoln,[12] agreed with Miller and dismissed the case, ruling that

> [i]t is time that members of the Negro race are accorded, without reservations and evasions, the full rights guaranteed them under the 14th amendment of the Federal Constitution. Judges have been avoiding the real issue too long. Certainly there was no discrimination against the Negro race when it

---

11. Jill Watts, Hattie McDaniel: Black Ambition, White Hollywood (2007).

12. *See CALIFORNIA: Victory on Sugar Hill*, Time Mag., Dec. 17, 1945, https://content.time.com/time/subscriber/article/0,33009,776487,00.html.

> came to calling upon its members to die on the battlefields in defense of this country in the war just ended.[13]

This was the first time a judge had ruled that a racially restrictive real covenant violated the 14th Amendment. Though the decision was appealed by the white homeowners, it also gave rise to more claims by Loren Miller and Thurgood Marshall, eventually leading to the more widely known and read case of *Shelley v. Kraemer*.

Beyond *Shelley*: Access to the American Dream in Suburbs like Levittown

As planned suburbs, or common schemes, became increasingly prevalent, they presented potentially lucrative business opportunities—the intentional planning and design of suburban neighborhoods was highly marketable and desirable. The Levitt family engaged in that very business, successfully establishing the first planned "Levittown" community in Long Island, New York, before building additional Levittowns in New York, Pennsylvania, New Jersey, and, eventually, Puerto Rico. The original Levittown in Long Island was marketed to veterans who would receive a subsidy from the government for the down payment on their new home. Marketing materials promoted the "American Dream." These neighborhoods were carefully crafted with curving streets to give them a "rural feel," with major roads being kept on the outskirts. Staggered houses meant that neighbors could never see inside each other's windows. Homes and common areas boasted manicured lawns and common areas. And rigid restrictions based on race deliberately excluded people of color from living in these neighborhoods. Though some covenants were designed specifically to exclude Black individuals and others were designed only to allow white families, the effect was the same: segregated, predominantly white neighborhoods. The American dream was at hand, affordable, and off limits to anyone who was not white. The

13. Hadley Meares, *The Short History of West Adams and Sugar Hill*, CURBED LA (Feb. 22, 2018), https://la.curbed.com/2018/2/22/16979700/west-adams-history-segregation-housing-covenants.

first Levittown in Long Island was so popular that what began as a plan to build 2,000 homes in 1947 turned into 17,000 homes built by 1951. The Levittown communities created in Pennsylvania and New Jersey continue to exist.

In the wake of *Corrigan v. Buckley*, the NAACP continued to search for plaintiffs to challenge the validity of racially restrictive covenants. *Shelley v. Kraemer*, which is read widely in both property and constitutional law classes, is considered a civil rights victory because the Court held that *judicial enforcement of a racially restrictive covenant qualifies as a state action, and accordingly, cannot be upheld.* (Notably, Justices Reed, Jackson, and Rutledge recused themselves from the case, likely because, as Justice Stevens (who had clerked for Justice Rutledge) has noted, each lived in homes with racially restrictive covenants.) Despite *Shelley*'s being regarded as a turning point in race relations in American legal history, its practical effect was less pronounced, as evidenced by the proliferation of racial segregation in residential communities in the mid-20th century. This was due, in large part, to the already established success of racially restrictive covenants, a tool that was widely used by realtors and developers and which homeowners were already accustomed to. Even though judicial enforcement of private discrimination constituted a state action, the existence of and compliance with racially restrictive covenants continued to have market value.

The holding in *Shelley v. Kraemer* is one of many examples in American legal history of how rules change but racial dynamics persist. Real change requires not only changes in policies and rules but also in values—in hearts and minds—and that often takes a generation or more. Accountability is the first step on the path to change, but accountability begins with knowledge. Although the Fair Housing Act of 1968[14] made racially restrictive covenants flatly illegal, many modern deeds still include racially restrictive language, and several state and local jurisdictions have commenced projects to research and amend deeds with racially restrictive covenants. Because these covenants are not enforced, and the residents who hold the deeds that contain them are often unaware of their existence, some may feel that the effort to amend such deeds is better spent elsewhere. However, given the importance of deeds

14. Fair Housing Act, 42 U.S.C. §§ 3604(a), (d).

in the eyes of the law, and the sacred status of memorialization of title in our system of laws, many may find the effort to be truly worthwhile.

Skills: Using Cases in Legal Analysis

The analysis section is the most important part of the IRAC. After refining and articulating a specific issue and synthesizing a rule, the only thing left is to attend to a legal analysis. The next chapter is devoted to the different tools that are available for crafting a strong and robust analysis section, but this chapter focuses on the most important analysis tool in the common law system: case comparison. Because the common law is made up of precedent cases, becoming skilled at comparing a novel fact pattern to already-decided cases in a clear, cogent, and organized way is essential. It is a deceptively simple skill because it is one that even the most experienced attorneys will continually refine, even throughout the later stages of their careers.

As you consider the following fact pattern, practice identifying the issues at hand, articulating the issue as specifically and precisely as possible, and responding with a rule statement that will prompt a thorough and robust legal analysis. After reading the fact pattern that relates to implied easements and notice, review some common responses made by first-year law students, and take the opportunity to distinguish the stronger analysis from the initial responses. Getting into the habit of editing your own work will help to improve and strengthen your legal writing skills.

> Agnes, a Black woman, has recently relocated from a densely populated, predominantly Black city to a large parcel of land adjacent to a lake in a predominantly white community. Agnes had always wanted private and direct access to recreational water and specifically selected that parcel because of its direct access to the water. Agnes purchased the property from Michael, who had split a large parcel of land that he owned, selling a portion of it to Agnes while retaining the rest for his own residential use. He owned the property on which his family had lived for generations. Michael's retained portion of the property did not have access to the lake. There was a gravel path running from

> Agnes's home on her parcel directly to the water which made it easier to carry recreational equipment to the shoreline.
>
> When summer arrived, a few months after Michael sold the property to Agnes, Michael walked across part of his property and part of Agnes's property with his small kayak before arriving at the gravel path that began at her house, which was his former boat house. The first time Michael entered Agnes's property with his kayak, Agnes was startled. He was not a complete stranger to Agnes because she had become acquainted with him during the real estate transaction, but she was surprised to see her neighbor so close to her home and clearly on her land. His hands full with a kayak and oar, Michael smiled, nodded, and bid "good morning" to Agnes. She returned the friendly greeting and went back to her day. Encouraged by Agnes's response, Michael continued to drag his kayak across the property to the gravel path regularly throughout the summer, so much that he wore a path in the grass and garden on Agnes's property.
>
> Though having morning coffee outside her house in her bathrobe had long been a dream of hers, Agnes began to have her morning coffee in her kitchen to avoid seeing Michael before she was dressed. Michael was an established and respected member of her new home community, and though she had not personally had any negative experiences, she was aware of a history of racial unrest in the area. Some years later, when Michael passed away, his son who inherited the property sought to establish an easement across Agnes's land. There was no language contained in the deed from Michael to Agnes referring to an easement.

In law school and in practice, the work of a lawyer is finding ways to compare the case law already decided to a novel set of facts at hand. Often, based on the hope that the administration of our laws would be race-neutral, many precedent cases did not explicitly address race and power dynamics between parties, such as the ones present in the preceding fact pattern. But regardless of whether the dynamics are named, they were/are present. And in many cases, those unnamed dynamics may have had/have an impact on the parties' rights in property.

Adhering to a rigid IRAC structure, a typical property student might respond to the prompt in the following way:

First Draft

> *The issue is whether Agnes's actions are sufficient to amount to notice and consent to Michael's use of the easement across her land such that a court may establish an easement implied by estoppel. When the owner of a burdened property, like Agnes, is aware of the consistent use and the extent to which the owner of the benefitted property, like Michael, relied on the use, and ending the right to use the easement would be a detriment to the benefitted property, an easement by estoppel may be implied. An easement by estoppel is created when no express easement exists. It must be implied by a court. The elements for an easement by estoppel require that the burdened estate permitted the initial entry and use, the benefitted estate reasonably and justifiably relied on permission not being revoked, the benefitted estate made a substantial change in position, and an injustice can only be avoided by implying an easement. Agnes "returned the friendly greeting" given by Michael when he initially entered her property. Michael continued to drag his kayak across her property. Agnes gave permission for initial entry and use of her property and Michael reasonably continued to rely on that permission. The first elements of an easement by estoppel are met.*

Though this initial draft was written by an individual well versed in the doctrine of easements, the analysis of rule applied to facts is lacking. This example highlights the importance of having a focused and specific issue statement followed by a responsive rule. That's because, while this draft gives the illusion that the writer was using the facts from the fact pattern, there is no analysis contained therein: *there is only a reordering of the facts provided in the fact pattern followed by a legal conclusion.*

Reflecting on the first draft may be easier to do if you insert it into the rigid IRAC structure. When performing this exercise and editing your work, it is important to use *only* the words contained in your draft, no matter how tempting it may be to edit in real time as you reflect.

Section	First Draft	Notes
Issue	The issue is whether Agnes's actions are sufficient to amount to notice and consent to Michael's use of the easement across her land such that a court may establish an easement implied by estoppel.	✓ Begins with "whether" → open-ended question ✓ Specific and focused ✓ Related to the facts at hand
Rule	When the owner of a burdened property, like Agnes, is aware of the consistent use and the extent to which the owner of the benefitted property, like Michael, relied on the use, and ending the right to use the easement would be a detriment to the benefitted property, an easement by estoppel may be implied. An easement by estoppel is created when no express easement exists. It must be implied by a court. The elements for an easement by estoppel require that the burdened estate permitted the initial entry and use, the benefitted estate reasonably and justifiably relied on permission not being revoked, the benefitted estate made a substantial change in position, and an injustice can only be avoided by implying an easement.	✓ Responsive to the issue × Too broad—listing the elements for an entire rule may be a red flag. × Too long—when the rule is longer than the analysis section, it may be a sign that the writer is seeking to demonstrate a *knowledge* of the rules rather than the ability to *use* the rules. *Remember: Anyone can look up the rules. It is the skill of a lawyer to provide analysis.*
Analysis	Agnes "returned the friendly greeting" given by Michael when he initially entered her property. Michael continued to drag his kayak across her property. Agnes gave permission for initial entry and use of her property and Michael reasonably continued to rely on that permission.	✓ Salient facts from the new fact pattern × No application × Premature conclusion Analysis should consist of rule + facts.
Conclusion	The first elements of an easement by estoppel are met.	

After completing this initial step, it is helpful to go line by line in the analysis and identify what has been done. It is common for students either to restate the rule or restate the facts from the novel fact pattern. Together, those two things may feel like rule plus facts, but, while they are adjacent to an analysis, they lack the actual application. Consider the stronger second draft below, in which the writer's thought process behind the organization of the facts and rules is more explicit. Many students skip the analysis because it seems too obvious or basic when it is, in fact, the most important legal skill. Having a model of a strong answer to refer to can help you to routinely conduct a strong analysis.

Second Draft

> *The first issue is whether Agnes's actions upon first seeing Michael on her property amount to an express permission for entry and use that can be reasonably and justifiably relied on for continuing use in the way they were by Michael without further discussion regarding rights in property. The standard for easement by estoppel requires that the benefited estate (Michael's) reasonably and justifiably relies on the initial permission to enter and use not being revoked. Absent an express agreement transferring a right in property, courts have historically been reluctant to require that property owners part with any interest in their property without the hallmarks of estoppel, including notice, reliance, and avoidance of injustice. Though Agnes returned Michael's greeting when she initially saw him on her property, she did so in a state of being startled. Basing initial permission for use and entry on an unplanned greeting for one day may be taking advantage of particular circumstances, but relying on that initial interaction in order to establish an easement that burdens Agnes's rights in her property is putting a great deal on a response to an unexpected greeting. Further, Michael was previously the owner of both his and Agnes's property, and when he severed the whole into two distinct parcels, Michael had the opportunity to reserve an easement*

for himself or to choose the parcel adjacent to the lake if he wanted to use it before he offered it for sale. He did neither. Rather, he created and sold a parcel with an expectation of a private and recreational water view before subverting that expectation a few months after the transfer of the property. The recreational nature of Michael's use does not indicate a reliance on the use that justifies changing the property rights of an owner of property in fee simple absolute. Accordingly, because Michael had the opportunity to seek explicit and informed permission to enter and use the path across Agnes's property and create an easement while being clear about the exchange of property rights and failed to do so, his recreational use of the property is insufficient to justify reliance sufficient for easement by estoppel.

Section	Second Draft	Notes
Issue	The first issue is whether Agnes's actions upon first seeing Michael on her property amount to an express permission for entry and use that can be reasonably and justifiably relied on for continuing use in the way they were by Michael without further discussion regarding rights in property.	✓ Open-ended question ✓ Specific about legal issue ✓ Specific about facts (and parties) ✓ Organized
Rule	The standard for easement by estoppel requires that the benefited estate (Michael's) reasonably and justifiably relies on the initial permission to enter and use not being revoked. Absent an express agreement transferring a right in property, courts have historically been reluctant to require that property owners part with any interest in their property without the hallmarks of estoppel, including notice, reliance, and avoidance of injustice.	✓ Responsive to the issue ✓ Specific about the facts ✓ Focused ✓ Contains the relevant part of the rule ✓ Demonstrates both knowledge of the rule *and an* understanding of how to use it

Analysis	Though Agnes returned Michael's greeting when she initially saw him on her property, she did so in a state of being startled. Basing initial permission for use and entry on an unplanned greeting for one day may be taking advantage of particular circumstances, but relying on that initial interaction in order to establish an easement that burdens Agnes's rights in her property is putting a great deal on a response to an unexpected greeting. Further, Michael was previously the owner of both his and Agnes's property and when he severed the whole into two distinct parcels, Michael had the opportunity to reserve an easement for himself or to choose the parcel adjacent to the lake if he wanted to use it before he offered it for sale. He did neither. Rather, he created and sold a parcel with an expectation of a private and recreational water view before subverting that expectation a few months after the transfer of the property. The recreational nature of Michael's use does not indicate a reliance on the use that justifies changing the property rights of an owner of property in fee simple absolute.	✓ Contains salient facts ✓ **Explains the relevance of the facts relative to the application of the rule.** ✓ Clear ✓ Organized ✓ Supports the rule with facts from the fact pattern × *Not* culturally responsive × Ignores race and power dynamics Consider the following: Agnes was a Black woman who moved from a predominantly Black, densely populated city to a predominantly white, residential community near a recreational lake. Michael's family had been in the community for generations and had severed his property and sold a parcel to Agnes, setting up a power dynamic in a real estate transaction that was imbued with race and history. In addition to being startled, Agnes was motivated to fit in with the culture of her new home and was unlikely to deny permission to Michael, given the dynamics between them as well as those reasonably perceived by Agnes in the community. *Policy Consideration: How should these race and power dynamics impact Agnes's rights in property?*

continued

continued

Conclusion	Accordingly, because Michael had the opportunity to seek explicit and informed permission to enter and use the path across Agnes's property and create an easement while being clear about the exchange of property rights and failed to do so, his recreational use of the property is insufficient to justify reliance sufficient for easement by estoppel.	✓ Very good, but there is always room to practice and improve. Always.

SUGGESTION FOR FURTHER READING

Richard Brooks & Carol Rose, Saving the Neighborhood: Racially Restrictive Covenants, Law, and Social Norms (2013).

FIVE

Access to Ownership

Mortgages, Foreclosures, Redlining, and Blockbusting

A nation of home owners, of people who own a real share in their own land, is unconquerable. You have the unique satisfaction of knowing that your institutions' business of financing homes over a period of 100 years have contributed inestimably to your country's strength.

—President Franklin Delano Roosevelt, Address to the Savings & Loan League, November 16, 1942[1]

During slavery, "Americans built a culture of speculation unique in its abandon."[2] That culture would drive cotton production up to the Civil War, and it has been a defining characteristic of American capitalism ever since. It is the culture of acquiring wealth without work, growing at all costs, and abusing the powerless. It is the culture that brought us the Panic of 1837, the stock-market crash of 1929, and the recession of 2008.

—Matthew Desmond[3]

---

1. Home Owners Hailed in Roosevelt Note: Make Nation "Unconquerable" He Tells Savings League, N.Y. Times, Nov. 17, 1942, at 35, https://timesmachine.nytimes.com/timesmachine/1942/11/17/85608627.html?pageNumber=35.

2. From Joshua Rothman, Flush Times and Fever Dreams (2012).

3. Interview with Matthew Desmond, The 1619 Project: Episode 2: The Economy That Slavery Built: In Order to Understand the Brutality of American Capitalism, You

Property ownership is central to the American story. It has long been held to be a part of the American dream. In art, literature, and popular culture, ownership of a home has been a hallmark of success and maturity. Given the magnitude of the investment involved in purchasing a home, a financial market to support investment in homes and other real property has developed. Where a home is often a major, stable, and important asset for an individual, real property and the value it holds also serve as the basis for healthy financial markets. In this chapter, we explore the relationship between individuals, banks, and the government to help us understand the basics of mortgages and the consequences for breach (foreclosure). Next we turn to the capital markets supporting the financial institutions that provide mortgages and the government programs that insure them. We also cover the (now defunct) federal Home Owners Loan Corporation (HOLC) and its color-coding of neighborhoods and its decisions about which home loans to insure during a time of exponentially increasing property values in U.S. history. The impact of this now-discontinued practice, known as "redlining," continues to have an effect on American communities—and, in fact, the 2008 financial crisis, precipitated in large part by mortgage defaults, disproportionately impacted those in "red" communities. Finally, this chapter explores the way that the government's involvement in insuring mortgages through HOLC and the way that it distributed funds through the G.I. Bill for down payments on real property intentionally excluded Black Americans from ownership at a crucial time in U.S. history, as well as how the effects of that exlusion are still felt today. We will see that, although many of the programs that excluded Black Americans from quality housing and promoted segregation are no longer legal, a number of U.S. cities in the United States continue to be segregated—exactly as they were designed to be.

Have to Start on the Plantation, N.Y. Times (Sep. 13, 2019), https://www.nytimes.com/2019/08/30/podcasts/1619-slavery-cotton-capitalism.html.

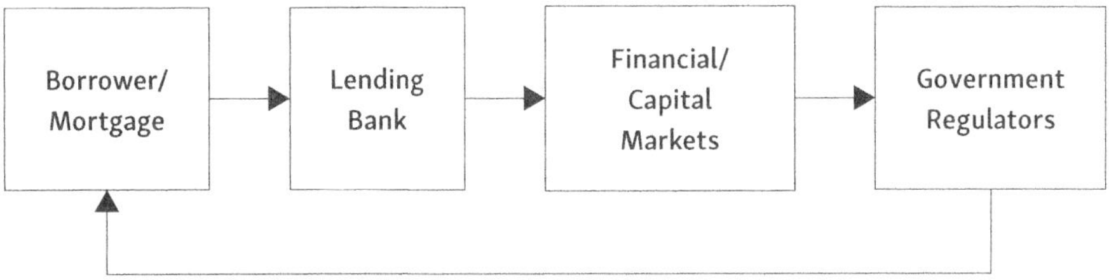

Mortgage Basics

There are numerous ways in which property is treated as exceptional under the law. When we consider how fundamentally important land and homes are to our individual and community identities, it makes sense that the law holds a special place and set of rules for real property. Whether we are talking about contracts, torts, civil procedure, or criminal law, the rules may be distinct when there is property involved. Mortgages are no different.

At its heart, a mortgage is a loan with collateral. What makes a mortgage distinct from other types of loans is that the collateral securing the loan is real property. Consider the following typical situation used to illustrate the concept of collateral: While Kavi is driving, without realizing it, they run out of fuel. Though Kavi is happily able to make it to the nearest fueling station, they quickly realize that they do not have the means to purchase any fuel: no money, no credit cards, no means of electronic payment. Kavi knows that if they can just take the car home, they can retrieve their wallet and pay for the fuel, but Kavi needs a loan to pay for the gas to get there. Kavi leaves their very valuable watch at the gas station with the attendant as collateral; the value of the watch is greater than the value of the fuel that Kavi is taking. The attendant is happy to make the loan because if Kavi does not return, then the attendant gets to keep the more valuable watch. If Kavi does return, then the attendant gets compensated for the loan (perhaps with interest). This basic transaction is a loan secured by collateral, where the loan is the value of the fuel to get Kavi home, and the collateral is the expensive watch.

Collateral, then is something that a borrower gives to a lender to ensure that they will repay the loan, that is, to *secure* the promise. Accordingly, when we speak about "secured transactions," we mean that there is some additional thing of value at stake. This security interest is important to both the borrower and the lender, and additional rules spring up to protect the interests of both parties and ensure that they treat each other, and each other's property, fairly.

What we commonly refer to as a "mortgage" is made of two components: (1) a note and (2) a mortgage. The "note" is the loan agreement. This is the document that outlines the essential terms of the contract, including who will borrow, what will be borrowed, how much will be borrowed, whether and how much interest will be charged, and the terms of repayment. The second component, the mortgage, is the security interest, and it is reserved for those occasions where the collateral securing the note is real property. The mortgage memorializes that the real property will be collateral for the note; if the borrower defaults on their promise to repay the loan, then the lender may *foreclose*, or take, the real property and sell it and use the proceeds to repay what is owed by the borrower. The mortgage contains details about the obligations of the borrower with regard to the duty of care to the property; if the real property is a security interest for the lender, then the lender wants to ensure that the value of the property is preserved and protected. These obligations include paying local real estate taxes, keeping the property physically maintained, and staying in compliance with local zoning laws and any private encumbrances (such as easements or covenants). All of these are aimed and ensuring that the value of the property is sufficient to repay the debt if the borrower should default.

What's in a NOTE?	What's in a MORTGAGE?
✓ Identity of borrower ✓ Identity of lender ✓ Amount of loan ✓ Interest charged/formula ✓ Repayment schedule	✓ Description of real property to serve as collateral or security ✓ Rights of foreclosure (power of sale, judicial sale, etc.) ✓ Duty of maintenance/care of property ✓ Title transfer details

Reflection:
Lessons from Behavioral Economics

Behavioral economics, a relatively new branch of economics made popular by Nobel Prize-winning economists like Daniel Khanemen, Amos Traversky, Richard Thaler, and Cass Sunstein, seeks to understand motives and incentives and shape policymaking accordingly. Some policies driven by these principles may be described as "padding the path of least resistance" in order to provide incentives for certain behavior. With that in mind, can you articulate what type of behavior is incentivized by lien-theory jurisdictions? Title-theory jurisdictions?

With regard to who holds title to the property during the life of the mortgage, or the loan, there are two prevailing theories in the United States: *lien theory* and *title theory*. The majority of states are lien-theory states. In lien-theory states, the borrower is the title holder or owner of the property and the lender has a security interest in the property. Accordingly, if the borrower defaults, when the lender forecloses on the property, title must be transferred to the lender. When the borrower fully pays the loan, no action is needed with regard to title in a lien-theory jurisdiction: the borrower just retains title. In this way, lien-theory states make it easier for borrowers to repay the loan; the administrative tasks of title transfer are reserved for when there is a default on the loan and the lender must foreclose. By contrast, in title-theory (also sometimes called "mortgage-theory") jurisdictions, title to the property is held by the lender until the final payment is made by the borrower, even in the very common circumstance in which the borrower is using or living on the property. If a borrower defaults on their loan, the lender already has title to the property and may sell and use the proceeds to satisfy the loan according to the mortgage. In title-theory jurisdictions, title, or ownership of the property, will only transfer when the loan has been fully repaid. Unlike in lien-theory jurisdictions, the administrative burden is placed on the fully compliant borrower who repays the loan, while the path is made easier for the foreclosing lender.

Lien Theory	Title Theory
Title to the mortgaged property is held by the borrower. A security interest, or lien, is held by the lender. No transfer necessary when loan repaid. Title must transfer in the event of foreclosure.	Title to the mortgaged property is held by the lender until the final payment of both interest and principal is made. Upon completion of the terms of the loan, transfer of title from lender to borrower will occur. In the event of foreclosure, no title transfer is necessary.

A jurisdiction's choice to follow lien theory or title theory can have major ramifications for borrowers. The choice sets a default position that results in a great deal less resistance for one party in the foreclosure process. Understanding the way these facially neutral tools can and have been used in the context of social and other governmental policies demonstrates the way that property law provides tools for change.

In her dissenting opinion in a case related to affirmative action, Justice Ketanji Brown Jackson saw fit to give a brief description of the history of the way the U.S. government has participated in excluding Black Americans from property ownership. Considering the importance of property ownership to our individual, national, and cultural identities, reflect on the importance of her inclusion of the history of property law in the opinion excerpted below. Justice Jackson cites and is influenced by Richard Rothstein's work *The Color of Law*,[4] which is not without its critics.[5] Understanding that Professor Rothstein's work is about government policy that existed in a larger social and psychological context around race is an essential part of understanding how the tools of the law may be used to make change in any direction.

---

4. Richard Rothstein, The Color of Law: A Forgotten History of How Our Government Segregated America (2017).

5. Special thanks to Professor Faisal Chaudhry for directing me to the work of Richard Walker, one of these critics. See Richard Walker, The New Deal Didn't Create Segregation, Jacobin (June 18, 2019), www.jacobin.com/2019/06/the-color-of-law-richard-rothstein-review.

STUDENTS FOR FAIR ADMISSIONS, INC. (SFFA) V. PRESIDENT & FELLOWS OF HARV. COLL.

143 S. Ct. 2141, 2264–68 (2023)

Justice Jackson, with whom Justice Sotomayor and Justice Kagan join, dissenting.

. . . .

"[A] page of history is worth a volume of logic." *New York Trust Co. v. Eisner*, 256 U.S. 345, 349, 41 S. Ct. 506, 65 L. Ed. 963, T.D. 3267 (1921). Many chapters of America's history appear necessary, given the opinions that my colleagues in the majority have issued in this case.
Justice Thurgood Marshall recounted the genesis:

> "Three hundred and fifty years ago, the Negro was dragged to this country in chains to be sold into slavery. Uprooted from his homeland and thrust into bondage for forced labor, the slave was deprived of all legal rights. It was unlawful to teach him to read; he could be sold away from his family and friends at the whim of his master; and killing or maiming him was not a crim. The system of slavery brutalized and dehumanized both master and slave." *Regents of Univ. of Cal. v. Bakke*, 438 U.S. 265, 387–388, 98 S. Ct. 2733, 57 L. Ed. 2d 750 (1978).

Slavery should have been (and was to many) self-evidently dissonant with our avowed founding principles. When the time came to resolve that dissonance, eleven States chose slavery. With the Union's survival at stake, Frederick Douglass noted, Black Americans in the South "were almost the only reliable friends the nation had," and "but for their help . . . the Rebels might have succeeded in breaking up the Union."[2] After the war, Senator John Sherman defended the proposed Fourteenth Amendment in a manner that encapsulated our Reconstruction Framers' highest sentiments: "We are bound by every obligation, by [Black Amerincas'] service on the battlefield, by their heroes who are buried in our

[2]. An Appeal to Congress for Impartial Suffrage, Atlantic Monthly (Jan 1867), in 2 The Reconstruction Amendments: The Essential Documents 324 (K. Lash ed. 2021) (Lash).

cause, by their patriotism in the hours that tried our country, we are bound to protect them an all their natural rights."[3]

To uphold that promise, the Framers repudiated this Court's holding in *Dred Scott v. Sandford*, 60 U.S. 393, 19 How. 393, 15 L. Ed. 691 (1857), by crafting Reconstruction Amendments, (and associated legislation) that transformed our Constitution and society.[4] Even after this Second Founding—when the need to right historical wrongs should have been clear beyond cavil—opponents insisted that vindicating equality in this manner slighted White Americans. So, when the Reconstruction Congress passed a bill to secure all citizens "the same [civil] right[s]" as "enjoyed by white citizens," 14 Stat. 27, President Andrew Johnson vetoed it because it "discriminat[ed] ... in favor of the negro."[5]

That attitude, and the Nation's associated retreat from Reconstruction, made prophesy out of Congressman Thaddeus Stevens's fear that "those States will all ... keep up this discrimination, and crush to death the hated freedmen."[6] And this Court facilitated that retrenchment.[7] Not just in *Plessy v. Ferguson*, 163 U.S. 537, 16 S. Ct. 1138, 41 L. Ed. 256 (1896), but "in almost every instance, the Court chose to restrict the scope of the second founding."[8] Thus, thirteen years pre-*Plessy*, in the Civil Rights Cases, 109 U.S. 3, 3 S. Ct. 18, 27 L. Ed. 835 (1883), our predecessors on this Court invalidated Congress's attempt to enforce the Reconstruction Amendments via the Civil Rights Act of 1875, lecturing that "there must be some stage ... when [Black Americans] tak[e] the rank of a mere citizen, and ceas[e] to be the special favorite of the laws." *Id.*, at 25. But Justice Harlan knew better. He responded: "what the nation, through Congress, had sought to accomplish in reference to [Black people] is—what had already been done in every State of the Union for

---

[3]. Speech of Sen. John Sherman (September 28, 1866) (Sherman), in id., at 276; see also W. Du Bois, Black Reconstruction in America 162 (1998) (Du Bois).

[4]. See Sherman 276; M. Curtis, No State Shall Abridge: The Fourteenth Amendment and the Bill of Rights 48, 71–75, 91, 173 (1986).

[5]. Message Accompanying Veto of the Civil Rights Bill (March 27, 1866), in Lash, 145.

[6]. Speech Introducing the [Fourteenth] Amendment (May 8, 1886), in id., at 159; see Du Bois 670–710.

[7]. E. Foner, The Second Founding 125–167 (2019) (Foner).

[8]. Id., at 128.

the white race—to secure and protect rights belonging to them as freemen and citizens; nothing more." *Id.*, at 61 (dissenting opinion).

Justice Harlan dissented alone. And the betrayal that this Court enabled had concrete effects. Enslaved Black people had built great wealth, but only for enslavers.[9] No surprise, then, that freedmen leapt at the chance to control their own labor and to build their own financial security.[10] Still, White southerners often "simply refused to sell land to blacks," even when not selling was economically foolish.[11] To bolster private exclusion, States sometimes passed laws forbidding such sales.[12] The inability to build wealth through the most American of means forced Black people into sharecropping roles, where they somehow always tended to find themselves in debt to the landowner when the growing seasons closed, with no hope of recourse against the ever-present cooking of the books.[13]

Sharecropping is but one example of race-linked obstacles that the law (and private parties) laid down to hinder the progress and prosperity of Black people. Vagrancy laws criminalized free Black men who failed to work for White landlords.[14] Many States barred freedmen from hunting or fishing to ensure that they could not live without entering de facto reenslavement as sharecroppers.[15] A cornucopia of laws (e.g. banning hitchhiking, prohibiting encouraging a laborer to leave his employer, and penalizing those who prompted Black southerners to migrate northward) ensured that Black people could not freely seek better lives else-

[9]. M. Baradaran, The Color of Money: Black Banks and the Racial Wealth Gap 9–11 (2017) (Baradaran).

[10]. Foner 179; see also Baradaran 15–16; I. Wilkerson, The Warmth of Other Suns: The Epic Story of Amercia's Great Migration 37 (2010) (Wilkerson).

[11]. Baradaran 18.

[12]. Ibid.

[13]. R. Rothstein, The Color of Law: A Forgotten History of How Our Government Segregated America 154 (2017) (Rothstein); Baradaran 33–34; Wilkerson 53–55.

[14]. Baradaran 20–21; Du Bois 173–179, 694–696, 698–699; R. Goluboff, The Thirteenth Amendment and the Lost Origins of Civil Rights, 50 Duke L.J. 1609, 1656–1659 (2001) (Goluboff); Wilkerson 152 (noting persistence of this practice "well into the 1940's").

[15]. Baradaran 20.

where.[16] And when statuses did not ensure compliance, state-sanctioned (and private) violence did.[17]

Thus emerged Jim Crow—a system that was, as much as anything else, a comprehensive scheme of economic exploitation to replace the Black Codes, which themselves had replaced slavery's form of comprehensive economic exploitation.[18] Meanwhile, as Jim Crow ossified, the Federal Government was "giving away land" on the western frontier, and with it "the opportunity for upward mobility and a more secure future," over the 1862 Homestead Act's three quarter-century tenure.[19] Black people were exceedingly unlikely to be allowed to share in those benefits, which by one calculation may have advantaged approximately 46 million Americans living today.[20]

Despite these barriers, Black people persisted. Their so called Great Migration northward accelerated during and after the First World War.[21] Like clockwork, American cities responded with racially exclusionary zoning (and similar policies).[22] As a result, Black migrants had to pay disproportionately high prices for disproportionately subpar housing.[23] Nor did migration make it more likely for Black people to access home ownership, as banks would not lend to Black people, and in the rare case banks would fund home loans, exorbitant interest rates were charged.[24] With Black people still locked out of the Homestead Act giveaway, it is no surprise that, when the Great Depression arrived, race-based wealth, health, and opportunity gaps were the norm.[25]

---

[16]. Goluboff 1656–1659 (recounting presence of these practices well into the 20th century); Wilkerson 162–163.

[17]. Rothstein 154.

[18]. C. Black, The Lawfulness of the Segregation Decisions, 69 Yale L. J. 421, 424 (1960); Foner 47–48; Du Bois 179, 696; Baradaran, 38–39.

[19]. T. Shanks, The Homestead Act: A Major Asset-Building Policy in American History, in Inclusion in the American Dream: Assets, Poverty and Public Policy, 23–25 (M. Sherraden ed 2005) (Shanks); see also Baradaran 18.

[20]. Shanks 32–37; Oliver & Shapiro 37–38.

[21]. Wilkerson 8–10; Rothstein 155.

[22]. Id., at 43–50; Baradaran 90–92.

[23]. Ibid.; Rothstein 172–173; Wilkerson 269–271.

[24]. Baradaran 90.

[25]. I. Katznelson, When Affirmative Action Was White: An Untold History of Racial Inequality in Twentieth-Century America 29–35 (2005) (Katznelson).

Federal and State Governments' selective intervention further exacerbated the disparities. Consider, for example, the federal Home Owners Loan Corporation (HOLC), created in 1933.[26] HOLC purchased mortgages threatened with foreclosure and issued new, amortized mortgages in their place.[27] Not only did this mean that recipients of these mortgages could gain equity while paying off the loan, successful full payment would make the recipient a homeowner.[28] Ostensibly to identify (and avoid) the riskiest recipients, the HOLC "created color-coded maps of every metropolitan area in the nation."[29] Green meant safe; red meant risky. And, regardless of class, every neighborhood with Black people earned the red designation.[30]

Similarly, consider the Federal Housing Administration (FHA), created in 1934 which insured highly desirable bank mortgages. Eligibility for this insurance required an FHA appraisal of the property to ensure a low default risk.[31] But nationwide, it was FHA's established policy to provide "no guarantee for mortgages to African Americans, or to whites who might lease to African Americans," irrespective of creditworthiness.[32] No surprise, then, that "[b]etween 1934 and 1968, 98 percent of FHA loans went to white Americans," with whole cities (ones that had a disproportionately large number of Black people due to housing segregation) sometimes being deemed ineligible for FHA intervention on racial grounds.[33] The Veterans Administration operated similarly.[34]

One more example: the Federal Home Loan Bank Board "chartered, insured, and regulated savings and loan associations from the early years of the New Deal."[35] But it did "not oppose the denial of mortgages to

---

[26]. D. Massey & N. Denton, American Apartheid: Segregation and the Making of the Underclass 51–53 (1993); Oliver & Shapiro 16–18.

[27]. Rothstein 63.

[28]. Id. at 63–64.

[29]. Id. at 64; see Oliver & Shapiro 16–18; Baradaran 105.

[30]. Rothstein 64.

[31]. Ibid.

[32]. Id., at 67.

[33]. Baradaran 108; see Rothstein 69–75.

[34]. Id., at 9, 13, 17.

[35]. Id., at 108.

African Americans until 1961" (and even then opposed discrimination ineffectively).[36]

The upshot of all this is that, due to government policy and choices, "[i]n the suburban-shaping years between 1930 and 1960, fewer than one present of all mortgages in the nation were issued to African Americans."[37] Thus, based on their race, Black people were "[l]ocked out of the greatest mass-based opportunity for wealth accumulation in American history."[38]

For present purposes, it is significant that, in so excluding back people, government policies affirmatively operated—one could say, affirmatively acted—to dole out preference to those who, if nothing else, were not Black. Those past preferences carried forward and are reinforced today by (among other things) the benefits that flow to homeowners and to the holders of other forms of capital that are hard to obtain unless one already has assets.[39]

This discussion of how the existing gaps were formed is merely illustrative, not exhaustive. I will pass over Congress's repeated crafting of family-, worker-, and retiree- protective legislation to channel benefits to White people, thereby excluding Black Americans from what was otherwise a "revolution in the status of most working Americans."[40] I will also skip over how the G.I. Bill's "creation of... middle-class America" (by giving $95 billion to veterans and their families between 1944 and 1971) was "deliberately designed to accommodate Jim Crow."[41] So, too, will I bypass how Black people were prevented from partaking in the consumer credit market—a market that helped White people who could access it build and protect wealth.[42] Nor will time and space permit my elaborating how local officials' racial hostility meant that even those benefits that Black people could formally obtain were unequally

---

[36]. Ibid.

[37]. R. Schragger, The Limits of Localism, 100 Mich. L. Rev. 371, 411, n. 144 (2001); see also Rothstein 182–183.

[38]. Oliver & Shapiro 18.

[39]. Id., at 43–44; Baradaran 109, 253–254; A. Dickerson, Shining a Bright Light on the Color of Wealth, 120 Mich. L. Rev. 1085, 1100 (2022) (Dickerson).

[40]. Katznelson 53; see id., at 22, 29, 42–48, 53–61; Rothstein 31, 155–156.

[41]. Katznelson 113–114; see id., at 113–141; see also, e.g., id., at 139–14 (Black veterans, North and South, were routinely denied loans that White veterans received); Rothstein 167.

[42]. Baradaran 112–113.

distributed along racial lines.[43] And I could not possibly discuss every way in which, in light of this history, facially race-blind policies *still* work race-based harms today (e.g., racially disparate tax system treatment; the disproportionate location of toxic-waste facilities in Black communities; or the deliberate action of governments at all levels in designing interstate highways to bisect and segregate Black urban communities).[44]

The point is this: Given our history, the origin of persistent race-linked gaps should be no mystery. It has never been a deficiency of Black Americans' desire or ability to, in Frederick Douglass's words "Stand on [their] own legs."[45] Rather, it was always simply what Justice Harlan recognized 140 years ago—the persistent and pernicious denial of "what had already been done in every State of the Union for the white race." *Civil Rights Cases*, 109 U.S., at 61 (dissenting opinion).

. . . .

History speaks. In some form, it can be heard forever. The race-based gaps that first developed centuries ago are echoes from the past that still exist today. By all accounts, they are still stark. . . .

NOTES ON *SFFA V. HARVARD*

1. Context Matters. In a case about affirmative action in higher education, why would Justice Jackson write so much about the ways in which Black Americans have interacted with property laws? Justice Thomas's concurring opinion is written, in many parts, as a response Justice Jackson's opinion. Justice Thomas and Justice Jackson frame their views of American history and their conclusions about how policy should respond to the modern race relations quite differently, but a careful read of both opinions reveals there is no disagreement about the facts of U.S. legal history. Each incorporates their individual experience into their legal analysis, as does every practicing lawyer. Whether one is a

---

[43]. Katznelson 22–23; Rothstein 167.

[44]. Id., at 54–56, 65, 127–131, 217; Stanford Institute for Economic Policy Research, Measuring and Mitigating Disparities in Tax Audits 1–7 (2023); Dickerson 1096–1097.

[45]. What the Black Man Wants: An Address Delivered in Boston, Massachusetts, on 26 January 1865, in 4 The Frederick Douglass Papers 68 (J. Blasssingame & J. McKivigan eds. 1991).

Supreme Court Justice or an intern working on a pro-bono case, each individual's experience adds a data point and fills our common law system with a much needed perspective.

2. Throughline in American History. Justice Jackson gives a very high-level overview of Black Americans' ownership rights, spanning from the time when this country was only a collection of British colonies to the mid-20th century. Though various components of this history, including slavery, Reconstruction, Jim Crow, and redlining, may be (and often are) viewed separately, Justice Jackson's organization of these components presents a wider perspective. The throughline in American history reveals a pattern of practices that reinforce the same biases in spite of changing rules and laws.

3. Law, Psychology, and Economics. Governments and policymakers around the world are increasingly embracing a behavioral economics approach to policymaking. This branch of economics challenges the foundations of traditional economics, which is based on the idea of a "rational person" who acts to maximize gain and minimize loss. As a discipline, behavioral economics seeks to understand the ways in which people are *not* rational but are instead driven by different parts of their psychology. It accounts for various cognitive biases, such as loss aversion and the endowment effect. But behavioral economics is but one subset of a new generation of approaches to economics. Heterodox economics takes various forms—it is a nimble and responsive approach to a rapidly changing world, and one that more boldly addresses questions of how rights in property may be impacted by identity.[6] Innovative scholars who study rights in property and heterodox economics argue that

> the essential disposition—the very *esprit*—of property as it is experienced in contemporary society is inherently raced and gendered because the relations among people in that society are, likewise, inherently raced and gendered. Because contemporary capitalism ... relies on the simple definition of property—because today's iteration of capitalism is focused on these valued resources—we must therefore conclude that all relations under such capitalism are raced and gendered.[7]

6. Shelley Cavalieri & Lua Kamal Yuille, The White Androcentric Disposition of Capitalist Property, 2 U.C. Berkeley J.L. & Polit. Econ. 252 (2022).

7. Id. at 253.

Given that policymakers are increasingly taking these insights into account, how may Justice Jackson's dissenting opinion, despite being dicta, impact policymaking?

A National Myth: De Facto Segregation

One of the realities of life in the United States is that the vast majority of residential communities are racially segregated. While many individuals may not think about this racial segregation at all, those that do may consider some of the causes to be related to private actions, or racial dynamics: de facto segregation. It is easy to overlook how the U.S. government, through executive agencies, legislation, and judicial opinions, has intentionally segregated communities by race. Its actions and policies were so powerful that even after they ended, the segregation they had created persisted. Recognizing racial segregation in the United States as de jure segregation, that is, segregation caused by a series of intentional government policies, is important context to understanding any potential responses.

Public Housing and Building Segregation

During the Great Depression of the 1930s, the federal government built public housing projects for middle class families, and many were designed to be segregated by race. Some of these housing projects even turned formerly integrated communities into segregated ones. Their original intended purpose was not to subsidize the cost of housing; rather, it was to provide a place to live for working class families who could afford to pay for housing but for whom none was available near their jobs and communities.[8]

The federal Public Works Administration (PWA) was created as part of a set of New Deal policies intended to address both a national housing shortage and to create construction jobs. President Franklin D. Roosevelt chose Secretary of the Interior Harold Ickes, a former leader of a chapter of the NAACP, to manage the PWA. Though Ickes personally

8. Rothstein, The Color of Law, supra note 4, at 18

believed in integration and had authorized the "neighborhood composition" rule, which prohibited a public housing project from altering the existing racial composition of the neighborhood it was built in, the PWA's objective was to explicitly segregate neighborhoods by race. In Cleveland, Ohio,[9] for example, the PWA built wholly separate housing projects for Black and white residents in a community that had previously been racially mixed, in defiance of the neighborhood composition rule. However, it was because of individuals like Secretary Ickes that public housing was made available to Black Americans in relative proportion to their population. In short, the goal of these programs was access and segregation, and the program was successful in both.

It should be noted that public housing as it existed around the time it was created was distinct in character and reputation from what it is now in the 21st century. Though public housing and subsidized housing are now synonymous, this was not so when it was created by the WPA. During the New Deal era, public housing was for well resourced middle-class families, and it often, especially in white housing projects, came with many resources and services that we associate with quality living. It was only later, when white families moved out of their white urban housing projects and into single-family homes in the suburbs, and when the demand for housing in the Black community was high, that the local services, subsidies, and reputations associated with public housing projects changed. A combination of federal, state, and local laws that made changes to municipal services, zoning policies (to increase population density), and other public services such as transportation, sanitation, education, and policing, all worked together to create a different type of neighborhood than the kind originally intended by public housing programs.

9. Near where the author was raised.

The Home Owners Loan Corporation and Color Coded Maps

The Home Owners Loan Corporation (HOLC) was created in June 1933 with the purpose of supporting individuals in purchasing real property and helping to prevent foreclosures. With the support of President Roosevelt, HOLC was created by Congress and accomplished its goals by refinancing mortgages that were currently in default and by insuring new mortgages. To do this while protecting its investments and mission, HOLC set out to rate neighborhoods based on their mortgage lending risk.

Grade	Color on Map	HOLC Designation
A	Green	Best
B	Blue	Still Desirable
C	Yellow	Declining
D	Red	Hazardous

> The Home Owners Loan Corporation's designations were *not* based on the likelihood of default but rather on the perceived risk that the value of property would decrease. According to HOLC, the mere presence of Black residents would negatively impact property values.

Because of the practice commonly referred to as "redlining," so called because of the way red lines were drawn around high-risk areas on maps, it was nearly impossible for Black Americans to purchase property at the time. Properties were rated and designated by HOLC based on their risk of decline in market value, not on their risk of default. Accordingly, Black families, despite being no more likely to default on mortgages than white families, were effectively excluded from the entire mortgage market, as the government would not insure mortgage loans on homes in the red-lined Black communities. This exclusion was occurring during a time in American history when homeownership rates were otherwise increasing exponentially due the affordability of single-family homes as well as federal, state, and local policies that encouraged white, middle-class families to move to suburban single-family homes—and it was the result of HOLC's intentional decision to protect its loans and investments by refusing to insure Black communities.

Speculators and investors understood this framework as an opportunity, and so the practice of "blockbusting" became commonplace in some areas. Blockbusting is when real estate agents, developers, or investors seek to purchase property below market value, and so they use tactics including hiring Black people to walk or drive through a neighborhood to convince white owners to sell their homes for less than market value based on the (false) fear that Black neighbors are entering the neighborhood and will change its character and diminish home values. Once the white homeowners sell to the developer at below-market prices, the developer, who now owns the whole "block," may build and resell at a higher price. This unethical practice was prevalent and very rarely censured, despite a highly regulated real estate licensing industry.

> Behavioral economists remind us that is much more difficult to establish a path than it is to maintain one. So, too, is it with the way we organize communities. With regard to both public housing and HOLC policies, the government's initial segregation took a great deal of resources to accomplish. But once established, our psychology and nature tends to maintain the status quo until some of us no longer even notice it. Even today, neighborhoods that HOLC designated "best" are still overwhelmingly white.

Though HOLC existed for roughly 20 years, the impact it had on the organization of the United States has been a lasting one. In some cases, HOLC would not insure mortgages on properties without racially restrictive real covenants. In the 1940s and 1950s, the G.I. Bill helped to continue to transform the homeownership landscape in the United States by providing more than four million home loans worth roughly \$33 million.[10] Black veterans, however, were largely unable to take advantage of this benefit because the loans were not provided for homes in

10. U.S. Dep't of Defense, 75 Years of the GI Bill: How Transformative It's Been, DEFENSE.GOV (Jan. 9, 2019), https://www.defense.gov/News/Feature-Stories/Story/article/1727086/75-years-of-the-gi-bill-how-transformative-its-been/.

Black neighborhoods, thanks to HOLC's mortgage-lending risk assessment practices, discussed above. The nation's economy was booming during this post-War period, and houses were affordable, particularly in light of government-insured home loans and down-payment assistance for veterans. Houses purchased during this period increased exponentially in value, allowing their owners the benefits of equity and generational wealth. Black families who were excluded from the homeownership market at that time were denied the opportunity to take advantage of the exponential growth in home values, leaving them with no opportunity to build equity in real estate that would result in generational wealth. Even after the Fair Housing Act was enacted and redlining and other forms of housing discrimination became illegal, this lack of wealth creation continued to prevent Black families from entering the real estate market.

Capital Markets and Subprime Mortgages (A Second Life for Red Lines)

The real estate market continues to be connected to American history, particularly as it relates to race relations and economics. Because of the exponential growth of property values during the second half of the 20th century, we, as a nation and a culture, came to view real estate as a very secure, dependable investment. At the beginning of the 21st century, capital markets around the world experienced their own exponential growth due to a number of factors, with the internet playing no small part in providing access to commerce for many individuals and developing nations that had not had it before. Consequently, global investors had an unprecedented amount of assets—a "giant pool of money."[11] Historically, one of the most attractive investments in the world had been U.S. real estate, and leading up to the financial crisis of 2008, that is exactly where the investors with their giant pool of money came looking.

In modern markets, when an individual seeks a mortgage-backed loan to purchase real estate, they seek out a lender, usually a bank, that inspects the property to ensure that its value is sufficient for a security

11. This American Life: The Giant Pool of Money, NPR (May 9, 2008) (podcast transcript), https://www.thisamericanlife.org/355/transcript.

interest. In addition to inspecting the property, a prudent lender also verifies that the borrower has sufficient sources of income or assets to keep current with the repayment schedule set forth in the note; this process normally includes verification of the borrower's employment, minimum savings, or credit score. This is all done to ensure that the borrower's risk of defaulting on the loan is low. Defaulting on a loan is difficult and expensive for all involved: the borrower does not want to lose their property, and the lender has to invest additional time, expense, and resources to reclaim the property through foreclosure to satisfy the debt. Verification that a borrower has the ability to repay the note is good practice that protects both the lender and the borrower; it supports the parties involved and the underlying financial systems by promoting stability.

It is rare in modern markets for the original lending institution to continue to hold the note and to collect payments from the borrower. Instead, the initial lender will transfer its rights under the loan, including the rights to foreclose and collect interest, to a financial institution that is engaged in the business of purchasing loans and bundling them together. This purchasing and bundling is called "securitization" because the resulting product—interest-bearing securities—is an investment: the purchaser collects the interest on those loans, which may have a higher rate of interest than the treasury bond rate. Government agencies rate the risk of these securities or investments, and so financial institutions that are in the business of bundling or securitizing these products seek high ratings so that they can market the investments.

When the global financial markets—the giant pool of money—experienced an exponential increase in demand for investments, some investment bankers began to offer mortgages with fewer and fewer verifications of borrower income and assets to help meet this demand. Because these unverified loans presented a higher risk of default, that is, they were "subprime," investment bankers bundled or securitized them with groups of non-high risk mortgages. Achieving just the right mix of risky subprime mortgages and "normal" mortgages to get an appropriate credit rating to attract investors became standard industry practice. Eventually, a new type of financial product known as a "collateralized debt obligation" (CDO) was born. In a CDO, many loans and other assets are pooled together, and the underlying assets (land, in the case of mortgages) serve as collateral in the event that the loans default. CDOs became highly rated and popular investments.

But there was a major problem. The rating agencies and investors in these products were making decisions based on their faith in a real estate and mortgage market that verified income and supported its borrowers; meanwhile, leading up to 2008, the standards for lending were dropping significantly. Eager to continue to create investments for the "giant pool of money," those seeking to "sell" loans turned to the areas that had been designated "hazardous" by HOLC—areas where individuals, most of whom were Black, had historically been excluded from participating in the real estate market as homeowners. So the inevitable happened: many borrowers defaulted on their loans, bringing financial markets to the brink of collapse. Many individuals who defaulted on their loans never had a reasonable chance of successfully repaying them to begin with. After defaulting, the banks foreclosed on their properties—but because of poor market conditions at the time, property values had dropped so low that even the foreclosure sale could not satisfy the amount that what was borrowed, leaving a great number of borrowers in debt even after foreclosure. In the aggregate, this caused investors in CDOs to lose not only their interest income but also their principal. It was this loss of principal—totaling billions of dollars—that led to the collapse of major investment banks and nearly the entire global financial system.

While the U.S. government's Troubled Asset Relief Program (TARP) helped to stabilize financial markets and allow large institutional investors to recover, many individuals continue to be in debt, a disproportionate number of whom live within the red lines drawn by HOLC.

Unforgetting Our History: The Panic of 1837 and Too Big to Fail (Part I)

Looking at the financial crisis in hindsight, it is evident that relying on the continued growth of the real estate market was a mistake. But back in 2008, even without the benefit of hindsight, those who looked carefully at the way mortgage backed securities were being collateralized and sold to satisfy the international appetite for investments could have turned to the lessons of history. Long before homes and land served as collateral for mortgages, people who were enslaved were used as collateral, as they were often the most valuable property owned and were much easier to buy and sell than land.[12] The desire to grow wealth at all costs produced a set of facts in the early 19th century that led to the Panic of 1837 and are eerily similar to those that led to the financial crisis of 2008.

In the early 19th century, technology was advancing, and it was during this time that the cotton gin was invented. The invention sparked a revolution in the cotton industry: "the gin broke the bottleneck, making it possible to clean as much cotton as you could grow."[13] Cotton was a lucrative crop, one that presented a promising opportunity to grow the economy of the then young nation (and which would eventually become a crucial cash crop in the American South). It only required land to grow it and labor to harvest it. Accordingly, the "United States solved its land shortage by expropriating millions of acres from Native Americans, often with military force, acquiring Georgia, Alabama, Tennessee, and Florida. It then sold that land on the cheap … to white settlers."[14] The labor needed to support the industry was supplied by people who were enslaved, and they came to be regarded as very valuable commodities.

In a time when land was not valuable and banks did not exist in the United States (and certainly the existing financial institutions that *did* exist were not regulated), people who were enslaved were used as collateral for mortgages. For many, they were the most valuable property and had the additional benefit of being easily alienable. The practice of using them as collateral was prevalent: Thomas Jefferson mortgaged 150 people he owned to Henderson, McCaul & Company; friends; and even a Dutch firm, in order to build Monticello.[15] This access to credit allowed banks to begin to establish themselves, and these early banks invested heavily in cotton. Farmed in the South, milled in the North, and exported abroad, cotton was the crop that established the American economy.[16] Though slavery had already been abolished on moral grounds in Europe by the mid-1830s, interactions between U.S. investors and European financial systems, including the British firm Baring Brothers,

12. Interview with Matthew Desmond, The 1619 Project: Episode 2, supra note 3.

13. Id. See also Bonnie Martin, Slavery's Invisible Engine: Mortgaging Human Property, 76 J.S. Hist. 817 (Nov. 2010).

14. Martin, Slavery's Invisible Engine, supra note 13.

15. Id. Between 1804 and 1860, the average price of men aged 21 to 38 sold in New Orleans grew from roughly $450 to $1200.

16. See generally id.

which financed the Louisiana Purchase, helped to support an industry built on the forced labor and abuse of people who were enslaved.[17]

And this is where the story really begins to echo what happened in 2008. Excitement about the financial returns on cotton and the market's hunger for investing in it did not last. Too much cotton was being produced, and demand could not keep up with the supply—resulting in lower prices, lower revenues, and decreasing values in farming investments. This then set off what is known as the Panic of 1837. By the time investors called in their debts, the farmers were already insolvent; even if the farmers sold all of their assets, they would not have enough money to pay back their debts. People who were bought for $2,000 were being sold at this time for $60. In the language of 2008, the assets backing these mortgages had become "toxic."[18]

This epidemic of insolvency might have caused a global financial collapse. "Because enslavers couldn't repay their loans, the banks couldn't make interest payments on their bonds. Shouts went up around the Western world, as investors began demanding that states raise taxes to keep their promises. After all, the bonds were backed by taxpayers."[19] Ultimately, the states did not foreclose on defaulting borrowers. Investors and bondholders filed lawsuits, but bankrupt states simply refused to pay their debts. The southern cotton industry simply removed itself from the global financial market. It was too big to fail.[20]

Sociologists, historians, and economists all note the strong parallels between the 1837 and 2008 financial crises: creation of a new financial product to obscure the undesirable morals underlying the system; promises of exponential returns on investment; speculation; misplaced faith in "the myth that some institution (cotton, housing) is unshakable; considered and intentional exploitation of [B]lack people; and impunity for the profiteers when it all falls apart."[21] Even skeptical individuals may find it difficult not to see similarities.

The job of lawyers is distinct from all other disciplines. In a common law system, we rely on precedent. For decades, the way that mortgages

---

17. See id.

18. Id.

19. Id.

20. Id. See also Edward E. Baptist, Half Has Never Been Told: Slavery and the Making of American Capitalism (2016).

21. Id.

and securities have been taught and learned has not fully accounted for their complicated history, that is, how they have shaped not only the country's economy but also the values that are imprinted in our legal system. Only by unforgetting this history and embedding it in our learning can we do better moving forward.

Skill: Comparing and Distinguishing Cases to Strengthen Legal Analysis

Both lawyers and law students may sometimes fall into the trap of thinking that knowing history and precedent and being able to restate them is sufficient for legal analysis. But, as we learned during our exploration of the subprime mortgage crisis, to predict what may occur, it is also crucial to think about the ways the salient facts at hand may relate to the previous outcome. In *assuming* that highly rated asset-backed securities would not default, investors failed to identify the salient facts—namely, what those ratings were based on, the high number of subprime mortgages bundled into the CDOs, and changes in demand. Though all of these things are much easier to see in hindsight, the 2008 financial crisis may still serve as a lesson for law students about the importance of seeking clarity and following logic and instincts to identify relevant facts.

Applying caselaw is the primary and most effective tool for crafting the analysis portion of the IRAC framework. Though mentioning the salient facts and holdings of very similar precedent cases may feel satisfying, it is the comparing and distinguishing of salient facts that is the heart of any legal analysis. While applying caselaw is the principal tool of lawyers practicing in a common law system like the United States, they can also use history and administrative proceedings for comparing and distinguishing the facts at hand. Consider the following primary source material:

Caselaw Summary: Commonwealth v. Freemont Inv. & Loan[22]

Freemont Investment & Loan made a number of subprime mortgages to borrowers in Massachusetts. When a large number of those borrowers defaulted, Freemont made an agreement with the Federal Deposit

22. 897 N.E.2d 548 (Mass. 2008).

Insurance Commission (FDIC) that they would no longer offer that type of loan. Freemont agreed that they would give the Attorney General of Massachusetts 90 days to inspect the terms of any loan and foreclosure and the opportunity to object during that period if the terms were unfair. The Commonwealth objected to nearly every foreclosure based on the terms of the loans, and the court enjoined Freemont from foreclosing on the properties. The court reasoned that Freemont knew or should have known by the terms and features of the loans that they were "doomed to foreclosure." Though the borrowers were not relieved of their obligations, Freemont was ordered to work on a reasonable payment plan with them. Freemont, in turn, argued that the terms of the loans were the industry norm at the time and that the court was applying a fairness standard retroactively and with the benefit of hindsight. The court held that the application of consumer protection statues that predate all of the loans have protected Massachusetts consumers, and while Freemont had proven that its activities were not prohibited, that is not the same as proving that they were permitted.

Caselaw Summary: United States Bank Nat'l Ass'n v. Ibanez[23]

Ibanez borrowed approximately $103,000 from Rose Mortgage, Inc., to finance the purchase of a new home. As was its practice, Rose Mortgage sold the Ibanez mortgage, but the assignment was left blank. When the Ibanez mortgage was transferred again and securitized and sold as part of collateralized debt obligation, the original assignment was also blank. When Ibanez defaulted on the loan, it was owned by U.S. Bank National, which sold the property at auction for approximately $94,000, an amount less than that of the loan outstanding. The court voided the foreclosure sale because of the lender's failure to prove a valid chain of title to the property.

> **Review**
>
> A *salient* fact is one on which the holding turns. If that fact were different, then the holding may have gone a different way.

23. 941 N.E.2d 40 (Mass. 2011).

When considering facts provided in a novel fact pattern, the first step is to isolate the salient facts from the precedent cases that you will be using. After isolating the salient facts, you should state them in a way that is concise, pointed, and focused on how they compare to your analysis of new facts. Spending too much time describing the case is unnecessary—recall that all lawyers, judges, and clients have access to the same cases. The most important thing is to plainly articulate how the salient facts you identified compare to the facts at hand. You can help to ensure a strong comparison by starting sentences with "Like ..." or "Unlike...." Use the following fact pattern to practice.

> Basile Borrower entered into a mortgage for $100,000 in order to purchase a house. Though the terms of the mortgage were standard for the industry at the time, the lender made no effort to ensure that Basile could repay the note; if it had, the lender would have found it nearly impossible for Basile to meet his repayment obligations with his current salary. The lender did verify that Basil had some assets that would help to delay a default, if needed. Promptly after purchasing the property, Basile depleted his savings to purchase a very expensive engagement ring. Shortly thereafter, Basile defaulted on the note. Snowdrop Mortgage Company entered into the mortgage agreement with Basile and promptly sold the loan to a larger bank. Though the paperwork was completed correctly, unbeknownst to everyone, the final page containing the assignment of the note had gotten stuck in the copy machine and was never recovered. When the note was securitized and included as part of a collateralized debt obligation investment, it was done without the original assignment. When Basile defaulted, it was Acme Bank Corp. that held the note. At foreclosure sale, Acme Bank Corp. sold the property for $70,000.

Practice your legal analysis skills by first isolating some salient facts. There may be multiple IRACs in your final product. Accordingly, it is acceptable for purposes of this exercise if your facts address different issues. Below you will see the difference between recalling/mentioning salient facts from precedent cases in your analysis and actually comparing the salient facts from precedent cases to to the novel facts you are given. Some students make the mistake of just stacking descriptions of precedent cases on top of facts from the novel fact pattern without bothering to compare them. But remember: making comparisons is the very crux of the legal analysis. Continually asking yourself "How is this the same?" and "How is this different?" and then applying those similarities and differences to the application of the rule is precisely what lawyers do.

Salient Facts Identified	Salient Facts Compared/Distinguished
In *Commonwealth v. Freemont Investment & Loan*, the lender made no effort to verify income or assets.	Like in *Commonwealth v. Freemont Investment & Loan*, the lender did not make an effort to verify income to ensure that Basile could repay the loan moving forward. *Unlike* in the *Freemont* case, however, the lender did verify assets to ensure that Basile would not default immediately. Basile's depleting his assets immediately after the verification may be accounted for in considering the responsibility of the parties.
In *United States Bank Nat'l Ass'n v. Ibanez*, the note was never assigned; when transferred there was no record of an assignment.	Unlike in the *Ibanez* case, though the assignment was missing from the file relating to the securitized loans, it was correctly completed by the parties at the closing of the transaction. The fact that the assignment was missing was unknown to the parties who had completed the associated administration.

Not only is practicing this skill in long form very helpful, but crafting your own fact patterns with materially different facts will assist your understanding and retention of the material. Considering the ways you might alter a fact pattern slightly to allow for some comparison and analysis without altering it so much that the precedent cases are rendered irrelevant is a helpful exercise. According to Bloom's Taxonomy,[24] working with material in this way is a high-order skill, and it is one that will help you to feel confident and comfortable when it comes time for exams.

24. See Ch. 3, supra.

SUGGESTIONS FOR FURTHER READING

Richard Rothstein, The Color of Law: A Forgotten History of How Our Government Segregated America (2017).

Mehrsa Baradaran, The Color of Money: Black Banks and the Racial Wealth Gap (2017).

Richard Thaler & Cass Sunstein, Nudge: Improving Decisions About Health, Wealth, and Happiness (2009).

Shelley Cavalieri & Lua Kamal Yuille, The White Androcentric Disposition of Capitalist Property (2002).

Edward E. Baptist, Half Has Never Been Told: Slavery and the Making of American Capitalism (2016).

Bonnie Martin, *Slavery's Impossible Engine: Mortgaging Human Property*, 76 J. S. Hist. 817 (Nov. 2010).

Ryan Best & Elena Mejia, *The Lasting Legacy of Redlining*, FiveThirtyEight (Feb. 9, 2022), https://projects.fivethirtyeight.com/redlining/.

Gene Denby & Shereen Marisol Meraji, *Code Switch: Location! Location! Location!*, NPR (April 11, 2018), https://www.npr.org/transcripts/601131468.

This American Life: The Giant Pool of Money, NPR (May 9, 2008) (podcast audio), https://www.thisamericanlife.org/355/the-giant-pool-of-money.

SIX

Zoning and Land Use

I became an expert in the language of fear. Couples locked arms or reached for each others' hands when they saw me. Some crossed to the other side of the street. People who were on conversations went mute and stared straight ahead, as though avoiding my eyes would save them.... I'd been walking the streets grinning good evening at people who were frightened to death of me. I did violence to them just by being....[1]

Zoning in Context

Protecting the rights of property owners to use and enjoy their property as they see fit is the central tenet of property law, and one that our country been considering and redefining throughout its history. With nuisance, we considered the ways that rights of use and enjoyment must be balanced against the same rights of nearby property owners. The courts' application of the reasonableness standard, which takes into consideration the usefulness of the nuisance-causing activity versus the gravity of the harm, among other factors, has revealed cultural biases and blind-spots in our common law. We also considered covenants, which bind owners of adjacent property and often involve a promise not to use the property in a certain way. This ability to restrict the way that a

1. From Claude M. Steele, Whistling Vivaldi: How Stereotypes Affect Us and What We Can Do (reprint ed. 2011).

neighbor may use their property becomes a (nonpossessory) interest in property itself. Given the importance of our property and our home to our identity, it makes sense that protection of these interests is a priority.

Unlike nuisance and covenants, zoning ordinances are not between private property owners but rather are creations of local governments. Because the government is restricting the use of private property, some private property owners view zoning as a form of "regulatory taking," as it diminishes some of their rights to do as they please with their owned property.[2] There is a great advantage in understanding all of these concepts before learning how they fit together. Zoning brings together many fundamental property-law concepts, and it has a profound impact not only on owners' use and enjoyment of property but also on the way that groups organize themselves: There are times zoning takes into consideration certain nuisance principles or seeks to minimize or avoid nuisance claims by organizing the use of property. Sometimes property owners purchase property in districts zoned in a particular way in the hope that the area will continue to be used in that way—very similar to a covenant or set of mutually enforceable covenants. And other times, property owners may feel so restricted by zoning regulations that they feel like they have lost a right in their property without just compensation. As we can see, zoning can take on the character of many concepts of property law, including but not limited to nuisance, real covenants, and takings.

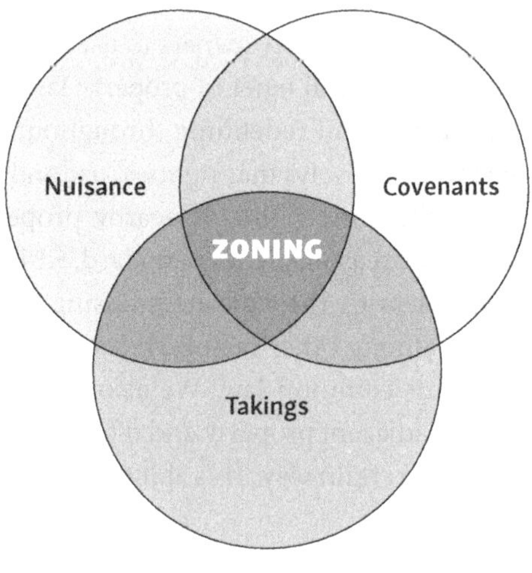

2. *See* Ch. 8, *infra*.

Zoning ordinances are all statutory in nature, that is, they are created by local governments. Each local jurisdiction in the United States has its own set of rules with regard to the bodies that create the ordinances, enforce them, and hear the appeals. The popular phrase "all politics are local" applies nowhere more than in the area of zoning. With certain exceptions for property in some unincorporated parts of counties that are not subject to zoning, the majority of real property in the United States exists within a jurisdiction and is accordingly subject to some oversight. Very often, zoning is an opportunity for local residents to use a democratic and legal process to establish and maintain the desired character of their local jurisdiction. It follows, then, that when change occurs and demographics shift, the democratic process can be stressed and tested in the context of zoning.[3]

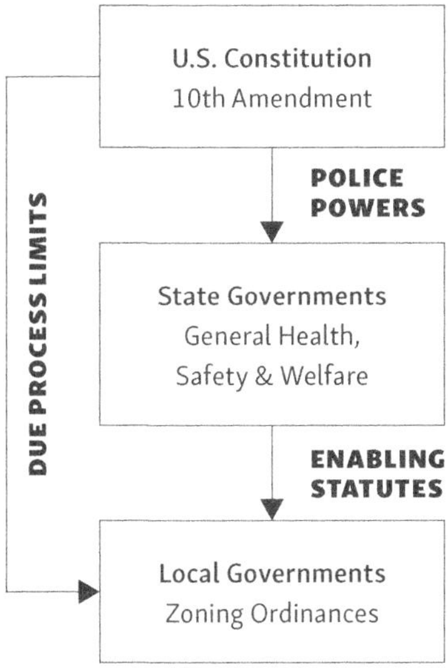

The 10th Amendment grants to the states any powers that it does not reserve for the federal government. States use these "police powers" to regulate behavior for the betterment of the general health, morals, safety, and welfare of the people within their territories. Using these powers, state legislatures enact "enabling statutes" that direct each local jurisdiction

3. Katherine Levine Einstein, David M. Glick, & Maxwell Palmer, Neighborhood Defenders (2019).

within the state to establish a set of rules related to zoning. The zoning ordinances control the use of real property in the local jurisdiction. Sometimes individual residents disagree with the local jurisdiction's zoning ordinances and petition the government on the basis that their federal constitutional rights are being violated. In this way, the U.S. Constitution *recognizes* the local jurisdiction's zoning authority (via the sovereign state's police powers) but also places *limits* on the local jurisdiction's authority.

The importance of zoning cannot be overstated. Where identity, property, and social values are closely connected, zoning is the key to controlling much of what can happen in each local jurisdiction. For those seeking to promote social justice, zoning is an impactful place to begin. In this chapter, we explore some of the history of the jurisprudence related to zoning and due process and also seek to understand some of the modern applications. Finally, keeping in mind the relationship between local services, identity, and social mobility—particularly in the historical context of government-sponsored segregation—this chapter underscores the connection between local tax bases and local services.

Zoning and Due Process

In 1917 the Supreme Court decided *Buchanan v. Warley*, a landmark case relating to zoning and due process that was largely ignored by many jurisdictions. As you read the case, consider the context in which it was decided as well as how some of the other areas in property law may have related to how property owners responded.

BUCHANAN V. WARLEY

245 U.S. 60 (1917)

MR. JUSTICE DAY delivered the opinion of the court.

Buchanan, the plaintiff in error, brought an action in the Jefferson Circuit Court of Kentucky for the specific performance of a contract for the sale of certain real estate situated in the City of Louisville at the corner of 37th Street and Pflanz Avenue. The offer in writing to purchase the property contained a proviso:

"It is understood that I am purchasing the above property for the purpose of having erected thereon a house which I propose to make my residence, and it is a distinct part of this agreement that I shall not be required to accept a deed to the above property or to pay for said property unless I have the right under the laws of the State of Kentucky and the City of Louisville to occupy said property as a residence." This offer was accepted by the plaintiff.

To the action for specific performance the defendant by way of answer set up the condition above set forth, that he is a colored person, and that, on the block of which the lot in controversy is a part, there are ten residences, eight of which at the time of the making of the contract were occupied by white people, and only two (those nearest the lot in question) were occupied by colored people, and that, under and by virtue of the ordinance of the City of Louisville, approved May 11, 1914, he would not be allowed to occupy the lot as a place of residence.

In reply to this answer the plaintiff set up, among other things, that the ordinance was in conflict with the Fourteenth Amendment to the Constitution of the United States, and hence no defense to the action for specific performance of the contract.

... The Court of Appeals of Kentucky, 165 Kentucky 559, held the ordinance valid and, of itself, a complete defense to the action.

The title of the ordinance is: "An ordinance to prevent conflict and ill-feeling between the white and colored races in the City of Louisville, and to preserve the public peace and promote the general welfare by making reasonable provisions requiring, as far as practicable, the use of separate blocks for residences, places of abode and places of assembly by white and colored people respectively."

By the first section of the ordinance, it is made unlawful for any colored person to move into and occupy as a residence, place of abode, or to establish and maintain as a place of public assembly, any house upon any block upon which a greater number of houses are occupied as residences, places of abode, or places of public assembly by white people than are occupied as residences, places of abode, or places of public assembly by colored people.

Section 2 provides that it shall be unlawful for any white person to move into and occupy as a residence, place of abode, or to establish and maintain as a place of public assembly any house upon any block upon which a greater number of houses are occupied as residences, places of abode or places of public assembly by colored people than are occupied as residences, places of abode or places of public assembly by white people.

....

The assignments of error in this court attack the ordinance upon the ground that it violates the Fourteenth Amendment of the Constitution of the United States, in that it abridges the privileges and immunities of citizens of the United States to acquire and enjoy property, takes property without due process of law, and denies equal protection of the laws.

....

We pass then to a consideration of the case upon its merits. This ordinance prevents the occupancy of a lot in the City of Louisville by a person of color in a block where the greater number of residences are occupied by white persons; where such a majority exists, colored persons are excluded. This interdiction is based wholly upon color—simply that and nothing more. In effect, premises situated, as are those in question, in the so-called white block are effectively debarred from sale to persons of color because, if sold, they cannot be occupied by the purchaser, nor by him sold to another of the same color.

This drastic measure is sought to be justified under the authority of the State in the exercise of the police power. It is said such legislation tends to promote the public peace by preventing racial conflicts; that it tends to maintain racial purity; that it prevents the deterioration of property owned and occupied by white people, which deterioration, it is contended, is sure to follow the occupancy of adjacent premises by persons of color.

The authority of the State to pass laws in the exercise of the police power, having for their object the promotion of the public health, safety, and welfare, is very broad, as has been affirmed in numerous and recent decisions of this court. Furthermore, the exercise of this power, embracing nearly all legislation of a local character, is not to be interfered with by the courts where it is within the scope of legislative authority and the means adopted reasonably tend to accomplish a lawful purpose. But it is equally well established that the police power, broad as it is, cannot justify the passage of a law or ordinance which runs counter to the limitations of the Federal Constitution; that principle has been so frequently affirmed in this court that we need not stop to cite the cases.

The Federal Constitution and laws passed within its authority are, by the express terms of that instrument, made the supreme law of the land. The Fourteenth Amendment protects life, liberty, and property from invasion by the States without due process of law. Property is more than the mere thing which a person owns. It is elementary that it includes the right to acquire, use, and dispose of it. The Constitution protects these essential attributes of property. *Holden v. Hardy*, 169 U.S. 366, 391. Property consists of the free use, enjoyment, and disposal of a person's acquisitions without control or diminution save by the law of the land. 1 Blackstone's Commentaries (Cooley's Ed.), 127.

True it is that dominion over property springing from ownership is not absolute and unqualified. The disposition and use of property may be controlled in the exercise of the police power in the interest of the public health, convenience, or welfare. Harmful occupations may be controlled and regulated. Legitimate business may also be regulated in the interest of the public. Certain uses of property may be confined to portions of the municipality other than the resident district, such as livery stables, brickyards and the like, because of the impairment of the health and comfort of the occupants of neighboring property. Many illustrations might be given from the decisions of this court, and other courts, of this principle, but these cases do not touch the one at bar.

The concrete question here is: may the occupancy, and, necessarily the purchase and sale of property of which occupancy is an incident, be inhibited by the States, or by one of its municipalities, solely because of the color of the proposed occupant of the premises? That one may dispose of his property, subject only to the control of lawful enactments curtailing that right in the public interest, must be conceded. The question now presented makes it pertinent to enquire into the constitutional right of the white man to sell his property to a colored man, having in view the legal status of the purchaser and occupant.

Following the Civil War, certain amendments to the Federal Constitution were adopted which have become an integral part of that instrument, equally binding upon all the States and fixing certain fundamental rights which all are bound to respect. The Thirteenth Amendment abolished slavery in the United States and in all places subject to their jurisdiction, and gave Congress power to enforce the Amendment by appropriate legislation. The Fourteenth Amendment made all persons born or naturalized in the United States citizens of the United States and of the States in which they reside, and provided that no State shall make or enforce any law which shall abridge the privileges or immunities of citizens of the United States, and that no State shall deprive any person of life, liberty, or property without due process of law, nor deny to any person the equal protection of the laws.

The effect of these Amendments was first dealt with by this court in *The Slaughter House Cases*, 16 Wall. 36. The reasons for the adoption of the Amendments were elaborately considered by a court familiar with the times in which the necessity for the Amendments arose and with the circumstances which impelled their adoption. In that case, Mr. Justice Miller, who spoke for the majority, pointed out that the colored race, having been freed from slavery by the Thirteenth Amendment, was raised to the dignity of citizenship and equality of civil rights by the Fourteenth Amendment, and the States were prohibited from abridging the privileges and immunities of such citizens, or depriving any person of life, liberty, or property without due process of law. While a principal purpose of the latter Amendment was to protect persons of color, the broad language used was deemed sufficient to protect all persons, white or black, against discriminatory legislation by the States. This is now the settled law. In many of the cases since arising, the question of color has not been involved, and the cases have been decided upon alleged violations of civil or property rights irrespective of the race or color of the complainant. In *The Slaughter House Cases*, it was recognized that *the chief inducement to the passage of the Amendment was the desire to extend federal protection to the recently emancipated race from unfriendly and discriminating legislation by the States.* [emphasis added—Ed.]

In *Strauder v. West Virginia*, 100 U.S. 303, this court held that a colored person charged with an offense was denied due process of law by a statute which prevented colored men from sitting on the jury which tried him. Mr. Justice Strong, speaking for the court, again reviewed the history of the Amendments, and, among other things, in speaking of the Fourteenth Amendment, said:

"It [the Fourteenth Amendment] was designed to assure to the colored race the enjoyment of all the civil rights that, under the law, are enjoyed by white persons, and to give to that race the protection of the general government in that enjoyment whenever it should be denied by the States. It not only gave citizenship and the privileges of citizenship to persons of color, but it denied to any State the power to withhold from them the equal protection of the laws, and authorized Congress to enforce its provisions by appropriate legislation. It ordains that no State shall make or enforce any laws which shall abridge the privileges or immunities of citizens of the United States.... It ordains that no State shall deprive any person of life, liberty, or property, without due process of law, or deny to any person within its jurisdiction the equal protection of the laws. What is this but declaring that the law in the States shall be the same for the black as for the white; that all persons, whether colored or white, shall stand equal before the laws of the States, and, in regard to the colored race, for whose protection the amendment was primarily designed, that no discrimination shall be made against them by law because of their color?...

"The *Fourteenth Amendment makes no attempt to enumerate the rights it designed to protect. It speaks in general terms, and those are as comprehensive as possible.* Its language is prohibitory, but every prohibition implies the existence of rights and immunities, prominent among which is an immunity from inequality of legal protection either for life, liberty, or property. Any State action that denies this immunity to a colored man is in conflict with the Constitution." [emphasis added—Ed.]

Again, this court, in *Ex parte Virginia*, 100 U.S. 339, 347, speaking of the Fourteenth Amendment, said:

"Whoever, by virtue of public position under a State government, deprives another of property, life, or liberty, without due process of law, or denies or takes away the equal protection of the laws, violates the constitutional inhibition, and, as he acts in the name and for the State and is clothed with the State's power, his act is that of the State."

In giving legislative aid to these constitutional provisions, Congress enacted in 1866, c. 31, § 1, 14 Stat. 27 [Rev.Stats., § 1978] that:

"All citizens of the United States shall have the same right in every State and Territory as is enjoyed by white citizens thereof to inherit, purchase, lease, sell, hold, and convey real and personal property."

And, in 1870, by c. 114, § 16, 16 Stat. 144 [Rev.Stats., § 1977] that:

"All persons within the jurisdiction of the United States shall have the same right in every State and Territory to make and enforce contracts, to sue, be parties, give evidence, and to the full and equal benefit of all laws and proceedings for the security of persons and property as is enjoyed by white citizens, and shall be subject to like punishment, pains, penalties, taxes, licenses and exactions of every kind, and no other."

In the face of these constitutional and statutory provisions, can a white man be denied, consistently with due process of law, the right to dispose of his property to a purchaser by prohibiting the occupation of it for the sole reason that the purchaser is a person of color intending to occupy the premises as a place of residence?

The statute of 1866, originally passed under sanction of the Thirteenth Amendment, 14 Stat. 27, and practically reenacted after the adoption of the Fourteenth Amendment, 16 Stat. 144, expressly provided that all citizens of the United States in any State shall have the same right to purchase property as is enjoyed by white citizens. Colored persons are citizens of the United States, and have the right to purchase property and enjoy and use the same without laws discriminating against them solely on account of color. *Hall v. DeCuir*, 95 U.S. 485, 508. *These enactments did not deal with the social rights of men, but with those fundamental rights in property which it was intended to secure upon the same terms to citizens of every race and color. Civil Rights Cases*, 109 U.S. 3, 22. [emphasis added—Ed.] The Fourteenth Amendment and these statutes enacted in furtherance of its purpose operate to qualify and entitle a colored man to acquire property without state legislation discriminating against him solely because of color.

....

In *Carey v. City of Atlanta*, 143 Georgia, 192, the Supreme Court of Georgia, holding an ordinance similar in principle to the one herein involved to be invalid, dealt with *Plessy v. Ferguson* and *The Berea College Case* in language so apposite that we quote a portion of it:

"In each instance, the complaining person was afforded the opportunity to ride, or to attend institutions of learning, or afforded the thing of whatever nature to which in the particular case he was entitled. The most that was done was to require him as a member of a class to conform with reasonable rules in regard to the separation of the races. In none of them was he denied the right to use, control, or dispose of his property, as in this case. Property of a person, whether as a member of a class or as an individual, cannot be taken without due process of law. In the recent case of *McCabe v. Atchison &c. Ry. Co.*, 235 U.S. 151, where the court had under consideration a statute which allowed railroad companies to furnish dining cars for white people and to refuse to furnish dining cars altogether for colored persons, this language was used in reference to the contentions of the attorney general: 'This argument with respect to volume of traffic seems to us to be without merit. It makes the constitutional right depend upon the number of persons who may be discriminated against, whereas the essence of the constitutional right is that it is a personal one.'...

"The effect of the ordinance under consideration was not merely to regulate a business or the like, *but was to destroy the right of the individual to acquire, enjoy, and dispose of his property.* Being of this character, it was void as being opposed to the due process clause of the constitution." [emphasis added—Ed.]

That there exists a serious and difficult problem arising from a feeling of race hostility which the law is powerless to control, and to which it must give a measure of consideration, may be freely admitted. But its solution cannot be promoted by depriving citizens of their constitutional rights and privileges.

As we have seen, this court has held laws valid which separated the races on the basis of equal accommodations in public conveyances, and courts of high authority have held enactments lawful which provide for separation in the public schools of white and colored pupils where equal privileges are given. But, in view of the rights secured by the Fourteenth Amendment to the Federal Constitution, such legislation must have its limitations, and cannot be sustained where the exercise of authority exceeds the restraints of the Constitution. We think these limitations are exceeded in laws and ordinances of the character now before us.

It is the purpose of such enactments, and, it is frankly avowed, it will be their ultimate effect, to require by law, at least in residential districts, the compulsory separation of the races on account of color. Such action is said to be essential to the maintenance of the purity of the races, although it is to be noted in the ordinance under consideration that the employment of colored servants in white families is permitted, and nearby residences of colored persons not coming within the blocks, as defined in the ordinance, are not prohibited.

The case presented does not deal with an attempt to prohibit the amalgamation of the races. The right which the ordinance annulled was the civil right of a white man to dispose of his property if he saw fit to do so to a person of color and of a colored person to make such disposition to a white person.

It is urged that this proposed segregation will promote the public peace by preventing race conflicts. Desirable as this is, and important as is the preservation of the public peace, this aim cannot be accomplished by laws or ordinances which deny rights created or protected by the Federal Constitution.

It is said that such acquisitions by colored persons depreciate property owned in the neighborhood by white persons. But property may be acquired by undesirable white neighbors or put to disagreeable though lawful uses with like results.

We think this attempt to prevent the alienation of the property in question to a person of color was not a legitimate exercise of the police power of the State, and is in direct violation of the fundamental law enacted in the Fourteenth Amendment of the Constitution preventing state interference with property rights except by due process of law. That being the case, the ordinance cannot stand. *Booth v. Illinois*, 184 U.S. 425, 429; *Otis v. Parker*, 187 U.S. 606, 609.

Reaching this conclusion, it follows that the judgment of the Kentucky Court of Appeals must be reversed, and the cause remanded to that court for further proceedings not inconsistent with this opinion.

Reversed.

NOTES ON *BUCHANAN V. WARLEY*

1. Effect of the Ruling. This case was not only a departure from precedent but also from the prevailing attitudes of the time. Local jurisdictions, particularly those that were reluctant to give up their property rights in people who were enslaved, were even more reluctant to give up the right to enact zoning ordinances that precluded Black Americans from living among white Americans. Even (and sometimes especially) in jurisdictions where slavery was not legal, racial segregation in housing, schooling, and almost every other aspect of daily life was accomplished through governmental and nongovernmental means. Despite its clear directive, many local jurisdictions simply ignored *Buchanan* and continued to pass and enforce zoning ordinances that segregated areas by race. Even jurisdictions that followed the letter of the law and found race-neutral ways to comply with the Court's decision and the 14th Amendment's due process provisions are still largely inaccessible to Black Americans. Consider low-density areas, for example. Because low-density areas have long been perceived as valuable, the goal of some zoning codes has been to limit development. Such codes serve to exclude people who do not have sufficient resources to afford property anywhere but in densely populated areas. In this way, the tools of zoning have been used creatively to segregate and exclude.

2. Relation to *Corrigan v. Buckley* (Covenants). In his opinion, Justice Day admits that promoting public peace and racial harmony is a desirable goal, but he also concedes that, because of the 14th Amendment, zoning ordinances are not an appropriate means of accomplishing that goal. In other words, the 14th Amendment applies only to state actions, not private ones. Shortly after *Buchanan* was decided, the Court upheld racially restrictive covenants between private property holders in *Corrigan v. Buckley*.[4]

3. De Facto v. De Jure Segregation. In his book *The Color of Law*, Richard Rothstein discusses at length the distinction between de facto and de jure segregation.[5] De facto segregation results from the decisions and choices private citizens make, for example, the way they choose to organize themselves. It is something that exists in practice. De jure segregation, in contrast, results from government policy. The zoning ordinance at issue in *Buchanan* is an example of de jure segregation that was dismantled by the Court, but many local jurisdictions continued to engage in de jure segregation by way of their own unconstitutional zoning ordinances. Why is it important to make this distinction? Are the effects of segregation the same regardless of how the segregation came into being? Though some believe that resources should be spent on assessing current circumstances and moving forward, others, including those who are interested in restorative justice, believe there is value in understanding history and taking accountability. Given the ways in which psychology, identity, and property ownership are so intimately connected, this difficult task seems worthwhile.

---

4. 271 U.S. 323 (1926). *See* Ch. 4, *supra*.

5. *See generally* RICHARD ROTHSTEIN, THE COLOR OF LAW: A FORGOTTEN HISTORY OF HOW OUR GOVERNMENT SEGREGATED AMERICA (2017).

Cumulative

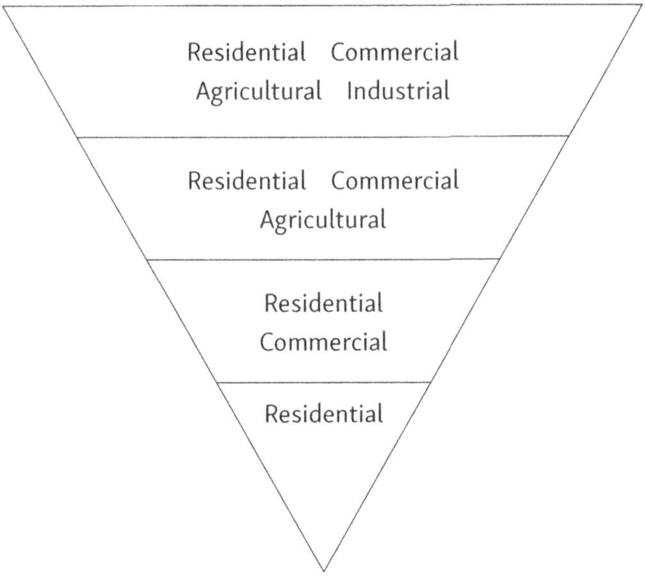

Non-Cumulative

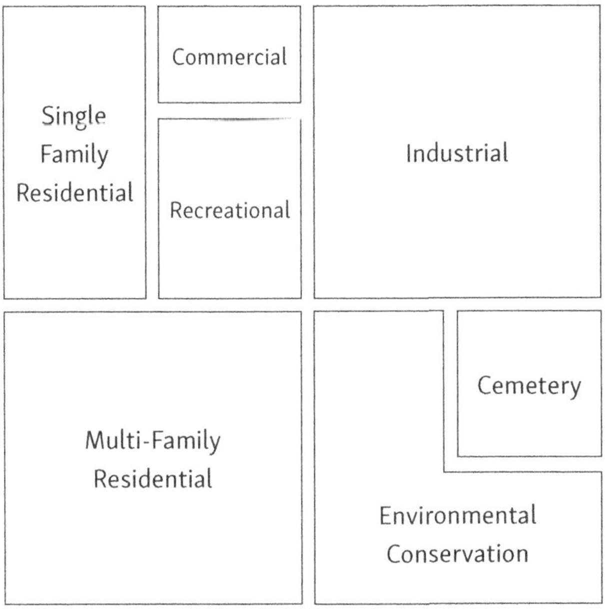

Zoning Basics

As the U.S. population grew, zoning regulations developed into more complex systems to accommodate the increasingly nuanced needs of communities. There are two main types of zoning ordinances: cumulative and noncumulative. Because the constitutionality of a cumulative zoning system was challenged (and upheld) in *Village of Euclid v. Ambler Realty Co.*,[6] cumulative zoning is sometimes referred to as "Euclidian" zoning.

In cumulative zoning, there is a hierarchy of uses—running from most restrictive (bottom/smallest part of the triangle) to least restrictive (top/largest part of the triangle); any use that is permitted in a less intensive zone is permissible in a more intensive zone. This contrasts with noncumulative zoning, which maintains a single use for each separately zoned area of a jurisdiction. In the *Euclid* case, a landowner sought relief following the village's passage of a zoning ordinance that limited the use of the owner's property—property that had been previously unrestricted and for which industrial development was planned. Ambler Realty sought to have the Village of Euclid's new zoning ordinance invalidated because it substantially diminished the value of the property. Ambler argued that the statute amounted to a taking of its rights in property without due process of law, in violation of the 14th Amendment. The Court upheld the zoning ordinance and, in doing so, gave local jurisdictions the authority and confidence to use their legislative powers as they saw fit for urban planning purposes. This landmark case helped to establish a culture of deference to local zoning laws.

While zoning ordinances may be either cumulative or noncumulative, local jurisdictions may regulate various aspects of property. The most common restrictions are related to area, use, and height. Each of these can be put into either a cumulative or noncumulative framework.

6. 272 U.S. 365 (1926).

Type of Restriction	Description
Use	How the property is being used: is it residential, commercial, industrial, agricultural, or hazardous? Some types of parcels, such as public parks or schools, may have restrictions not only on their use but also on their proximity to other types of uses. These restrictions may be general or specific and define, in a granular way, the *type* of use that is permitted (e.g., single family residence).
Area	Area restrictions relate to the structures on the property and how they relate to the boundaries. There may be required setbacks (a minimum distance that structures must be from the property line) or minimum lot sizes.
Height	Height restrictions relate to the permissible height of structures on the property.

Each is a tool for a zoning board to work with in crafting a package of rules that relates to property within its jurisdiction. A zoning board may divide the locality as it sees fit, and so long as it adheres to the process outlined in the enabling statute, which often includes periods of public notice and comment, it is unlikely to violate due process requirements. In this way, zoning boards have become powerful forces in structuring the way we live.

Defining Exclusionary Zoning

The Fair Housing Act of 1968 expressly prohibits municipalities and other local government entities from discriminating on the basis of race, color, religion, sex, disability, familial status, or national origin.[7] Despite the protections the act affords to individuals in protected classes, the nature of zoning is very local—and very personal. Because income level is not a protected class, many jurisdictions have found ways to use the tools of their zoning codes to exclude poor people and families from desirable areas (note that family status is one of the constitutionally protected classes). And because effecting these regulations in the name of

7. 42 U.S.C. §§ 3601–19.

protecting property values is facially neutral, property owners may take issue with the notion that such policies disproportionately impact Black communities that have been excluded from real property ownership throughout American history.

One tool of local jurisdictions that has recently been receiving significant attention is single-family zoning. When a local jurisdiction demands that all the residences in a municipality be single-family homes or have a minimum lot size, it effectively excludes populations that do not have the wealth or resources to purchase property in these areas. In this way, local jurisdictions can preserve the character of their localities, which all too often means perpetuating racial segregation.[8]

In the landmark case *Moore v. City of East Cleveland*,[9] the Supreme Court examined an ordinance that went beyond requiring single-family zoning. Though the Court determined that the ordinance violated the Due Process Clause, it is interesting to note that it was not the ordinance itself but rather its strict definition of "family" that it found to be unconstitutional. Note also that in its opinion in *Moore*, the Court cites its decision in *Village of Belle Terre v. Boraas*,[10] where it upheld the constitutionality of a statute that defined "family" as "one or more persons related by blood, adoption, or marriage, living and cooking together as a single housekeeping unit" or two people unrelated by blood or marriage. In *Boraas*, the Village objected to a group of unrelated students' living together in a house in violation of the statute. Ultimately, the Court upheld the zoning ordinance on the grounds that the students did not constitute a family and the ordinance was appropriately created through and related to the police powers. As you read *Moore*, consider what you know about modern neighborhoods and their organization.

---

8. *See generally* John Infranca, *Singling Out Single-Family Zoning*, 111 Geo. L. Rev. 659 (Apr. 2023).

9. 431 U.S. 494 (1977).

10. 416 U.S. 1 (1974).

MOORE V. CITY OF EAST CLEVELAND

431 U.S. 494 (1977)

MR. JUSTICE POWELL announced the judgment of the Court, and delivered an opinion in which MR. JUSTICE BRENNAN, MR. JUSTICE MARSHALL, and MR. JUSTICE BLACKMUN joined.

East Cleveland's housing ordinance, like may throughout the country, limits occupancy of a dwelling unit to members of a single family. § 1351.02. But the ordinance contains an unusual and complicated definitional section that recognizes as a "family" only a few categories of related individuals. The East Cleveland ordinance defines "family" to include, in addition to the spouse of the "nominal head of the household," the couple's childless unmarried children, but only one dependent child (married or unmarried) having dependent children, and one parent of the nominal head of the household or of his or her spouse. Thus, an "extended family" is authorized in only the most limited sense, and "family" is essentially confined to parents and their own children. Appellant grandmother was charged with violating the ordinance because John, Jr., lived with her at the same time her other grandson, Dale, Jr., was also living in the home; the latter is classified as an "unlicensed roomer" authorized by the ordinance to live in the house.

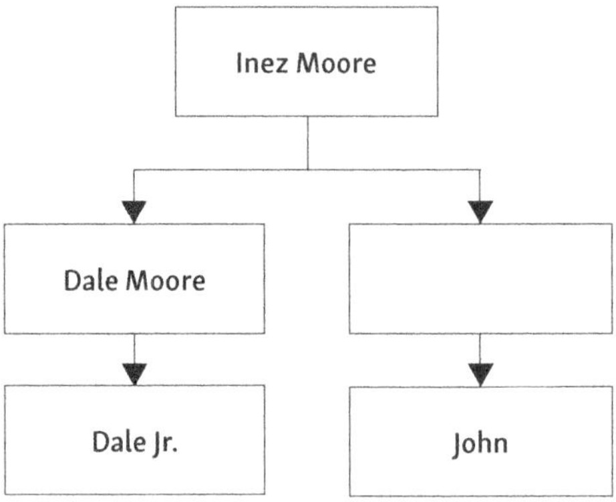

Because her family, living together in her home, fits none of those categories, appellant stands convicted of a criminal offense. The question in this case is whether the ordinance violates the Due Process Clause of the Fourteenth Amendment.

I

Appellant, Mrs. Inez Moore, lives in her East Cleveland home together with her son, Dale Moore, Sr., and her two grandsons, Dale, Jr., and John Moore, Jr. The two boys are first cousins, rather than brothers;

we are told that John came to live with his grandmother and with the elder and younger Dale Moores after his mother's death.

In early 1973, Mrs. Moore received a notice of violation from the city, stating that John was an "illegal occupant" and directing her to comply with the ordinance. When she failed to remove him from her home, the city filed a criminal charge. Mrs. Moore moved to dismiss, claiming that the ordinance was constitutionally invalid on its face. Her motion was overruled, and, upon conviction, she was sentenced to five days in jail and a $25 fine. The Ohio Court of Appeals affirmed after giving full consideration to her constitutional claims, and the Ohio Supreme Court denied review. We noted probable jurisdiction of her appeal, 425 U.S. 949 (1976).

II

The city argues that our decision in *Village of Belle Terre v. Boraas*, 416 U.S. 1 (1974), requires us to sustain the ordinance attacked here. Belle Terre, like East Cleveland, imposed limits on the types of groups that could occupy a single dwelling unit. Applying the constitutional standard announced in this Court's leading land use case, *Euclid v. Ambler Realty Co.*, 272 U.S. 365 (1926), we sustained the Belle Terre ordinance on the ground that it bore a rational relationship to permissible state objectives.

But one overriding factor sets this case apart from *Belle Terre*. The ordinance there affected only unrelated individuals. It expressly allowed all who were related by "blood, adoption, or marriage" to live together, and, in sustaining the ordinance, we were careful to note that it promoted "family needs" and "family values." 416 U.S., at 9. East Cleveland, in contrast, has chosen to regulate the occupancy of its housing by slicing deeply into the family itself. This is no mere incidental result of the ordinance. On its face, it selects certain categories of relatives who may live together and declares that others may not. In particular, it makes a crime of a grandmother's choice to live with her grandson in circumstances like those presented here.

When a city undertakes such intrusive regulation of the family, neither *Belle Terre* nor *Euclid* governs; the usual judicial deference to the legislature is inappropriate. "This Court has long recognized that freedom of personal choice in matters of marriage and family life is one of the liberties protected by the Due Process Clause of the Fourteenth Amendment." 414 U.S. 632, 639–640 (1974). A host of cases, tracing their lineage to *Meyer v. Nebraska*, 262 U.S. 390, 399–401 (1923), and *Pierce v. Society of Sisters*, 268 U.S. 510, 534–535 (1925), have consistently acknowledged a "private realm of family life which the state cannot enter." *Prince v. Massachusetts*, 321 U.S. 158, 166 (1944). *See, e.g., Roe v. Wade*, 410 U.S. 113, 152–153 (1973); *Wisconsin v. Yoder*, 406 U.S. 205, 231–233 (1972); *Stanley v. Illinois*, 405 U.S. 645, 651 (1972); *Ginsberg v. New York*, 390 U.S. 629, 639 (1968); *Griswold v. Connecticut*, 381 U.S. 479 (1965); *id.*, at 495–496 (Goldberg, J., concurring); *id.*, at 502–503 (WHITE, J., concurring); *Poe v. Ullman*, 367 U.S. 497, 542–544, 549–553 (1961) (Harlan, J., dissenting); *cf. Loving v. Virginia*, 388 U.S. 1, 12 (1967); *May v. Anderson*, 345 U.S. 528, 533 (1953); *Skinner v. Oklahoma ex rel. Williamson*, 316 U.S. 535, 541 (1942). Of course, the family is not beyond regulation. *See Prince v. Massachusetts, supra*, at 166. But when the government intrudes on choices concerning family living arrangements, this Court must examine carefully the importance of the governmental interests advanced and the extent to which they are served by the challenged regulation. *See Prince v. Massachusetts, supra*, at 166.

When thus examined, this ordinance cannot survive. The city seeks to justify it as a means of preventing overcrowding, minimizing traffic and parking congestion, and avoiding an undue financial burden on East Cleveland's school system. Although these are legitimate goals, the ordinance before us serves them marginally, at best. For example, the ordinance permits any family consisting only of husband, wife, and unmarried children to live together, even if the family contains a half dozen licensed drivers, each with his or her own car. At the same time, it forbids an adult brother and sister to share a household, even if both faithfully use public transportation. The ordinance would permit a grandmother to live with a single dependent son and children, even if his school-age children number a dozen, yet it forces Mrs. Moore to find another dwelling for her grandson John, simply because of the presence of his uncle and cousin in the same household. We need not labor the point. Section 1341.08 has but a tenuous relation to alleviation of the conditions mentioned by the city.

III

....

Understanding those reasons requires careful attention to this Court's function under the Due Process Clause. Mr. Justice Harlan described it eloquently:

"Due process has not been reduced to any formula; its content cannot be determined by reference to any code. The best that can be said is that through the course of this Court's decisions it has represented the balance which our Nation, built upon postulates of respect for the liberty of the individual, has struck between that liberty and the demands of organized society. If the supplying of content to this Constitutional concept has of necessity been a rational process, it certainly has not been one where judges have felt free to roam where unguided speculation might take them. The balance of which I speak is the balance struck by this country, having regard to what history teaches are the traditions from which it developed, as well as the traditions from which it broke. That tradition is a living thing. A decision of this Court which radically departs from it could not long survive, while a decision which builds on what has survived is likely to be sound. No formula could serve as a substitute, in this area, for judgment and restraint."

"... [T]he full scope of the liberty guaranteed by the Due Process Clause cannot be found in or limited by the precise terms of the specific guarantees elsewhere provided in the Constitution. This 'liberty' is not a series of isolated points pricked out in terms of the taking of property; the freedom of speech, press, and religion; the right to keep and bear arms; the freedom from unreasonable searches and seizures; and so on. It is a rational continuum which, broadly speaking, includes a freedom from all substantial arbitrary impositions and purposeless restraints, ... and which also recognizes what a reasonable and sensitive judgment must, that certain interests require particularly careful scrutiny of the state needs asserted to justify their abridgment." *Poe v. Ullman, supra* at 367 U.S. 542–543 (dissenting opinion).

Substantive due process has at times been a treacherous field for this Court. There are risks when the judicial branch gives enhanced protection to certain substantive liberties without the guidance of the more specific provisions of the Bill of Rights. As the history of the *Lochner* era demonstrates, there is reason for concern lest the only limits to such judicial intervention become the predilections of those who happen at the time to be Members of this Court. That history counsels caution and restraint. But it does not counsel abandonment, nor does it require what the city urges here: cutting off any protection of family rights at the first convenient, if arbitrary boundary—the boundary of the nuclear family.

Appropriate limits on substantive due process come not from drawing arbitrary lines, but rather from careful "respect for the teachings of history [and] solid recognition of the basic values that underlie our society." *Griswold v. Connecticut*, 381 U.S., at 501 (Harlan, J., concurring). *See generally Ingraham v. Wright*, 430 U.S. 651, 672–674, and nn. 41, 42 (1977); *Joint Anti-Fascist Refugee Committee v. McGrath*, 341 U.S. 123, 162–163 (1951) (Frankfurter, J., concurring); *Lochner v. New York*, 198 U.S. 45, 76 (1905) (Holmes, J., dissenting). Our decisions establish that the Constitution protects the sanctity of the family precisely because the institution of the family is deeply rooted in this Nation's history and tradition. It is through the family that we inculcate and pass down many of our most cherished values, moral and cultural.

Ours is by no means a tradition limited to respect for the bonds uniting the members of the nuclear family. The tradition of uncles, aunts, cousins, and especially grandparents sharing a household along with parents and children has roots equally venerable and equally deserving of constitutional recognition. Over the years, millions of our citizens have grown up in just such an environment, and most, surely, have profited from it. Even if conditions of modern society have brought about a decline in extended family households, they have not erased the accumulated wisdom of civilization, gained over the centuries and honored throughout our history, that supports a larger conception of the family. Out of choice, necessity, or a sense of family responsibility, it has been common for close relatives to draw together and participate in the duties and the satisfactions of a common home. Decisions concerning childrearing, which *Yoder*, *Meyer*, *Pierce* and other cases have recognized as entitled to constitutional protection, long have been shared with grandparents or other relatives who occupy the same household—indeed who may take on major responsibility for the rearing of the children. Especially in times of adversity, such as the death of a spouse or economic need, the broader family has tended to come together for mutual sustenance and to maintain or rebuild a secure home life. This is apparently what happened here.

Whether or not such a household is established because of personal tragedy, the choice of relatives in this degree of kinship to live together may not lightly be denied by the State. *Pierce* struck down an Oregon law requiring all children to attend the State's public schools, holding that the Constitution "excludes any general power of the State to standardize its children by forcing them to accept instruction from public teachers only." 268 U.S., at 535. By the same token, the Constitution prevents East

Cleveland from standardizing its children—and its adults—by forcing all to live in certain narrowly defined family patterns.

Reversed.

MR. JUSTICE BRENNAN, with whom MR. JUSTICE MARSHALL joins, concurring.

I join the plurality's opinion. I agree that the Constitution is not powerless to prevent East Cleveland from prosecuting as a criminal and jailing a 63-year-old grandmother for refusing to expel from her home her now 10-year-old grandson who has lived with her and been brought up by her since his mother's death when he was less than a year old. I do not question that a municipality may constitutionally zone to alleviate noise and traffic congestion and to prevent overcrowded and unsafe living conditions, in short, to enact reasonable land use restrictions in furtherance of the legitimate objectives East Cleveland claims for its ordinance. But the zoning power is not a license for local communities to enact senseless and arbitrary restrictions which cut deeply into private areas of protected family life. East Cleveland may not constitutionally define "family" as essentially confined to parents and the parents' own children. The plurality's opinion conclusively demonstrates that classifying family patterns in this eccentric way is not a rational means of achieving the ends East Cleveland claims for its ordinance, and further that the ordinance unconstitutionally abridges the "freedom of personal choice in matters of... family life [that] is one of the liberties protected by the Due Process Clause of the Fourteenth Amendment." *Cleveland Board of Education v. LaFleur*, 414 U.S. 632, 639–640 (1974). I write only to underscore the cultural myopia of the arbitrary boundary drawn by the East Cleveland ordinance in the light of the tradition of the American home that has been a feature of our society since our beginning as a Nation—the "tradition" in the plurality's words, "of uncles, aunts, cousins, and especially grandparents sharing a household along with parents and children...." *Ante*, at 504. The line drawn by this ordinance displays a depressing insensitivity toward the economic and emotional needs of a very large part of our society.

In today's America, the "nuclear family" is the pattern so often found in much of white suburbia. J. Vander Zanden, Sociology: A Systematic Approach 322 (3d ed. 1975). The Constitution cannot be interpreted, however, to tolerate the imposition by government upon the rest of us of white suburbia's preference in patterns of family living. The "extended family" that provided generations of early Americans with social services and economic and emotional support in times of hardship, and was the beachhead for successive waves of immigrants who populated our cities, remains not merely still a pervasive living pattern, but, under the goad of brutal economic necessity, a prominent pattern—virtually a means of survival—for large numbers of the poor and deprived minorities of our society. For them, compelled pooling of scant resources requires compelled sharing of a household.

The "extended" form is especially familiar among black families. We may suppose that this reflects the truism that black citizens, like generations of white immigrants before them, have been victims of economic and other disadvantages that would worsen if they were compelled to abandon extended, for nuclear, living patterns. Even in husband and wife households, 13% of black families compared with 3% of white families include relatives under 18 years old, in addition to the couple's own children. In black households whose head is an elderly woman, as in this case, the contrast is even more striking: 48% of such black households, compared with 10% of counterpart white households, include related minor children not offspring of the head of the household.

I do not wish to be understood as implying that East Cleveland's enforcement of its ordinance is motivated by a racially discriminatory purpose: the record of this case would not support that implication. But the prominence of other than nuclear families among ethnic and racial minority groups, including our black citizens, surely demonstrates that the "extended family" pattern remains a vital tenet of our society. It suffices that, in prohibiting this pattern of family living as a means of achieving its objectives, appellee city has chosen a device that deeply intrudes into family associational rights that historically have been central, and today remain central, to a large proportion of our population.

Moreover, to sanction the drawing of the family line at the arbitrary boundary chosen by East Cleveland would surely conflict with prior decisions that protected "extended" family relationships. For the "private realm of family life which the state cannot enter," recognized as protected in *Prince v. Massachusetts*, 321 U.S. 158, 166 (1944), was the relationship of aunt and niece. *See also Wisconsin v. Yoder*, 406 U.S. 205, 232–233 (1972). Indeed, in *Village of Belle Terre v. Boraas, Village of Belle Terre v. Boraas*, 416 U.S. 1 (1974), the case primarily relied upon by the appellee, actually supports the Court's decision. The Belle Terre ordinance barred only unrelated individuals from constituting a family in a single-family zone. The village took special care in its brief to emphasize that its ordinance did not in any manner inhibit the choice of *related* individuals to constitute a family, whether in the "nuclear" or "extended" form. This was because the village perceived that choice as one it was constitutionally powerless to inhibit. Its brief stated: "Whether it be the extended family of a more leisurely age or the nuclear family of today, the role of the family in raising and training successive generations of the species makes it more important, we dare say, than any other social or legal institution.... *If any freedom not specifically mentioned in the Bill of Rights enjoys a 'preferred position' in the law, it is most certainly the family.*" (Emphasis supplied.) Brief for Appellants in No. 73-191, O.T. 1973, p. 26. The cited decisions recognized, as the plurality recognizes today, that the choice of the "extended family" pattern is within the "freedom of personal choice in matters of ... family life [that] is one of the liberties protected by the Due Process Clause of the Fourteenth Amendment." 414 U.S., at 639–640.

Any suggestion that the variance procedure of East Cleveland's Housing Code assumes special significance is without merit. This is not only because this grandmother was not obligated to exhaust her administrative remedy before defending this prosecution on the ground that the single-family occupancy ordinance violates the Equal Protection Clause. *Euclid v. Ambler Realty Co.*, 272 U.S. 365 (1926), the leading case in the zoning field, expressly held that one attacking the constitutionality of a building or zoning code need not first seek a variance. *Id.*, at 386. Rather, the matter of a variance is irrelevant also because the municipality is constitutionally powerless to abridge, as East Cleveland has done, the freedom of personal choice of related members of a family to live together. Thus, the existence of the variance procedure serves to lessen neither the irrationality of the definition of "family" nor the extent of its intrusion into family lifestyle decisions.

....

NOTES ON *MOORE V. CITY OF EAST CLEVELAND*

1. Individual Property Rights and Zoning. In property law, there is frequently something to negotiate with regard to the hallowed rights of property owners being diminished in order to live in harmony with a larger community. In particular, owner-occupied residential property is the most protected type of property. Inez Moore, having refused to remove her grandson from her home, was subject to criminal charges and served a sentence of five days in jail. While great deference is given to zoning ordinances and the power of local governments, does this type of criminal enforcement seem proportionate to and in line with the way that others with different racial identities might have been treated for being in violation of the zoning ordinance?

2. Whose Family? A Culturally Competent Analysis. Note that the majority opinion expands on the rights of the family and constitutional protections for privacy rights but does not mention race. Not until Justice Brennan's concurring opinion, joined by Justice Marshall, is the notion of race raised. The understanding that Black and immigrant families especially may have needs and cultures different from the norms of the white nuclear family that are enshrined in the common law is an important part of this decision that is not in the majority opinion.[11]

Property Tax Revenue and Local Services

The impacts of exclusionary zoning regulations compound because of the way that local, or ad valorem, taxes function. Local governments collect tax based on the value of the properties in the jurisdiction, generally as a percentage of the property's assessed value. Accordingly, jurisdictions with high property values will have a high property tax base and collect a large income. Wise zoning boards are acutely aware of this when making choices about ordinances, particularly as different types of uses (residential, commercial, and industrial) may be subject to different types of tax. Those who live in areas with high property values generally have sufficient income to fund healthy local services: schools, sanitation, police, transportation, and public parks are often funded, in part, by local jurisdictions.

11. *See generally* Angela Onwuachi-Willig, *Extending the Normativity of the Extended Family: Reflections on* Moore v. City of East Cleveland, 85 FORDHAM L. REV. 2655 (2017), https://ir.lawnet.fordham.edu/flr/vol85/iss6/11.

On the opposite end of the spectrum are low-income jurisdictions, which have low property values, a lower tax base, and, consequently, less available funding for municipal services. These areas may struggle to fund the very same local services that are provided in high-tax jurisdictions. Combine this with a system that encourages large polluters to establish themselves near areas that are often more densely populated, and what you get is a spiral that makes it very difficult for individuals to escape the cycle of poverty.[12] For those who are interested in social justice and finding ways to use the law to effect lasting change in communities, identifying ways to change some of the systems and structures related to zoning is an impactful starting point.

A number of state and local jurisdictions have undertaken efforts to study ways of amending their zoning laws to change the existing paradigm. Though zoning is a creature of local law, the federal government has become involved by creating a grant program that incentivizes jurisdictions to reform their exclusionary zoning policies.

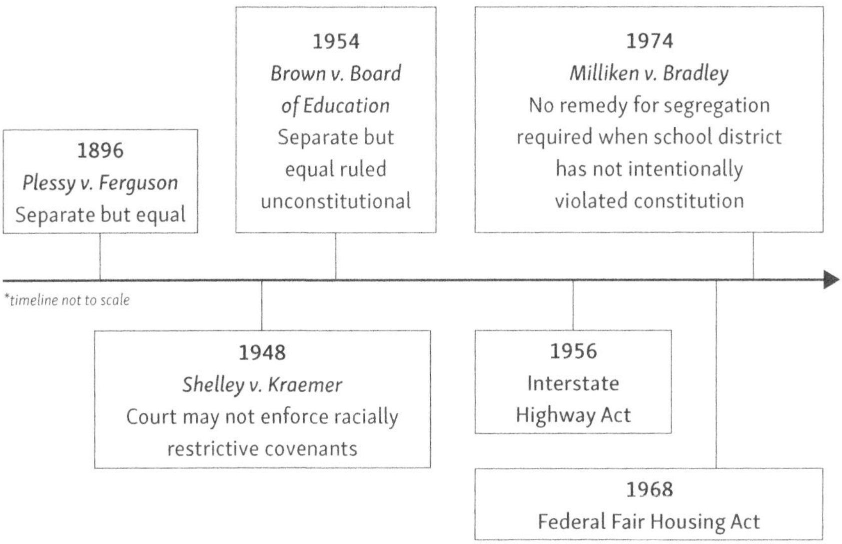

12. William Fischel, The Homevoter Hypothesis: How Home Values Influence Local Government Taxation, School Finance, and Land-Use Policies (2005).

Prioritizing Local Control

In considering whether local zoning ordinances have exceeded the limits set by the 14th Amendment's Due Process Clause, federal courts have historically granted great deference to local governments. When we study the history of segregation, we often learn how Supreme Court jurisprudence evolved from its upholding of the "separate but equal" doctrine in *Plessy v. Ferguson*,[13] to its overturning of *Plessy* in *Brown v. Board of Education of Topeka*,[14] where it held race-based segregation in public schools to be unconstitutional. *Brown* would serve as an important catalyst for the civil rights movement and desegregation in other areas.

In our history books, this story of evolving Supreme Court jurisprudence often culminates in the passage of civil rights legislation. However, in inspecting the reasons why the public education system continues to be largely segregated despite the decision in *Brown*, it is important to understand how local control interacts with those holdings. Consider the syllabus from *Milliken v. Bradley*, a 5–4 decision authored by Chief Justice Burger. Bear in mind that a syllabus is not part of the Court's official opinion but rather is provided by the Court to give a brief (in comparison to the opinion) summary of the case and to outline the reasoning that led to the holding.

MILLIKEN V. BRADLEY

418 U.S. 717 (1974)

Respondents brought this class action, alleging that the Detroit public school system is racially segregated as a result of the official policies and actions of petitioner state and city officials, and seeking implementation of a plan to eliminate the segregation and establish a unitary nonracial school system. The District Court, after concluding that various acts by the petitioner Detroit Board of Education had created and perpetuated school segregation in Detroit, and that the acts of the Board, as a subordinate entity of the State, were attributable to the State, ordered the Board to submit Detroit-only desegregation plans. The court also ordered the state officials to submit desegregation plans encompassing the

13. 163 U.S. 537 (1896).

14. 347 U.S. 483 (1954).

three-county metropolitan area, despite the fact that the 85 outlying school districts in these three counties were not parties to the action and there was no claim that they had committed constitutional violations. Subsequently, outlying school districts were allowed to intervene, but were not permitted to assert any claim or defense on issues previously adjudicated or to reopen any issue previously decided, but were allowed merely to advise the court as to the propriety of a metropolitan plan and to submit any objections, modifications, or alternatives to any such plan. Thereafter, the District Court ruled that it was proper to consider metropolitan plans, that Detroit-only plans submitted by the Board and respondents were inadequate to accomplish desegregation, and that, therefore, it would seek a solution beyond the limits of the Detroit school District, and concluded that "[s]chool district lines are simply matters of political convenience, and may not be used to deny constitutional rights." Without having evidence that the suburban school districts had committed acts of *de jure* segregation, the court appointed a panel to submit a plan for the Detroit schools that would encompass an entire designated desegregation area consisting of 53 of the 85 suburban school districts plus Detroit, and ordered the Detroit Board to acquire at least 295 school buses to provide transportation under an interim plan to be developed for the 1972–1973 school year. The Court of Appeals, affirming in part, held that the record supported the District Court's finding as to the constitutional violations committed by the Detroit Board and the state officials; that, therefore, the District Court was authorized and required to take effective measures to desegregate the Detroit school system; and that a metropolitan area plan embracing the 53 outlying districts was the only feasible solution and was within the District Court's equity powers. But the court remanded so that all suburban school districts that might be affected by a metropolitan remedy could be made parties and have an opportunity to be heard as to the scope and implementation of such a remedy, and vacated the order as to the bus acquisitions, subject to its reimposition at an appropriate time.

Held: The relief ordered by the District Court and affirmed by the Court of Appeals was based upon erroneous standards, and was unsupported by record evidence that acts of the outlying districts had any impact on the discrimination found to exist in the Detroit schools. A federal court may not impose a multidistrict, area-wide remedy for single-district *de jure* school segregation violations where there is no finding that the other included school districts have failed to operate unitary school systems or have committed acts that effected segregation within the other districts, there is no claim or finding that the school district boundary lines were established with the purpose of fostering racial segregation, and there is no meaningful opportunity for the included neighboring school districts to present evidence or be heard on the propriety of a multidistrict remedy or on the question of constitutional violations by those districts. Pp. 737–753.

(a) The District Court erred in using as a standard the declared objective of development of a metropolitan area plan which, upon implementation, would leave "no school, grade or classroom ... substantially disproportionate to the overall pupil racial composition" of the metropolitan area as a whole. The clear import of *Swann v. Board of Education*, 402 U.S. 1, is that desegregation, in the sense of dismantling a dual school system, does not require any particular racial balance. Pp. 739–741.

(b) While boundary lines may be bridged in circumstances where there has been a constitutional violation calling for inter-district relief, school district lines may not be casually ignored or treated as a mere administrative convenience; substantial local control of public education in this country is a deeply rooted tradition. Pp. 741–742.

(c) The inter-district remedy could extensively disrupt and alter the structure of public education in Michigan, since that remedy would require, in effect, consolidation of 54 independent school districts historically administered as separate governmental units into a vast new super school district, and, since—entirely apart from the logistical problems attending large-scale transportation of students—the consolidation would generate other problems in the administration, financing, and operation of this new school system. Pp. 742–743.

(d) From the scope of the inter-district plan itself, absent a complete restructuring of the Michigan school district laws, the District Court would become, first, a *de facto* "legislative authority" to resolve the complex operational problems involved, and thereafter a "school superintendent" for the entire area, a task which few, if any, judges are qualified to perform, and one which would deprive the people of local control of schools through elected school boards. Pp. 743–744.

(e) Before the boundaries of separate and autonomous school districts may be set aside by consolidating the separate units for remedial purposes or by imposing a cross-district remedy, it must be first shown that there has been a constitutional violation within one district that produces a significant segregative effect in another district; *i.e., specifically, it must be shown that racially discriminatory acts of the state or local school districts, or of a single school district have been a substantial cause of inter-district segregation.* [emphasis added—Ed.] Pp. 744–745.

(f) With no showing of significant violation by the 53 outlying school districts and no evidence of any inter-district violation or effect, the District Court transcended the original theory of the case as framed by the pleadings, and mandated a metropolitan area remedy the approval of which would impose on the outlying districts, not shown to have committed any constitutional violation, a standard not previously hinted at in any holding of this Court. P. 745.

(g) Assuming, *arguendo,* that the State was derivatively responsible for Detroit's segregated school conditions, it does not follow that an inter-district remedy is constitutionally justified or required, since there has been virtually no showing that either the State or any of the 85 outlying districts engaged in any activity that had a cross-district effect. Pp. 748–749.

(h) An isolated instance of a possible segregative effect as between two of the school districts involved would not justify the broad metropolitan-wide remedy contemplated, particularly since that remedy embraced 52 districts having no responsibility for the arrangement and potentially involved 503,000 pupils in addition to Detroit's 276,000 pupils. Pp. 749–750.

Reversed and remanded.

▲ ▼ ▲

In his dissent, Justice White wrote, "The core of my disagreement is that deliberate acts of segregation and their consequences will go unremedied, not because a remedy would be infeasible or unreasonable in terms of the usual criteria governing school desegregation cases, but because an effective remedy would cause what the Court considers to be undue administrative inconvenience to the State."[15] Justice White, skeptical of the majority and seeking more wholesale change, further stated,

15. *Milliken,* 418 U.S. at 763.

> [R]emedies calling for school zoning, pairing, and pupil assignments, become more and more suspect as they require that schoolchildren spend more and more time in buses going to and from school and that more and more educational dollars be diverted to transportation systems. Manifestly, these considerations are of immediate and urgent concern when the issue is the desegregation of a city school system where residential patterns are predominantly segregated and the respective areas occupied by blacks and whites are heavily populated and geographically extensive. Thus, if one postulates a metropolitan school system covering a sufficiently large area, with the population evenly divided between whites and Negroes and with the races occupying identifiable residential areas, there will be very real practical limits on the extent to which racially identifiable schools can be eliminated within the school district. It is also apparent that the larger the proportion of Negroes in the area, the more difficult it would be to avoid having a substantial number of all-black or nearly all-black schools.[16]

In this way, we see that despite civil rights-related legislative victories and legislatures' intent to desegregate schools, the constitutional framework of local zoning ordinances and local control continues to perpetrate segregated systems. In a separate dissenting opinion in *Milliken*, in addition to mourning the direction of progress on the issue of race relations, Justice Marshall makes a structural argument for state-level involvement where school districts are concerned.[17] Given the history of state-level involvement in education policy, his argument is pragmatic and informed, and it indicates that the majority, whether conscious of it or not, may be driven by forces other than concern for administrative burdens.

---

16. *Id.* at 764.
17. *Id.* at 796.

Skill: Statutory Construction Arguments

In the event that a statute is ambiguous, or subject to more than one reasonable interpretation, you have several tools of statutory construction at your disposal to determine and argue the meaning of the statute. As Justice Burger stated in his dissent in *Moore v. City of East Cleveland*: "[This] Court will not pass upon a constitutional question although properly presented by the record, if there is also present some other ground upon which the case may be disposed of.... Thus, if a case can be decided on either of two grounds, one involving a constitutional question, the other a question of statutory construction or general law, the Court will decide only the latter."[18]

Understanding how to use the construction of a statute to frame a legal argument is a high-order and nuanced legal-analysis skill. Among the most common tools used in a statutory-construction or interpretation analysis are (1) a textual review of the statute, (2) existing legal interpretations of the statute, and (3) context and structure of the statute. Each of these tasks requires close reading, prolonged attention to detail, and the ability to toggle between large policy concepts and granular words (sometimes punctuation!).

Textual Review

When determining the plain meaning of a statute or what was intended by the legislature, it is important to keep in mind the diligence with which laws are written. In the best iteration of the legislative process, words are carefully chosen and debated so that they accurately reflect the desired outcome of the entire legislative process. Where there are terms of art, many statutes will have a "definitions" section in which relevant terms will be clearly defined for a particular chapter. This section may be particularly important when the codified definition is distinct from the common usage of a term. For example, in *Moore*, it was not the substantive provision of the zoning ordinance that violated due process but rather the specific definition of "family" as applied to the chapter of the

18. 431 U.S. at 526 (quoting Justice Brandeis's concurrence in *Ashwander v. TVA*, 297 U.S. 288, 347 (1936)).

ordinance. Paying close attention to the particulars of how the definitions of words and phrases are codified for the statute is often vital.

Many courts hold that the "plain meaning" of a statute, if it is clear and unambiguous, requires no further analysis or investigation. But whether something is ambiguous is itself subject to interpretation. Particularly with circumstances that lend themselves to different cultural interpretations, a court's willingness to entertain more than one reasonable interpretation strengthens the common law as a whole. Specific or industry-defined terms should be treated with caution.

Statutes often use general terms, and sometimes these general terms include a few examples. Interpreting what is included with a general term should involve a close reading of the word and associated punctuation as well as a reasonable reading of the context. A zoning statute describing use restrictions may describe "dangerous or hazardous activity, such as disposal of industrial waste...." Understanding the structure of the sentence and the context of the property are both necessary to construe what other type of activity fits within the meaning of the statute. Similarly, when an enumerated list is provided, there may be a negative implication, that is, that activities *not* on the list are not contemplated. For example, a zoning statute expressly permitting "domestic animals: cats, dogs, fish, rabbits, and turtles" may not permit teacup pigs. If, however, a statute begins an enumeration with the word "including," then it may be construed to include similar animals. For example, a zoning statute expressly permitting "domestic animals *including* cats, dogs, fish, rabbits, and turtles" may more likely permit teacup pigs. In addition, the *ejusdem generis* ("of the same kind") principle of statutory interpretation can also help in interpreting lists with specific examples. This principle states that where general words follow specific words, the general words are limited to things in the same group as the specific words. For example, "domestic animals, *such as* dogs, cats, fish, and others" might indicate that a rabbit, turtle, and teacup pig are permitted, but a water buffalo is not. The chart below contains a number of common terms appearing in statutes that may prove useful in a close reading.[19]

19. The Writing Center, Geo. Univ. L. Center, *A Guide to Reading, Interpreting, and Applying Statutes* (2017).

Terms	Function
And v. Or	"And" typically signifies a conjunctive list, meaning each condition in the list must be satisfied, while "or" typically signifies a disjunctive list, meaning satisfying any one condition in the list is sufficient
May v. Shall	Generally, "shall" signifies that certain behavior is mandated by the statute, while "may" grants the agent some discretion
Unless Except	These terms usually signify an exception to the statute
Subject to ... Within the meaning of For the purposes of	These terms may limit the scope of the statute, or may indicate that a certain part of the statute is controlled or limited by another section or statute
If ... then ... Upon Before/After Provided that ...	Generally, these terms indicate that for one part of a statute to take effect, a precondition or requirement must be satisfied
Notwithstanding	Literally, "in spite of," this term usually signifies that a certain term or provision is not controlled or limited by other parts of the statute, or by other statutes
Each/Only Every/Any/All	These terms commonly limit the class of objects that are either included in or excluded from the statute

Legal Interpretation

Many statutes and rules have been subject to interpretation either by courts or administrative agencies, and when completing a legal analysis, you should give deference to, or at least acknowledge, the already existing interpretations. Agency regulations may sometimes be found in the Code of Federal Regulations and should be given particular deference.[20]

20. *See generally* Chevron U.S.A., Inc. v. NRDC, Inc., 467 U.S. 837 (1984) (statutes); Auer v. Robbins, 519 U.S. 452 (1997) (agency regulations).

Context and Structure

A statute should be construed according to the plain meaning of its individual provisions but also viewed in the context of the whole statute. In addition, the context of the area of the law and structure of rules surrounding that area cannot be ignored. Particularly in a statute-heavy area like zoning (the zoning ordinances serving as the statutes), where statutes may have been enacted and amended over a long period by different parties with shifting values, it is important to understand the statute's context and structure and make reasonable choices about its interpretation.

There are different theories of statutory construction, each with its own benefits and pitfalls. *Textualists*, who adhere only to the text of a statute, limit their interpretations to what appears within the four corners of the document. This method may make for predictable interpretations, but because statutes are often written broadly, those interpretations sometimes fall short of the intent of the drafters and the expectations of the affected communities and parties. Instead of adhering strictly to a statute's text, *intentionalists* look closely at the intent of those who drafted it. Understanding the motivation, purpose, and intent of a statute is what informs the interpretation of intentionalists. *Pragmatists* interpret statutes with the least amount of adherence to the actual text. They consider contemporary context, practical application, fairness, justice, and equity. This approach may not only make for unpredictable interpretations but also may reflect the biases of the one engaged in the interpretation.

When working on the analysis portion of the IRAC framework, a statutory construction argument will be difficult to accomplish effectively but may still be well worth the effort, in the right context.

SUGGESTIONS FOR FURTHER READING

Derrick Bell, Silent Covenants: Brown v. Board of Education and the Unfulfilled Hopes for Racial Reform (2004).

Lawrence T. Brown, The Black Butterfly: The Harmful Politics of Race and Space in America (2022).

Katherine Levine Einstein, David M. Glick, & Maxwell Palmer, Neighborhood Defenders (2019).

William A. Fischel, The Homevoter Hypothesis: How Home Values Influence Local Government Taxation, School Finance, and Land-Use Policies (2005).

M. Nolan Gray, Arbitrary Lines: How Zoning Broke the American City and How to Fix It (2022).

John Infranca, *Singling Out Single-Family Zoning*, 111 Geo. L. Rev. 659 (Apr. 2023).

Cecilia Rouse et al., *Exclusionary Zoning: Its Effect on Racial Discrimination in the Housing Market*, The White House (June 17, 2021), https://www.whitehouse.gov/cea/written-materials/2021/06/17/exclusionary-zoning-its-effect-on-racial-discrimination-in-the-housing-market/.

Claude Steele, Whistling Vivaldi: How Stereotypes Affect Us and What We Can Do (reprint ed. 2011).

Beverly Daniel Tatum, Why Are All the Black Kids Sitting Together in the Cafeteria? And Other Conversations About Race (1997).

SEVEN

Takings

The Takings Clause of the Fifth Amendment, applicable to the States through the Fourteenth Amendment, provides: "Nor shall private property be taken for public use, without just compensation." The Founders recognized that the protection of private property is indispensable to the promotion of individual freedom. As John Adams tersely put it, "Property must be secured, or liberty cannot exist." This Court agrees, having noted that protection of property rights is "necessary to preserve freedom" and "empowers persons to shape and to plan their own destiny in a world where governments are always eager to do so for them."

—Chief Justice John Roberts[1]

Our national transportation system represents one of the great accomplishments in the history of this country.... But we can't ignore the basic truth that some of the planners and politicians behind [highway] projects built them directly through the heart of vibrant, populated communities—sometimes in an effort to reinforce segregation. Sometimes because the people there had less power to resist. And sometimes as part of a direct effort to replace or eliminate Black neighborhoods.

—U.S. Secretary of Transportation Pete Buttigieg[2]

1. Writing for the majority in *Cedar Point Nursery v. Hassid*, 141 S. Ct. 2063 (2021), citing *Murr v. Wisconsin*, 137 S. Ct. 1933 (2017).

2. Transcript: *Secretary Pete Buttigieg Remarks on Launch of Reconnecting Communities Program—Birmingham, Alabama*, U.S. Dep't of Transp. (June 30, 2022), https

Legislation can always be changed. It's very hard to tear down a bridge once it's up.

—Robert Moses, Urban Planner and Primary Architect of the New York State Parkway System

Eminent Domain: Government-Sponsored Dispossession of Property

Since the time of the founding of the United States, protection of property interests has been held sacred. When the Fifth Amendment was enacted as part of the Bill of Rights, it was not lightly that Congress took the power to take private property for public use, even when "just compensation" was offered. History suggests, however, that Black property owners have been disproportionately burdened by the state's use of its powers of condemnation. This chapter broadly reviews the fundamentals and vocabulary of eminent domain before inspecting the way the Takings Clause has particularly impacted Black property owners at pivotal points in history.

After exploring the distinctions between the components of the Takings Clause, with a particular focus paid to the different forms "public use" has taken, the chapter moves on to an examination of regulatory and per se takings. In going over some of the arguments for different types of takings, this chapter reviews cases with fact patterns very similar to those explored in different sections of the book that dealt with the right to exclude.

Finally, this chapter examines the history of urban planning and the way federal infrastructure projects have used the power of eminent domain to accomplish goals. Taking into particular account the arguments that justified the takings, this chapter seeks to identify patterns in American history regarding the treatment and relative ownership rights of Americans based on their racial identity.

://www.transportation.gov/briefing-room/transcript-secretary-pete-buttigieg-remarks-launch-reconnecting-communities-program.

Fifth Amendment Components and Basics

The Takings Clause of the Fifth Amendment states "nor shall private property be taken for public use, without just compensation." These 12 words grant the U.S. government great power to impact the organization of communities and encourage migration patterns.

The jurisprudence around takings has been separated into *per se takings*, when land is physically taken from owners, and *regulatory takings*, when government action limits the rights of property owners to such a degree that the owners are entitled to compensation for the loss of a right in an interest in property. Any interest in property is subject to a taking: the state take may take the entire ownership interest or just a right to use (an easement). Regulatory takings may be divided into two subcategories: *total regulatory takings*, in which some set of government rules deprive private property of all economic value,[3] and *partial regulatory takings*, whose specific rules are difficult for courts to articulate because they are complex and closely related to specific facts and circumstances. But the general idea of a partial regulatory taking is that government rules have limited the use and enjoyment (and value) of property to some extent.

The word "condemn" is used to describe the process of the taking. Although it has a negative connotation in common language, the term does not have this connotation in the context of takings. It only describes the process of the government's using its power of *eminent domain*, or *taking* (these are interchangeable terms). Federal, state, or local government may exercise this power.

When the state (any level of government) seeks to take private property through its power of eminent domain, it must establish a public use for the taking. It is often the case that if a state is using this power, it is because a private owner has already refused an offer to sell the property without the invocation of the Fifth Amendment. Accordingly, private property owners may seek to understand the underlying reasons for and often find ways to undermine the state's taking. Disputes about whether the proposed use of the property is sufficient to justify the taking is an often litigated subject. Courts have sometimes taken the words "public use" to mean "public benefit" and asked if there is a way for the larger

---

3. *See* Lucas v. S.C. Costal Council, 505 U.S. 1003 (1992).

community to benefit from the taking. This approach supports the underlying justification for power to begin with: a sacrifice of one to support many.

Public Use: Who Benefits?

As in all areas of the law, the perspectives of parties may vary greatly and be informed by their experience. It is the judiciary's job to resolve disputes in ways that are just and fair and that provide predictability and stability in the form of precedent. In short, though courts rule on disputes between individual parties, in a way, larger cultural values are imprinted in their decisions and the precedents they set. Nowhere is this truer than a court's deciding whether a "public use" is sufficient to justify a taking. In particular, courts have often used the concept of *urban renewal* to justify taking property from private individuals. When property is deemed to be "blighted," local governments have an interest in improving the area. In this way, public use becomes public benefit. In *Berman v. Parker*,[4] the local government, in accordance with an urban renewal plan to redevelop an entire blighted area of downtown Washington, D.C., sought to acquire a non-blighted department store located in that blighted area through the power of eminent domain. The department store objected because it was neither blighted nor a problematic part of the community. The plaintiff objected to the taking of the property solely for the "beautification" and redevelopment of the area, but a unanimous Supreme Court held that there was nothing in the Fifth Amendment that precluded the taking.

Context Consideration

Berman v. Parker was decided in Washington, D.C., in 1954. Two years later, in 1956, the federal legislature passed the Interstate Highway Act (discussed below), which used the power of eminent domain with unprecedented frequency. Urban planners, with deliberate and often open intent, used the act and the Fifth Amendment together with confidence to effect segregation and to demolish undesirable Black communities.

4. 348 U.S. 26 (1954).

Though the plaintiff in *Berman* did not prevail, the decision both affected the jurisprudence of the Supreme Court, which was expanding the state's power of eminent domain at the time, and made an impression on future justices. In *Kelo v. City of New London*,[5] a well-documented and publicized case, plaintiffs sought to enjoin the City of New London, Connecticut, from using the power of eminent domain to effect an urban renewal plan. Though the plaintiffs ultimately did not prevail, Justice Thomas's dissent cited *Berman* and looked at the justification of urban renewal through a racial lens.

As you read the following excerpt from Justice Thomas's dissent in *Kelo*, consider the changes that occurred in race relations from 1954 (when *Berman* was decided) to 2005 (when *Kelo* was decided). In those intervening years, the state's power of eminent domain had expanded and been used a great deal, but Justice Thomas believed that a shift in cultural values had also occurred during that time which necessitated a change in course. Pay attention to the ways in which Justice Thomas crafts a public-policy argument in his dissenting opinion.

KELO V. CITY OF NEW LONDON

545 U.S. 469, 505, 521–22 (2005)

Justice Thomas, dissenting.

Long ago, William Blackstone wrote that "the law of the land ... postpone[s] even public necessity to the sacred and inviolable rights of private property." 1 Commentaries on the Laws of England 134–135 (1765) (hereinafter Blackstone). The Framers embodied that principle in the Constitution, allowing the government to take property not for "public necessity," but instead for "public use." Defying this understanding, the Court replaces the Public Use Clause with a "'[P]ublic [P]urpose'" (or perhaps the "Diverse and Always Evolving Needs of Society" (capitalization added)), a restriction that is satisfied, the Court instructs, so long as the purpose is "legitimate" and the means "not irrational[]".... This deferential shift in phraseology enables the Court to hold, against all common sense, that a costly urban-renewal project whose stated purpose is a vague promise of new jobs and increased tax revenue, but which is also suspiciously agreeable to the Pfizer Corporation, is for a "public use."

5. 545 U.S. 469 (2005).

I cannot agree. If such "economic development" takings are for a "public use," any taking is, and the Court has erased the Public Use Clause from our Constitution. I do not believe that this Court can eliminate liberties expressly enumerated in the Constitution and therefore join her dissenting opinion. Regrettably, however, the Court's error runs deeper than this. Today's decision is simply the latest in a string of our cases construing the Public Use Clause to be a virtual nullity, without the slightest nod to its original meaning. In my view, the Public Use Clause, originally understood, is a meaningful limit on the government's eminent domain power. Our cases have strayed from the Clause's original meaning, and I would reconsider them.

....

IV

The consequences of today's decision are not difficult to predict, and promise to be harmful. So-called "urban renewal" programs provide some compensation for the properties they take, but no compensation is possible for the subjective value of these lands to the individuals displaced and the indignity inflicted by uprooting them from their homes. Allowing the government to take property solely for public purposes is bad enough, but extending the concept of public purpose to encompass any economically beneficial goal guarantees that these losses will fall disproportionately on poor communities. Those communities are not only systematically less likely to put their lands to the highest and best social use, but are also the least politically powerful. If ever there were justification for intrusive judicial review of constitutional provisions that protect "discrete and insular minorities," *United States v. Carolene Products Co.*, 304 U.S. 144, 152, n. 4, 82 L. Ed. 1234, 58 S. Ct. 778 (1938), surely that principle would apply with great force to the powerless groups and individuals the Public Use Clause protects. The deferential standard this Court has adopted for the Public Use Clause is therefore deeply perverse. It encourages "those citizens with disproportionate influence and power in the political process, including large corporations and development firms," to victimize the weak....

Those incentives have made the legacy of this Court's "public purpose" test an unhappy one. In the 1950's, no doubt emboldened in part by the expansive understanding of "public use" this Court adopted in *Berman*, cities "rushed to draw plans" for downtown development. B.

Frieden & L. Sagalyn, Downtown, Inc. How America Rebuilds Cities 17 (1989). "Of all the families displaced by urban renewal from 1949 through 1963, 63 percent of those whose race was known were nonwhite, and of these families, 56 percent of nonwhites and 38 percent of whites had incomes low enough to qualify for public housing, which, however, was seldom available to them." *Id.*, at 28. Public works projects in the 1950's and 1960's destroyed predominantly minority communities in St. Paul, Minnesota, and Baltimore, Maryland. *Id.*, at 28–29. In 1981, urban planners in Detroit, Michigan, uprooted the largely "lower-income and elderly" Poletown neighborhood for the benefit of the General Motors Corporation. J. Wylie, Poletown: Community Betrayed 58 (1989). Urban renewal projects have long been associated with the displacement of blacks; "[i]n cities across the country, urban renewal came to be known as 'Negro removal.'" Pritchett, The "Public Menace" of Blight: Urban Renewal and the Private Uses of Eminent Domain, 21 Yale L. & Pol'y Rev. 1, 47 (2003). Over 97 percent of the individuals forcibly removed from their homes by the "slum-clearance" project upheld by this Court in *Berman* were black. 348 U.S., at 30, 99 L. Ed. 27, 75 S. Ct. 98. Regrettably, the predictable consequence of the Court's decision will be to exacerbate these effects....

NOTES ON *KELO V. CITY OF NEW LONDON*

1. Slum Clearance. Justice Thomas refers to the "slum-clearance" project in *Berman*, and he offers statistics relating to the ways in which Black communities have been disproportionately dispossessed of property at the hands of the state through its use of the power granted by the Fifth Amendment. Many states justified these takings based on the nuisance created by these slums, when, in fact, the housing conditions of these predominantly Black neighborhoods, whether public housing or not, were largely a result of government policy.[6]

2. Gentrification. Whether by taking or by private action, slum clearance and urban renewal has been the recent trend in American cities. While the suburbs, created and popularized in the mid-20th century, had made it possible for white Americans to build equity in real property, the newer generation of property owners is returning to urban cen-

---

6. *See* Ch. 6, *supra*.

ters. This migration back to cities has impacted urban property values, rendering some neighborhoods unaffordable for the nonwhite communities, particularly Black communities, that had been living there. The psychology of developing neighborhoods in formerly blighted areas is familiar to developers (as noted by Justice Thomas). Upon gentrification of neighborhoods, what recourse is there for individuals who suffer loss of community?

3. A Political Question. The *Kelo* case received a great deal of media attention, both while and after it was litigated.[7] Unlike *Berman*, which was decided by a unanimous Court, Kelo was a 5–4 decision, split along ideological lines. As was frequently the case in that era, Justice Kennedy was the swing vote. The conservative and dissenting Justices (Rehnquist, O'Connor, Scalia, and Thomas) felt strongly about the protection of property rights, whereas the majority found a way to prioritize the good of the many over the good of the few and give deference to local governments to use the power of takings as they saw fit. Though cases are not decided on ideology alone, in *Kelo*, the logic of the majority and dissenting opinions is consistent. Still, there is room on each side to consider the ways the identity of the parties may impact the determination of who is in the best position to decide the best interests of the property at issue.

Per Se Takings vs. The Right to Exclude: A Case Comparison of *Cedar Point Nursery v. Hassid* and *State v. Shack*

Unlike law students, courts are not bound to stay within the lines of doctrine when deciding how to respond to the parties before them. Consider the similar facts of two cases decided under different theories of law—*State v. Shack*, which was decided by the New Jersey Supreme Court in 1971, and *Cedar Point Nursery v. Hassid*, which was decided by the U.S. Supreme Court in 2021. Both cases involved the rights of property owners of agricultural land who were engaged in disputes with government agencies hoping to provide services to migrant workers living

7. The movie *Little Pink House*, based on the book of the same title and starring Catherine Keener, was based on the *Kelo* fact pattern and trial.

on their property. In the 40 intervening years, take note of the factors that have changed—and those that have not.

State v. Shack 58 N.J. 297 (1971)	Cedar Point Nursery v. Hassid 141 S. Ct. 2063 (2021)
✓ Agricultural Property Owner (Tedesco) hires migrant farm workers ✓ Individual (Shack) seeks access to farm and migrant workers in accordance with government-sanctioned mandate (Farmworkers Division of Camden Regional Legal Services) ✓ Relevant State Statute—Trespass[8] × Holding: No Right to Exclude	✓ Agricultural Property Owner (Cedar Point Nursery) hires migrant farm workers ✓ Individuals (Organizers) seek access to farm and migrant workers in accordance with government-sanctioned mandate (United Farm Workers) ✓ Relevant State Regulation—Right to Access for Unionization[9] × Holding: Per Se Taking

In light of their similar fact patterns, consider not only that the outcomes of these cases were distinct but also that they were considered under wholly different theories. Where *State v. Shack* is frequently read by law students as an example of the limits of a property owner's right to exclude, it also begins to acknowledge the humanity and rights of the migrant worker. The litigant, Shack, is not a migrant worker himself but rather a worker for a government sponsored agency, which is an important part of the court's policy-centered analysis: if the legislature prioritized the care of migrant workers, it would not make sense to exclude those workers from the property of the private owner. This is an example of an effective policy argument (that uses the concept of federal preemption).

In contrast, *Cedar Point Nursery v. Hassid*, deals with the theory of eminent domain. Knowing that there would be no right to exclude the union, lawyers for the petitioner advanced an argument based on a different theory: a right in property had been taken by the government and, accordingly, just compensation was required pursuant to the Fifth Amendment. The regulations at issue in *Cedar Point Nursery* are funda-

8. N.J.S.A. 2A:170-31.

9. Cal. Code Regs., tit. 8, § 20900(e)(1)(c).

mentally distinct from those in *State v. Shack*. A product of the farm workers movement, the regulations in California guarantee to organizers the rights of access to property and migrant workers. The holding in *Cedar Point Nursery* does not change that, but it seeks something in return: compensation for the loss of a property right. Note that the migrant worker has lost their central place in this argument. In a trespass statute, there is room for a policy analysis concerning the rights and human dignity of migrant workers and the rights they might enjoy to invite guests onto the premises on which they temporarily reside. But in an argument focusing on compensation for the loss of property rights, there is no opportunity to consider the dignity and humanity and rights of migrant farmworkers—it simply isn't the issue.

Urban Planning and Eminent Domain: Intentional Efforts to Dispossess, Segregate, and Exclude

The Interstate Highway Act became public law in 1956 and authorized $26 billion to construct a forty-one-thousand mile network of highways to connect major cities across the United States.[10] This happened during a time in American history when the suburbs were flourishing as a result of the trend of using zoning ordinances and racially restrictive covenants to maintain segregated communities. As upper- and middle-class white families continued to use government assistance to invest in home ownership outside of the city, migration to the suburbs changed the national culture. The federal government's investment in roads connecting the suburbs to cities ensured that white suburban families could continue to access high-paying jobs in urban centers, even as suburban areas flourished with commerce to support those family members who did not travel into the city on a daily basis. Prior to this time, people lived near where they worked and mostly relied on public transportation. The aggregate migration to the suburbs resulted in an increase in dependence on automobiles for access to urban centers, and the Interstate Highway Act was passed to facilitate that transition.

10. Federal Highway Act of 1956, Pub. L. No. 627, 70 Stat. 374 (1956).

At the same time, the American civil rights movement was gaining traction. The migration of Black Americans from the Jim Crow South to cities in the North and West had changed the demographics of the country. These individuals had moved in search of a better life, only to find that government-sponsored segregation was still the norm in their new homes. Policies like redlining, racially restrictive covenants, and explicit rules in federal public housing programs ensured the perpetuation of racial segregation. The passage of the Interstate Highway Act gave planners and builders the opportunity to connect the new white suburbs with the city centers where the jobs were and to effect "slum clearance" of blighted areas. These highways were intentionally built for the convenience suburban dwellers, allowing them to efficiently travel to the city without having to be exposed to low-income, "slum," and "blighted" neighborhoods. A few urban planners had an outsize influence not only in their area but also on others who crafted plans and designs throughout the country.

> Robert Moses, an influential New York public official who shaped urban development and public works projects both in New York and around the country, was a leader among those who believed infrastructure projects and physical barriers would be effective, semipermanent barriers to access for poor people of color.[72] He took great pains to build New York's roads and highways in a way that would limit the ability of poor people of color to visit the parks and beaches he built.[73] For example, Moses instructed the highway engineers to build the bridges across the Southern State Parkway with one foot less clearance than the bridges on the Hutchinson, Saw Mill, and Bronx River Parkways.[74] The clearance was intentionally too low for buses coming from New York City to pass, as he believed Black and Puerto Rican New Yorkers would most

[72]. *See* Robert A. Caro, The Power Broker: Robert Moses and the Fall of New York (1974) (discussing Robert Moses's role in building highways and other infrastructure across New York State).

[73]. *Id.*

[74]. *See id.* at 8, 318 (noting that Moses built every mile of parkway in New York and that he attempted to limit bus access to parks by "poor and lower-middle-class families" by having "bridges across his new parkways [built] low—too low for buses to pass").

> likely use buses to access the beach.[75] As a result, bus trips to the beach would have to be made on local roads, making the trips "discouragingly long and arduous."[76] The law already prohibited commercial traffic, including trucks and buses, from using all the American parkways.[77] When asked why he made the bridges low, Moses replied, "*Legislation can always be changed; It's very hard to tear down a bridge once it's up.*"[78] [emphasis added—Ed.] In communities of color around the country, highways were designed to be walls, wedges and extractors. They became the embodiment of a norm of exclusion authored by the state."[79], [11]

With the support of the federal government and a national infrastructure project, Black neighborhoods were intentionally destroyed. According to Professor Deborah Archer, Moses and other engineers came to think of their imperative from the federal government as "killing two birds with one stone"—improving efficiency and traffic conditions for suburban white communities and removing undesirable populations.[12]

As Professor Archer points out in her work, large Black communities in major metropolitan areas were decimated, including in Miami, Florida (I-95 was designed to run through the center of Overtown, considered to be the center of economic and cultural life for Black people living in Miami);[13] Birmingham, Alabama (I-59 was built to separate and preserve the character of the white neighborhood of College Hills by creating a buffer between it and the nearby Black neighborhoods after a racial

---

[75]. *See id.* at 318–19, 513 (discussing the steps Moses took to limit access of beaches and pools for Blacks and Puerto Ricans, whom Moses "classed with" Blacks).

[76]. *Id.* at 318.

[77]. Thomas J. Campanella, *Robert Moses and His Racist Parkway, Explained*, Bloomberg Citylab (July 9, 2017, 11:03 AM CDT), https://www.citylab.com/transportation/2017/07/how-lowdid-he-go/533019/ [https://perma.cc/4Y3Z-M6CB].

[78]. Matthew Noah Smith, *Reliance Structures: How Urban Public Policy Shapes Human Agency*, *in* The Palgrave Handbook of Philosophy and Public Policy 809, 812 (David Boonin ed., 2018) (quoting Campanella, *supra* note 77).

[79]. *Id.* at 813.

11. Deborah N. Archer, *"White Men's Roads through Black Men's Homes": Advancing Racial Equity through Highway Reconstruction*, 73 Vanderbilt L. Rev. 1259, 1275–76 (2020), https://scholarship.law.vanderbilt.edu/vlr/vol73/iss5/1.

12. *Id.* at 1276–77.

13. *Id.* at 1278–81.

zoning law was struck down, and I-65 was built to follow the boundaries created by racial zoning ordinances and separate the Black neighborhood of Enon Ridge from the white neighborhood of Fountain Heights, following a number of violent incidents targeting Black families in response to an increase in the latter's Black population);[14] Atlanta, Georgia (I-20 was built along racial zoning lines that were ruled impermissible and city officials explicitly stated that the route was to be the boundary between Black and white neighborhoods);[15] and Los Angeles, California (where the Sugar Hill neighborhood,[16] which had prevailed in its action regarding racially restrictive covenants, was condemned by the government for the purpose of creating the Santa Monica Freeway—a project unanimously approved by the California Highway Commission over community protests). Around the country, countless Black communities were intentionally divided or destroyed after being condemned under the authority of the Fifth Amendment and for the purposes set forth in the Interstate Highway Act.

The impact of the power of eminent domain in making possible the construction of the roads and highways demanded by Interstate Highway Act was seismic, and it changed the course of race relations in the United States. And yet it is not the only example of the condemnation of Black property in our country's history. Long before the Interstate Highway Act, at a time when New York City was mostly confined to the southern tip of the island of Manhattan, there was Seneca Village, an integrated yet predominantly Black community. The community was home to churches and one of the few schools available to Black children. Compared to other Black residents of New York City, the residents of Seneca village tended to be more economically stable and successful, and many owned their homes. But in 1853, the New York State Legislature set aside property to create a park that would be held for public use and used the power of eminent domain to condemn Seneca Village, which was subsequently razed. Its remnants lie underneath Central Park today.

Apart from using the government-sanctioned power of eminent domain, the United States has a history, sometimes more recent than we like to admit, of destroying Black enclaves and communities when they

14. *Id.* at 1281–84.

15. *Id.* at 1284–86.

16. *See* Ch. 4, *supra*.

become successful. The race riots in Tulsa, Oklahoma, and the fates of numerous Black towns like Oscarville, Georgia, which now lies under Lake Lanier, and Klwaliga (Benson), Alabama, which lies submerged under Lake Martin, are but two examples that are seldom remembered in our history.

Skill: Public Policy Arguments

When dealing with constitutional questions and rights of property, there are often major issues at stake. Understanding best practices for including a strong policy argument in the analysis section of your IRAC takes practice. Though it is rare that a policy argument should be the only part of a legal analysis, using policy to support a case analysis or to make a compelling argument when application of the rule does not yield clear results can be very helpful. Modeling policy arguments after judicial opinions is a good starting point. The chart below includes some examples of common frameworks for policy arguments in legal analyses.

Type of Policy Argument	Description
Arc of History	Reviewing legal history on a subject and putting the facts at hand into the context of a larger historical framework can be a very effective tool for a policy analysis. Justice Marshall often did this very effectively with race relations, skillfully weaving this approach with a normative one (see below).
Judicial Administration	Courts respond well to arguments about how a decision may impact a rule. In particular, the demands of the practical administration of courts are at issue here. In those areas that require a heavily fact-based analysis, it may make sense to make this type of argument: that is, to raise the issue of the type of burden it would present for courts to have to navigate a rule in a particular way every time an issue arises.

Normative Approach	Normative arguments demonstrate how the application of a rule may promote or undermine a shared societal value. *Representation on the bench is essential here*: the intricacies of the shared values often at issue in these cases may vary in the finer points across different communities and cultures. Though normative arguments may be read to be political in nature, they need not be. These types of arguments have historically been based in "morals," driven by an altruistic view of the world, or related to social utility of rules and incentives. Some normative arguments may relate to corrective justice, which, as mentioned above, may be woven together with an "arc of history" type of argument.
Institutional Competence	This type of argument identifies the branch of government that is best suited to deal with the type of issue at hand. Where most legal arguments are written in briefs and memoranda that come before the judiciary, an argument may be made that the legislature or executive branch, which may have fact-finding authority and resources or different designated powers, is the more appropriate body for policymaking than the court.
Law and Economics	Arguments centering around law and economics are growing in popularity as the field of economics evolves and becomes increasingly involved in policymaking. Often historically related to efficiencies, new arguments about law and economics make room for more nuanced considerations, including what kinds of applications may serve as incentives and deterrents. Like law, economics is not a fixed discipline and has room for cultural responsiveness and competency when done well.

There are as many types of policy-based arguments as there are individuals willing to make them. This guide merely provides a framework of some of the most commonly used types. Primary authority is rarely used to support policy-based arguments; accordingly, it is seldom central to the legal analysis but can nevertheless be a compelling complement.

SUGGESTIONS FOR FURTHER READING

Deborah Archer, "*White Men's Roads through Black Men's Homes": Advancing Racial Equity through Highway Reconstruction*, 73 Vanderbilt L. Rev. 1259, 1275–76 (2020), https://scholarship.law.vanderbilt.edu/vlr/vol73/iss5/1.

Robert A. Caro, The Power Broker: Robert Moses and the Fall of New York (1974).

Highway Robbery: Transportation Racism and New Routs to Equity (Robert Bullard, Glenn Johnson, & Angel Torres eds., 2004).

EIGHT

Fair Housing, Leaseholds, and Power Dynamics

"Equal justice under law is a farce" without lawyers for the poor. Any lay person would find "completely unreasonable" the idea that a lease for an apartment has a warranty requiring that the place be "livable." If the landlord doesn't fulfill "all of his bargain," then why should the tenant have to fulfill all of his?

—Judge James Skelly Wright[1]

Our working hypothesis is that the algorithms are often simply trying to maximize price. Presumably, whoever is designing the algorithm is unaware of the racial consequence of this single-minded focus on profitability. But they need to understand that there is this racial dynamic, that the proxy variables they're using—in all likelihood, that's where the discrimination is. In some sense, there's effectively redlining of the reddest sort going in through the code.

—Bobby Bartlett, U.C. Berkeley[2]

---

1. Comments on *Saunders v. First National Realty Corp.*, excerpted from an interview broadcasted in a 1971 program titled "Some Are More Equal Than Others." *See* Richard H. Chused, Javins (a.k.a. Saunders) v. First National Realty Corporation, *in* PROPERTY STORIES 173 (Gerald Korngold & Andrew Morriss, eds., 2d ed. 2009).

2. Professor Bartlett "led the research providing some of the first large-scale evidence for how artificial intelligence creates discrimination in mortgage lending." *See* Charlton McIlwain, *AI Has Exacerbated Racial Bias in Housing. Could It Help Eliminate It Instead?*, MIT TECH. REV. (Oct. 20, 2020), https://www.technologyreview.com/2020/10/20/1009452/ai-has-exacerbated-racial-bias-in-housing-could-it-help-eliminate-it-instead/.

When Ownership Is Not an Option

This text has placed a great deal of emphasis on the many ways that Black Americans have been denied ownership rights in property throughout the course of this country's history. The alternative to owning property is to rent property; renters help property owners (landlords) to build equity in their property. This chapter examines the impact of the Fair Housing Act on discrimination and racial steering-policies that served to perpetuate segregation in communities. After reviewing the framework and structure of a housing discrimination claim under the Fair Housing Act, this chapter explores the Department of Housing and Urban Development's (HUD) more modern efforts to weed out housing discrimination in algorithm-based advertising.

But housing discrimination does not end when a leasehold is secured. And so this chapter continues by reviewing some basic information about different types of leaseholds, all the while keeping in mind the underlying power dynamics of the landlord–tenant relationship. The chapter concludes by revisiting a classic case in the canon of property law, *Javins v. First National Realty Corp.*,[3] which marked a turning point in U.S. legal history by establishing implied terms in all lease contracts. A brief description of the context surrounding *Javins* and stories about the individuals involved is intended to add nuance and depth to the meaningfulness of the court's holding.

Finally, the chapter includes a sample integrated question set from the NextGen Multistate Bar Exam on the topic of leaseholds, along with some advice about how to prepare for this type of integrated question.

Discrimination Claims under the Civil Rights Act's Fair Housing Act

The 1960s civil rights era culminated with the passage of a package of legislation related to civil rights. The Fair Housing Act was one of the last pieces of legislation passed in that package. Pursuant to 42 U.S.C. § 1982, "all citizens in the United States shall have the same right, in every State and Territory, as is enjoyed by white citizens thereof to inherit, purchase,

3. 428 F.2d 1071 (1970).

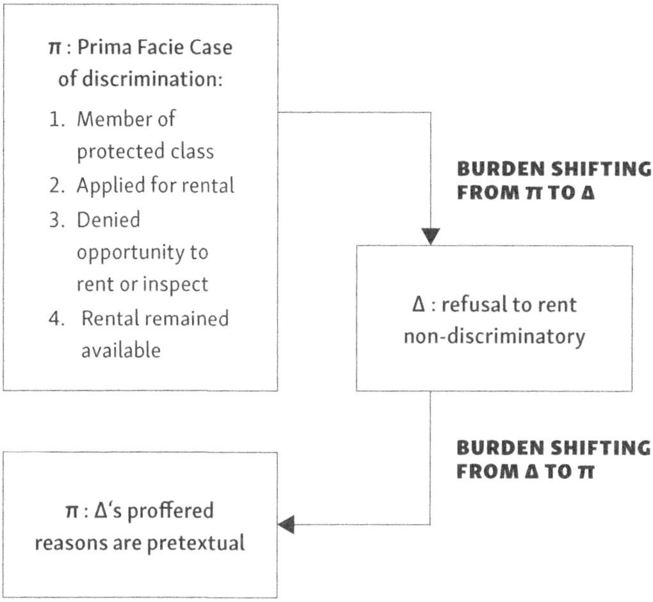

lease, sell, hold or convey real and personal property." The Fair Housing Act provides additional protections intended to ensure that people are not discriminated against in the search for housing, negotiated with unfairly, or told that an apartment is not available based on their membership in one or more protected classes.[4] Together, these protections were intended to ensure that people would be treated fairly under the law and not be denied housing based on their immutable characteristics.

The structure of litigation relating to a discrimination claim is laid out by the Fair Housing Act. Pay close attention to the shifting of burdens and consider what evidentiary task is required of each of the parties. When legislatures weigh in on which party has the burden of proof and by which standard, lawyers may glean a great deal about the intent of the policy at hand. Burden-shifting and standards of proof are tools that legislatures have at their disposal to put their thumb on the scales of justice when a case comes before a court. Keeping that in mind, consider the structure for a claim of discrimination under the Fair Housing Act.[5]

4. 42 U.S.C. § 3604

5. Diagram based on *Asbury v. Brougham*, 866 F.2d 1276 (1989).

Consider the burdens on the parties and the evidence that one would have to present to satisfy those burdens. In *Asbury v. Brougham*,[6] a case often read by first-year law students, the plaintiff had a set of facts demonstrating that housing discrimination had occurred; she was able to meet the burden and prevail on the merits of her claim. Though the case is often lauded as a victory, scores of students fail to consider how uncommon the plaintiff's circumstances were: she had a white sister-in-law who was willing to be a "secret shopper" on her behalf, and she had an uncanny ability to collect and organize data. Additionally, it is uncommon for a party claiming discrimination to have the patience and resources required to prevail in a protracted appeal. What is reasonable to ask of a party who is being denied housing?

The term "racial steering" describes the actions of those who direct people to particular residential areas based on their race. It is accomplished either by encouraging people of the same race to establish enclaves or by guiding only those people who belong to a specific racial group to properties in a particular area. Another way to accomplish racial steering is to deny all but one option for residence to a group based on its protected status. Though this type of discrimination does not involve overt violence, its impact—creating or maintaining segregated communities—is undesirable and, accordingly, a violation of the Fair Housing Act.

Algorithms in Advertising and Discrimination

Though real estate professionals and those engaged in advertising are aware of the rules just discussed, the modern practice of using algorithms to create targeted advertising has revived the racial-steering problem. In 2019, the Department of Housing and Urban Development, the administrative agency created by the Fair Housing Act, filed a complaint against Facebook for its advertising practices. Facebook's use of data algorithms to organize and produce various desirable and targeted "audiences" for their advertisers amounted to racial steering. In 2021, a new complaint was filed against Meta, and in June 2022, Meta settled. As

6. *Id.*

you read about the complaint and settlement agreement below, consider the history of segregation, racial steering, and what the next frontier of housing discrimination might be.

PRESS RELEASE: *JUSTICE DEPARTMENT SECURES GROUNDBREAKING SETTLEMENT AGREEMENT WITH META PLATFORMS, FORMERLY KNOWN AS FACEBOOK, TO RESOLVE ALLEGATIONS OF DISCRIMINATORY ADVERTISING*[7]

Lawsuit is the Department's First Case Challenging Algorithmic Discrimination Under the Fair Housing Act; Meta Agrees to Change its Ad Delivery System

The Department of Justice announced today that it has obtained a settlement agreement resolving allegations that Meta Platforms Inc., formerly known as Facebook Inc., has engaged in discriminatory advertising in violation of the Fair Housing Act (FHA). The proposed agreement resolves a lawsuit filed today in the U.S. District Court for the Southern District of New York alleging that Meta's housing advertising system discriminates against Facebook users based on their race, color, religion, sex, disability, familial status and national origin. The settlement will not take effect until approved by the court.

Among other things, the complaint alleges that Meta uses algorithms in determining which Facebook users receive housing ads, and that those algorithms rely, in part, on characteristics protected under the FHA. This is the department's first case challenging algorithmic bias under the Fair Housing Act.

Under the settlement, Meta will stop using an advertising tool for housing ads (known as the "Special Ad Audience" tool) that, according to the department's complaint, relies on a discriminatory algorithm. Meta also will develop a new system to address racial and other disparities caused by its use of personalization algorithms in its ad delivery system for housing ads. That system will be subject to Department of Justice approval and court oversight.

This settlement marks the first time that Meta will be subject to court oversight for its ad targeting and delivery system.

---

7. Press Release No. 22-650, U.S. Dep't of Justice, Office of Pub. Affairs (June 22, 2022), https://www.justice.gov/opa/pr/justice-department-secures-groundbreaking-settlement-agreement-meta-platforms-formerly-known.

"As technology rapidly evolves, companies like Meta have a responsibility to ensure their algorithmic tools are not used in a discriminatory manner," said Assistant Attorney General Kristen Clarke of the Justice Department's Civil Rights Division. "This settlement is historic, marking the first time that Meta has agreed to terminate one of its algorithmic targeting tools and modify its delivery algorithms for housing ads in response to a civil rights lawsuit. The Justice Department is committed to holding Meta and other technology companies accountable when they abuse algorithms in ways that unlawfully harm marginalized communities."

"When a company develops and deploys technology that deprives users of housing opportunities based in whole or in part on protected characteristics, it has violated the Fair Housing Act, just as when companies engage in discriminatory advertising using more traditional advertising methods," said U.S. Attorney Damian Williams for the Southern District of New York. "Because of this ground-breaking lawsuit, Meta will—for the first time—change its ad delivery system to address algorithmic discrimination. But if Meta fails to demonstrate that it has sufficiently changed its delivery system to guard against algorithmic bias, this office will proceed with the litigation."

"It is not just housing providers who have a duty to abide by fair housing laws," said Demetria McCain, the Principal Deputy Assistant Secretary for Fair Housing and Equal Opportunity at the Department of Housing and Urban Development (HUD). "Parties who discriminate in the housing market, including those engaging in algorithmic bias, must be held accountable. This type of behavior hurts us all. HUD appreciates its continued partnership with the Department of Justice as they seek to uphold our country's civil rights laws."

United States' Lawsuit

The United States' complaint challenges three key aspects of Meta's ad targeting and delivery system. Specifically, the department alleges that:

- Meta enabled and encouraged advertisers to target their housing ads by relying on race, color, religion, sex, disability, familial status and national origin to decide which Facebook users will be eligible and ineligible to receive housing ads.
- Meta created an ad targeting tool known as "Lookalike Audience" or "Special Ad Audience." The tool uses a machine-

learning algorithm to find Facebook users who share similarities with groups of individuals selected by an advertiser using several options provided by Facebook. Facebook has allowed its algorithm to consider FHA-protected characteristics—including race, religion and sex—in finding Facebook users who "look like" the advertiser's source audience and thus are eligible to receive housing ads.

- Meta's ad delivery system uses machine-learning algorithms that rely in part on FHA-protected characteristics—such as race, national origin and sex—to help determine which subset of an advertiser's targeted audience will actually receive a housing ad.

The complaint alleges that Meta has used these three aspects of its advertising system to target and deliver housing-related ads to some Facebook users while excluding other users based on FHA-protected characteristics.

The department's lawsuit alleges both disparate treatment and disparate impact discrimination. The complaint alleges that Meta is liable for disparate treatment because it intentionally classifies users on the basis of FHA-protected characteristics and designs algorithms that rely on users' FHA-protected characteristics. The department further alleges that Meta is liable for disparate impact discrimination because the operation of its algorithms affects Facebook users differently on the basis of their membership in protected classes.

Settlement Agreement

These are the key features of the parties' settlement agreement:

- By Dec. 31, 2022, Meta must stop using an advertising tool for housing ads known as "Special Ad Audience" (previously called "Lookalike Audience"), which relies on an algorithm that, according to the United States, discriminates on the basis of race, sex and other FHA-protected characteristics in identifying which Facebook users will be eligible to receive an ad.
- Meta has until December 2022 to develop a new system for housing ads to address disparities for race, ethnicity and sex between advertisers' targeted audiences and the group of Facebook users to whom Facebook's personalization algo-

rithms actually deliver the ads. If the United States concludes that this new system sufficiently addresses the discriminatory disparities that Meta's algorithms introduce, then Meta will fully implement the new system by Dec. 31, 2022.

- If the United States concludes that Meta's changes to its ad delivery system do not adequately address the discriminatory disparities, the settlement agreement will terminate and the United States will litigate its case against Meta in federal court.
- The parties will select an independent, third-party reviewer to investigate and verify on an ongoing basis whether the new system is meeting the compliance standards agreed to by the parties. Under the agreement, Meta must provide the reviewer with any information necessary to verify compliance with those standards. The court will have ultimate authority to resolve disputes over the information that Meta must disclose.
- Meta will not provide any targeting options for housing advertisers that directly describe or relate to FHA-protected characteristics. Under the agreement, Meta must notify the United States if Meta intends to add any targeting options. The court will have authority to resolve any disputes between the parties about proposed new targeting options.
- Meta must pay to the United States a civil penalty of $115,054, the maximum penalty available under the Fair Housing Act.

The Justice Department's lawsuit is based in part on an investigation and charge of discrimination by HUD, which found that all three aspects of Meta's ad delivery system violated the Fair Housing Act. When Facebook elected to have the HUD charge heard in federal court, HUD referred the matter to the Justice Department for litigation....

NOTES ON *UNITED STATES V. META PLATFORMS*

1. Data and Property. There is a very good chance that data from every reader of this book has contributed to these algorithms. Outside of housing discrimination and property law, there are a host of ethical questions about the collection, sale, and use of data. Many people consider their personal data to be their property, but the prevailing view is that data does not have value to advertisers until it is aggregated and anonymized.

2. Deterrents. Given the history of racial steering and segregation in this country and the nature of the complaint, is Meta's civil penalty sufficient? Does Meta's size and annual revenues factor into your determination about what would be an effective deterrent? How would you determine an appropriate remedy? What is the goal of the remedy?

Personal Reflection on Segregation

In order to consider policy from all perspectives, it is essential to bring your own experiences. As a property professor with an interest in tax policy, I have done a great deal of critical thinking about the ill effects of segregation and the ways in which segregation has perpetuated a sometimes dehumanizing hierarchy among races. I need no convincing.

There are times that I have experiences that stop me in my tracks and help me to see all my rationally, legally informed perspectives in a new light. I am South Asian, and a very particular kind who can identify as both Indian and Pakistani (it's not that common, trust me). Once, when I found myself traveling to a different city, I visited its South Asian district. Not only is the racial enclave South Asian, but there are separate sections for the Pakistani and Indian populations. Being in that part of town, surrounded by the sounds and smells of Americans who are South Asian, helped me to experience a unique sense of belonging.

Some of the holidays I celebrate revolve around a fast. Many are afterthoughts to the populations of tax lawyers and academics that I spend most of my days with, so the chance to be surrounded by others who are also experiencing hunger, and the anticipation and sacrifice of a fast, in solidarity with me makes me appreciate the ability to have a space segregated by specific community. On some days there are fasts for the Indian/Hindu side, and other days for the Pakistani/Muslim side. For me, the important part is the ability to be in close community.

As I reflect on my gratitude for those communities and my academic feelings about the history of segregation in our country, there is one large distinction that comes to mind: CHOICE. The ability to choose where to live and to come and go as one pleases—that is the right in property that is worth protecting.

Leasehold Basics

Even after a lease is obtained, unequal power dynamics persist and barriers to dignity remain. In this section, after briefly reviewing basic types of leaseholds, we examine the story behind a case that is canon in property law: *Javins v. First National Realty Corp.*[8] It is one of many cases in which the law does not bother with distinctions between doctrinal areas; accordingly, it is important to understand the way that concepts from contracts interact with interests in property. For the purposes of this section, however, the focus will be the history, context, and story surrounding the case, in order that it may inform a view of what a right to habitability really means in context.

To begin, leaseholds can be broken into four general types. Each type should be considered through the context of the power dynamics that surround it: in particular, how the lease is formed, how it is terminated, and how much notice a tenant must be given before being evicted or removed from the leased premises. In addition, whether the property is alienable speaks to the strength of the interest in property. An interest in property is alienable (transferable) if it is devisable (meaning the holder can leave it to another person by way of a will), inheritable (a person may receive the interest in property either by a will or by intestate succession), or capable of being transferred by sale or by gift.

8. 428 F.2d 1071.

Type of Leasehold	Features
Term of Years	The most common and predictable form of lease. Though it is called a term of years, it can be for any length of time so long as the period is defined. Those with a rental period of more than one year must be in writing in order to be in compliance with the statute of frauds. The notice of termination is the lease itself, which defines the state and end date of the rental agreement. The interests of both the landlord and the tenant are alienable.
Periodic Tenancy	Often after a term of years expires, the tenant will continue to pay rent to the landlord, who will continue to accept the payments. Without an express end date, this becomes a periodic tenancy. The payment period becomes the rental period: for example, if rent is paid monthly, a periodic tenancy is described as a "month-to-month" lease. Notice of at least one rental period must be given to terminate, though each jurisdiction may have more specific rules about termination. The modern trend is one that gives deference and increased notice to a tenant before being evicted, particularly from a residential tenancy. Interests in periodic tenancy are alienable subject to the same termination requirements.
Tenancy at Will	There is no written agreement in a tenancy at will, and the tenant may be evicted at any time according to the common law. In some jurisdictions, mandatory minimum notice requirements provide some protections for residential tenants. Because of the "handshake agreement" nature of these tenancies, they are not alienable.
Tenancy at Sufferance/ Holdover Tenancy	To call this a "tenancy" is a misnomer. A tenant at sufferance, or a "holdover tenant," has no legal right to be there. A holdover tenant is distinct from a trespasser because a holdover tenant did once have a legal right to be there but has since relinquished that right. There must be more than a de minimis presence (it has to be more than a tenant moving out and leaving some of their belongings behind in the formerly leased premises). As this is not an interest in property, it is not alienable.

Implied Warranty of Habitability: The Untold Story of *Javins v. First National Realty Corp.*

Once a lease is secured, the potential for abuse of power dynamics does not dissipate. A legal framework has developed to support tenants—particularly those in low-income housing, who, due to generations of government-sponsored policy and private discrimination, tend to be disproportionately Black and brown—when the conditions of their leased premises fall below habitable standards. Professor Richard H. Chused provides some important context around the case in an article he first published in 2004.[9] Consider the introduction:

> [T]he tenants living in the Clifton Terrace Apartments who had refused to pay their rent because of the terrible conditions in the three building complex were asked to collect evidence of housing code violations and bring their exhibits to court. They brought bags of mouse feces, dead mice, roaches and pictures of their apartments to the courtroom, which was filled with tenants from the buildings. A housing inspector was also there, carrying a pile of paper that, according to Fleming [the tenants' lawyer—Ed.], "stood at least one and one-half feet high," memorializing well over one thousand citations for code violations. Herman Miller, the lawyer for Sidney Brown's First National Realty Corporation which owned Clifton Terrace, moved to bar the introduction of any evidence of code violations on the ground that it would inflame the jury. Fleming, of course, vehemently opposed Miller's motion. Judge Fickling, in accordance with the longstanding refusal of courts to allow tenants to raise defenses in eviction cases, then barred introduction of the evidence, entered judgements for possession as a matter of law and dismissed the jury.[3]

9. Richard H. Chused, Javins (*a.k.a.* Saunders) v. First National Realty Corporation, 11 Geo. J. of Poverty L. & Pol'y 208 (Winter 2004) (later reprinted in *Property Stories*, *supra* note 1).

[3]. Since no facts were left to be determined—everyone agreed that rent had not been paid—there was nothing left for the jury to do. Traditionally, the court decides legal issues and the jury resolves factual disputes.

These events turned out to be the beginning of what turned out to be a very long saga. Eventually, in *Javins v. First National Realty Corporation*,[4] the United States Circuit Court of Appeals for the District of Columbia Circuit became the first tribunal to unequivocally hold that a warranty of habitability was implied in all residential leases and that tenants could set off damages for violation of that warranty defensively in eviction cases. But the propriety of Judge Fickling's decision took four years to resolve. During that time Clifton Terrace became the object of enormous coverage in the press, City Hall politicians took center stage in the controversy for a time, plans to sell the building to a non-profit corporation for remodeling emerged, collapsed and reemerged, Sidney Brown was sent to jail for a brief period, the city erupted in major civil disturbances and the tenants continued to suffer under terrible living conditions.

The acrimonious quality of the trial between Brown and his tenants typified many of the events surrounding the litigation of *Javins*, arguably the most influential landlord-tenant case of the twentieth century. The tenants were largely poor and black residents of Washington, D.C.—a city rife with racial unrest and protest. The efforts of some tenants living in Clifton Terrace to alleviate hundreds of housing code violations in their apartments included sit-ins at the offices of Corporation Counsel of the city and of the Secretary of the Department of Housing and Urban Development, as well as a rent strike. It was the rent strike, and the resulting actions brought by the landlord to obtain possession of the apartments from the non-paying tenants that eventually led to the *Javins* decision.

Protest and unrest in this epoch went far beyond sit-ins and rent strikes. June 17, 1966, the date the striking tenants' effort to avoid eviction from the Clifton Terrace Apartments were first frustrated in Landlord and Tenant Court, was only ten months after the Watts area of Los Angeles went up in flames in an outburst of black anger, ten days after civil rights worker

[4]. 428 F.2d 1071, 138 U.S. App. D.C. 369 (D.C. Cir. 1970), rev'g *Saunders v. First National Realty Corp.*, 245 A.2d 836 (D.C. App. 1968). The proceeding in the Landlord and Tenant Division of the D.C. Court of General Sessions resulted in no published opinion.

James Meredith was shot by a sniper in a failed assignation attempt while on a "March Against Fear" from Memphis to Jackson, five days after the start of the first of two civil disturbances that summer in Chicago, and the same day Stokely Carmichael, chairman of the Student Non-Violent Coordinating Committee, made his famous "Black Power" speech in Greenwood, Mississippi. And these same tenants lost their appeal before the District of Columbia Court of Appeals on September 23, 1968, only a few months after Dr. Martin Luther King, Jr. was assassinated and parts of Washington, D.C., including areas on 14th Street north and south of Clifton Terrace, went up in flames. By the time the United States Circuit Court of Appeals issued its now famous decision in 1970, old downtown Washington had begun a steady decline....

The *Javins* story, therefore, is full of the raw passion of actors convinced of the righteousness of their positions. Reconstructing the tale requires more than a review of the changes *Javins* made in landlord-tenant law, though that material will be covered. The meaning and impact of the case can be grasped only if some of the emotions of its actors and the passions of their historical moment can be recaptured....[10]

Implied Terms in Lease Contracts

The *Javins* decision revolutionized something that may be taken for granted today: the right to live in a habitable place. As this decision indicates, the foundations of landlord–tenant law had been established when possession of *land* was being transferred. In Washington, D.C., in the 1970s and, indeed, in an urbanized society, the real property was hardly relevant. Instead, housing was a package of services, including the right to possession, ventilation, plumbing, pest control, and all of the conveniences we expect from a residence. Incorporating by reference already existing housing codes and consumer protection statutes is an example of the way that contract law works to support questions related to interests in real property, which require special protections.

10. (Some citations omitted—Ed.)

Furthermore, although a lease is a contract, it is distinct from other types of contracts because the subject of the lease is an interest in real property. In contracts, some terms are implied, including good faith and fair dealing, and the warranty of merchantability (when one of the parties qualifies as a merchant). In the context of leaseholds, this case borrows from the doctrine of contract law while staying grounded in the concept of treating rights in property with special care and attention. Given the history, context, and facts at hand, the circumstances implied a warranty of habitability in the contract's terms. Implied terms, particularly those related to human dignity and which have sprung from history in the way that the implied warranty of habitability has, are generally not subject to waiver. Once the law establishes that implied in every lease is a promise that the leased premises will be kept in a habitable condition, landlords and tenants may not contract around that. While there is some debate about free markets and laissez-faire economics, the importance of the *Javins* decision, and of many state jurisdictions that have enacted statutory support in its wake, is the requirement that a minimum standard of habitability be implied in all lease contracts.[11]

Freedom of contract continues to be essential. And while parties may agree to various terms and be specific with regard to their agreements, careful lawyers will be sure to balance the freedom of contract against the polices that underlie the implied warranties, particularly as they relate to interests in use and enjoyment of property (like habitability).

Independent Covenants → Dependent Covenants

The relationship of the covenants is another area of contract law that is important for understanding the implications of *Javins* as it relates to interests in real property. Prior to *Javins*, the covenants of the parties to the contract—the landlord and tenant—were independent. Each person signing the contract was agreeing to perform on their promises, regardless of the actions of the other (this, too, was a vestige of the agrarian leaseholds from which landlord-tenant law had evolved). But in *Javins*, covenants that were previously independent became dependent. As a

11. *Contract Remedy for the Slum Dweller*, Javins v. First National Realty Corporation, 428 F.2d 1071 (D.C. Cir. 1970), 1970 Wash. U. L. Q. 499 (1970).

practical matter, this change supports tenants: if a landlord does not fulfill their promise to provide habitable premises, then a tenant is relieved of their obligation in the same proportion. This has not come to mean that a tenant is not obligated to pay *any* rent if the landlord does not repair something in the leased space; indeed, courts have, since *Javins*, established formulas for percent abatements for certain violations of housing codes. But this change is a vast improvement over the reality tenants faced in the era before *Javins*, when they were liable to pay rent regardless of the state of the property. One only needs to look to the procedural history of *Javins*, which describes how tenants were evicted immediately for nonpayment of rent, without being allowed to defend against the landlord's eviction by citing various housing code violations as the reason for their nonpayment.

Understanding the stories of the individuals on both sides of the lease is vitally important. Loss of habitability may often mean loss of income and ability to pay rent. For the same reasons that consumer-protection statutes are applied to leaseholds, housing courts also need to be able to uncover the facts and circumstances of the individuals impacted by housing violations in order to come to a resolution that comports with justice. It has repeatedly been established in our system of law that residential property is a fundamental human right, one that is essential to not only our identity but also to the way we function in society. *Javins* adapted principles of contract law to account for this.

Since the time *Javins* was decided, jurisdictions have established, both by statute and common law, a more complex set of available remedies for tenants when a landlord is in breach of their duty. These remedies reflect the modern way of living in which a leasehold has taken on the features of a contract for a package of housing services rather than a transfer of interest in real property. Understanding the ways that a landlord and tenant may need to balance their duties to one another with regard to the lease is constantly changing and the work of a lawyer. The framework for dealing with accountability when something does not go according to the plan described in the lease requires balancing the interests of the contracting parties as well as the rights of the property holders. Accordingly, when establishing a remedies paradigm, which may include partial rental abatement, repair and deduct, and other solutions, lawyers and courts will be well served to keep in mind the priority of interests to be protected while conducting their analysis.

Skill: Sample NextGen Bar Exam Integrated Question Set: Overview

In July 2023, the National Conference of Bar Examiners (NCBE) released a sample set of questions for the NextGen bar exam. Three main types of tasks will be included on this exam: multiple-choice questions, integrated question sets, and longer writing tasks.[12]

Task	Approximate Percent Allocation	Description
Multiple-Choice Questions	~ 50%	These multiple-choice questions will have between four and six answer options with one or more correct answers. Some responses may receive partial credit.
Integrated Question Sets	Slightly > 33%	Each integrated question set centers around a common fact scenario. It may include a variety of materials, such as legal resources and supplemental documents. It will contain a combination of multiple-choice and short-answer responses, and it will test knowledge of doctrinal law as well as skills in drafting, editing, client counseling, and dispute resolution.
Longer Writing Tasks	~ 25%	There will be two longer writing tasks in this section of the exam. One of these tasks will include a set of multiple choice questions followed by a longer writing assignment. These tasks will be designed to evaluate lawyering skills in realistic situations that new lawyers should be able to accomplish.

12. *NextGen Bar Exam Sample Questions*, NEXTGEN BAR EXAM, https://nextgenbarexam.ncbex.org/nextgen-sample-questions/#ftoc-heading-12 (last visited March 4, 2024).

Sample NextGen Bar Exam Integrated Question Set: Practice

Below is the first sample NextGen bar exam integrated question set provided by the NCBE. Note the extent to which the answers provided require a mix of substantive knowledge, skills, lawyering experience regarding client representation. Students enhance these skills by integrating their identities and personal experiences into how they learn and practice the law.

Integrated Question Set 1

Your law firm encourages you to take on pro bono cases. Recently, you agreed to take on a pro bono case through your local bar's volunteer lawyers program in which you represent a tenant whose apartment has flooded. The following is an excerpt from your notes from the initial interview with the client:

Notes from the Initial Interview

During a recent hurricane, a lot of water entered the client's apartment. The apartment has carpet throughout, which was completely soaked. The property manager refuses to do anything about the flooding and said that the lease the client signed makes this the client's responsibility. The property manager also claims that the client did not take proper precautions before the storm, which made the flooding worse. The client disagrees. After the storm, the property manager recommended that the client buy a water pump and some fans to "dry things out." The client tried this, but it didn't fix the problem. The apartment is still wet and smells "unbearably bad." The client can't afford to try to fix it anymore. The client does not want to move but can't keep on living in these conditions.

The client is in a month-to-month lease. The lease identifies the landlord as "Rentals LLC." The lease was signed by both your client and the property manager, who signed as "the Managing and Sole Member of Rentals LLC." The lease includes the following provision:

Condition of the Premises

Landlord ("Rentals LLC") makes no covenants or warranties about the condition of the leased premises and disclaims all responsibility for the condition of the leased premises. Tenant agrees to be solely responsible for maintaining the condition of the leased premises. Tenant waives any and all rights to the contrary, including but not limited to a right to bring a claim related to the habitability of the leased premises.

The lease does not include any provision on what damages may be available in the event of breach. Your jurisdiction has a residential landlord-tenant statute that applies to the lease. The following is an excerpt from that statute:

6-20-5 Landlord's Duty to Maintain Premises; Prohibited Conduct

(a) Subject to subsections (b) and (c), a landlord has a nonwaivable duty to maintain the premises in a habitable condition, including making necessary repairs. The duty includes but is not limited to a requirement that the landlord ensure that the premises ... have effective waterproofing and weather protection of the roof and exterior walls, including windows and doors.... Tenants have a cause of action for breach of this duty, with remedies as set forth in §6-20-10 [Tenant Remedies]. This cause of action supplants any common-law claims for breach of the landlord's implied warranty of habitability.

(b) The landlord's duty in subsection (a) is relieved if the uninhabitable condition of the premises was caused by an unreasonable act or omission of the tenant, the tenant's immediate family member, or the tenant's guest.

(c) If the premises are substantially damaged by a fire, other casualty, or natural disaster and continued occupancy of the unit is unlawful or dangerous or requires repairs that can be made only if the tenant vacates the premises, the landlord may terminate the lease by giving the tenant reasonable written notice.

(d) Any provision in a lease that purports to waive the landlord's duty in subsection (a) is unenforceable. If the landlord seeks to enforce such a provision or accepts the tenant's voluntary compliance with such a provision, the tenant has a cause of action in the amount of three times the periodic rent. This cause of action accrues irrespective of any claim the tenant may have for breach of the duty described in subsection (a).

Integrated Question 1

Which of the following is an accurate application of Section 6-20-5 to the facts? **Select one.**

A. The section allows the landlord to enforce the lease provision, making the client responsible for repairs, but the tenant may seek damages of three times the periodic rent.
B. The section makes the lease provision unenforceable but does not decide the issue of which party is responsible for which portion of the repairs.
C. The section makes the lease provision unenforceable and makes the landlord responsible for the full extent of the repairs.
D. The section does not decide the issue of the lease provision's enforceability but establishes the landlord's negligence per se.

Question 1 Answer

The correct answer is (B). Section 6-20-5(d) makes the lease provision unenforceable, but §6-20-5(b) relieves the landlord's duty to maintain the premises in a habitable condition if the uninhabitable condition was caused by an act or omission of the tenant or a tenant's guest or family member. (A) is incorrect because, as noted above, §6-20-5(d) of the statute makes the lease provision unenforceable. (C) is incorrect because the statute does not necessarily make the landlord responsible for the full extent of the repairs; as noted above, §6-20-5(b) makes the tenant responsible in certain circumstances. (D) is incorrect because, as noted above, §6-20-5(d) of the statute makes the lease provision unenforceable. Although §6-20-5(a) establishes a landlord's duty to provide habitable premises, it does not establish negligence per se.

Integrated Question 2

Section 6-20-5 of the statute does not define the term "habitable." A partner at your firm has asked a law clerk to determine the jurisdiction's meaning of the term for the purposes of potential litigation, and the law clerk has asked you for guidance.

Advise the law clerk on two specific legal sources that are the most likely to provide a controlling definition of the term "habitable."

Question 2 Representative Correct Answers

- State statute that defines the term as it is used in this statute, such as a "definitions" subsection within the same statutory scheme.
- High court decision in this state interpreting "habitable" as it is used in this statute.
- Appellate court decision in this state interpreting "habitable" as it is used in this statute.
- State regulatory or administrative source if an administrative agency regulates the area and has provided a definition.

Integrated Question 3

You receive an email from your client. In the email, the client asks you "whether it would be a good idea to sue." You begin your reply to the client by explaining that litigation will consume the client's personal time and will almost certainly take longer to resolve than reaching a settlement before litigation. You consider what other risks your client would face in litigation.

Considering your client's objectives and the applicable statute, describe two other potential risks of filing a claim or claims on the client's behalf.

Question 3 Representative Correct Answers

- The landlord may be able to use subsection (c) of the statute to terminate the lease, if it is necessary for the client to vacate in order to repair the flood damage.
- Termination of the lease could also be a concern based on the month-to-month status of the lease (regardless of the statutory provision). Termination is a risk for this client even if the jurisdiction has a statute that prohibits a landlord from terminating in retaliation for filing a complaint.
- Even if the client remains in the apartment, a lawsuit will further sour the client's relationship with the landlord.
- The landlord might counterclaim and allege that the client was negligent, which could open the client up to potential liability.
- Litigation, particularly about your home, can be extremely stressful and frustrating.

Integrated Question 4

After discussing your research with the client and assisting the client in setting goals, you contact the property manager on the client's behalf and attempt to negotiate a settlement. The property manager agrees to replace the carpet but refuses to refund any of the client's past rent or to pay any of the client's costs. Eventually, negotiations break down, and you prepare to draft a complaint on behalf of the client.

Which of the following facts provide the most support to a cause of action under § 6-20-5(d)? **Select two.**

A. The lease provides that the client "waives any ... right to bring a claim related to the habitability of the leased premises."
B. The apartment has an unbearably bad smell.
C. The property manager claims that the client did not take proper precautions to prevent flood damage.
D. The client bought a water pump and fans at the property manager's recommendation.
E. The client cannot afford to make any other repairs.
F. The flooding was caused by a hurricane.

Question 4 Answer

The correct answers are (A) and (D). Section 6-20-5(d) states that any provision in a lease prohibited by subsection (a) is unenforceable. If the landlord seeks to enforce the provision or accepts the tenant's voluntary compliance with the provision, the tenant has a cause of action in the amount of three times the periodic rent. (A) is correct because the lease's inclusion of a provision that violates this statute is relevant to a request for damages under § 6-20-5(d). (D) is also correct because the fact that the client bought a water pump and fans at the property manager's recommendation is evidence that Rentals LLC is seeking to enforce the prohibited provision. The client's purchase of the water pump and fans at the property manager's recommendation is relevant and supportive even if it is not dispositive. (B), (E), and (F) are incorrect because none of these options is relevant to the lease's inclusion of a provision that violates the statute or Rentals LLC's attempt to enforce the provision. (C) raises an issue that, if true, would be relevant but not favorable to the client. **Partial credit is available for this answer.**

Integrated Question 5

Your legal research since the initial client interview supports a finding that the condition of the client's apartment after the storm fell below the standard of habitability in the jurisdiction. In addition, your factual investigation has established the following:

- There was nothing that Rentals LLC could reasonably have done to prevent the flooding from the hurricane.
- The client spent money on fans and a water pump.
- Since the client notified the property manager about the flood five months ago, the client has continued paying monthly rent in full.

List two claims you could bring on behalf of your client to seek the greatest possible damages for your client. For each claim, describe what remedy you will seek in the complaint. If the remedy is uncertain, describe the information you need to determine the appropriate remedy.

Question 5 Representative Correct Answers

- **Breach of § 6-20-5(a)**—I'm going to need to determine remedies through the remedies provision. [We don't know what it would cover, though possibilities could be the fans/pump and the rental value.]
- **Breach of § 6-20-5(d)**—The remedy is three times the monthly periodic rent. I'm going to need to determine what the client's monthly rent payment is.

Integrated Question 6

Your firm has had some experience with Rentals LLC. The company does not always show up in court to defend small claims against it, and you are concerned that it might be difficult to collect a future judgment against the company.

List two factual issues you could investigate to help determine whether the LLC's veil can be pierced to collect a future judgment from the property manager personally. In your jurisdiction, the test for piercing the veil of an LLC is the same as the test for piercing the veil of a corporation.

For example, in a torts matter, a factual issue that might require investigation is "whether the plaintiff lost wages as a result of the accident."

Question 6 Representative Correct Answers

- Whether any commingling of the company's assets and the property manager's assets occurred.
- Whether the company maintained adequate business records, to the extent the company was required to keep business records.
- Whether the company disregarded legal formalities, to the extent that the company was required to follow formalities.
- Whether the property manager was so inseparable from the company as to be its "alter ego."
- Whether the property manager used the company as an agent.
- Whether the property manager intended to use the company to perpetrate a fraud.
- Whether the company was undercapitalized.[13]

---

13. ©2023 National Conference of Bar Examiners. Reprinted with permission from the National Conference of Bar Examiners. The National Conference of Bar Examiners did not review the contents of this book and does not endorse any views expressed by the author.

NINE

Returning to Basics

What Can Be Owned

Even after the period of conquest and colonization of the New World and the abolition of slavery, whiteness was the predicate for attaining a host of societal privileges, in both public and private spheres. Whiteness determined whether one could vote, travel freely, attend schools, obtain work, and indeed, defined the structure of social relations along the entire spectrum of interactions between the individual and society. Whiteness then became status, a form of racialized privilege ratified in law. Material privileges attendant to being white inhered in the status of being white. After the dismantling of legalized race segregation, whiteness took on the character of property in the modern sense in that relative white privilege was legitimated as the status quo.

—Cheryl I. Harris[1]

1. From Cheryl I. Harris, *Whiteness as Property*, 106 Harv. L. Rev. 1707, 1745 (June 1993).

Race and Intellectual Property

This book began with an inquiry about what can be owned and the extent to which there can be property interests in human bodies. An examination of the legal history of the United States reveals that owning (some) people in order to build an economic and political order is in our very foundations. These chapters have explored various incidents of ownership, including the right to exclude and the rights of use and enjoyment, as well as some tensions regarding the taking of private property for public use and the greater good. In so many different areas of property law doctrine, value judgments, cultural norms, and biases are baked into the rules, often without any notice.

As commerce and technology evolve, so does our common law. As transportation and the internet make our world smaller, and as our collective conscience and social and cultural awareness grow, our rules must respond to these changing physical, social, and psychological boundaries. Yet, despite the rapid growth and reinvention of so many paradigms, many tenets of the doctrine of property law that are attached to our intimate psychology can be preserved: the desire to keep what is yours, the right to profit from your property, and the right to control the fruits of your own labor, for example. Accordingly, our law and policy has formalized the protection of these rights. As valuable property increasingly became intangible and technology grew more complex, our laws evolved to protect creativity and incentivize innovation.

Protections for intellectual property fall into three main categories, all defined by federal statute (though there are state statues on point): patent, copyright, and trademark. Some may believe that this area of the law is "race neutral," but this chapter will show this to be far from the case. Due to the specialized nature of the law of intellectual property,[2] this chapter uses very broad strokes to inspect some ways in which racial dynamics have impacted its application. The chapter begins with an examination of patent law, presenting two similar fact patterns describing situations where human tissue was extracted to create useful cell lines that were subsequently patented. An inspection of the legal processes surrounding these cases reveals a great deal about access to justice and its relation to racial identity in the United States. Next, the chapter offers

2. An entire course may be offered on each of these three areas of the law.

a brief examination of the legislative history and timing of the requirement in copyright law that an artistic work must be affixed to a tangible medium in order to be eligible for copyright protection. Then the chapter looks at *Matal v. Tam*,[3] a complex trademark case decided by the Supreme Court in 2017, in which the Court examined (and ultimately discarded) the "disparagement clause." The case helps to demonstrates how the various levels of appeals courts consider and deal with difficult or uncomfortable racially charged language.

To conclude the chapter and the entire book, in lieu of a skill, the chapter offers a very brief introduction to the tenets of a new doctrine: critical race theory. Despite some recent rhetoric, critical race theory is a separate doctrine that contains its own structure, tenets, and scholarship. This work has inspected *history*—and though it has at times taken a critical perspective of the long view of history, the doctrine of critical race theory (CRT) has not been invoked or introduced writ large. This distinction is important. And so, for those students who are interested in learning how distinguished legal scholars have been using the tools of the law to view and dismantle systemic racism, it seems fitting to end this work with a description of the doctrine of CRT.

	What Is Protected	Nature of Protection
Patent	Invention or process that is (1) novel, (2) non-obvious, (3) useful, and (4) patentable	Exclusive right to use or profit for 20 years from the date of the patent. After expiration of the patent, the subject goes into the public domain.
Copyright	Artistic, literary, or intellectually created works that are original and affixed in a medium	In general, copyright protection lasts for the life of the author + 70 years.
Trademark	A word, phrase, or design that identifies goods and services	Trademarks may be registered or unregistered. Actions relating to brand dilution and competition may be initiated regardless of the status of the trademark.

3. 582 U.S. 218 (2017).

A patent is granted by the U.S. Patent and Trademark Office (USPTO). The holder of a patent has exclusive rights to use the subject of the patent for 20 years. Inventions or processes are subjects of patents, which are designed to help ensure that innovators can profit from their creativity in order to encourage invention. Patents are registered, and they become part of the public domain after they expire. Holders of patents may license the rights they hold under the patent—a frequent occurrence in the pharmaceutical industry—so that the public may benefit from the invention and the creator may enjoy a financial reward for their invention.

Case Comparison: *Moore v. Regents of the University of California*[4] and Henrietta Lacks

Consider the stories of John Moore (*Moore v. Regents*) and Henrietta Lacks. Both stories relate to patents and human bodies and have generally the same outcome. As you read and consider the nature of how these stories have (or have not) permeated our legal system and popular culture, try to think critically and introspectively about any biases that may be at work—your own and the ones that exist writ large.

These stories have some remarkably similar basic facts, yet there are some distinctions in their respective tones and outcomes. Practice rewriting these facts in ways that may be persuasive with changing goals in mind. Each party sought recognition for their contributions to a useful cell line, but the Lacks family also wanted recognition of the ways that Black bodies have been used without consent throughout history, and they wanted historical wrongs to be addressed. Applying the tools and frameworks we covered in this text, how would you rewrite these facts to be more or less objective? What types of persuasive policy arguments could be made to support these parties?

4. 51 Cal. 3d 120 (1990).

John Moore	Henrietta Lacks
John Moore, a white man, initiated this action based on his belief that he had property rights in the unique tissue that was removed from his body and which was the basis of a patented and profitable cell line. Mr. Moore was treated by doctors in California for cancer, and he consented to having his spleen removed in accordance with his care. But he was unaware of his doctors' plans and financial interest in his extracted tissue. His doctors had formulated a plan, which they carried out, to use his tissue to create a cell line, named the "Mo" cell line for Moore, that was eventually the subject of a lucrative patent. In his brief, Mr. Moore made an argument that it was the uniqueness of his cells, like his likeness, that was his property. Without this unique set of cells, he argued, the cell line that the doctors created would not be possible, and accordingly, he was due some compensation. In considering his case, a sympathetic and passionate court decided not to extend the tort of conversion to Mr. Moore's extracted cells. Over outrage at the lack of disclosure and consent, the court decided that on balance the pursuit of medical advances and work of physicians to develop cell lines was more important.	Henrietta Lacks, a Black woman, was diagnosed with an aggressive cervical cancer from which she died at age 31. She was treated at one of the few hospitals that would treat Black people in 1951, Johns Hopkins. During Ms. Lacks's treatment and before her death, doctors at the hospital, without her knowledge and consent, took cells from her body, which they found to have an extraordinary capacity to survive and reproduce (they were "immortal"). These features of Ms. Lacks's cells made them particularly well suited for medical research, and the cell line, named "HeLa" for Henrietta Lacks, was duplicated and used around the world for key discoveries in many fields of medicine, without the knowledge or consent of the family. Once Henrietta Lacks's descendants discovered the cell line was still in use, a media storm ensued. Rebecca Skloot authored a book, which was followed by podcasts, documentaries, and an HBO special about the family's journey.

Did Copyright Kill Jazz?

Copyright protections are intended to protect creative and artistic works. There is a long history of the dominant culture's finding ways to appropriate the creativity and culture of colonized people in fashion,[5] art,[6] cuisine,[7] literature,[8] and almost every artistic endeavor. There are simple ways to resolve nuanced questions about how to draw the line between appropriation and appreciation. Whether the act of borrowing from one culture and using it as a source of inspiration to create a wholly new product is done with respect and with proper credit and resources given to the right individuals or groups can be in the eye of the beholder.

Law and policy does not shudder in the face of nuanced questions. The history of music in particular is rife with examples of white individuals appropriating Black creators, with white-owned entities profiting as a result. The structure of copyright rules has contributed to this dynamic where Black creators have been unable to reap the financial benefits of their creations. Consider the following excerpt from an article by Candace G. Hines:[9]

> The Black musical tradition works in a "trope of revision," that is, it is a highly creative tradition that builds and improves upon the music within its community.[5] Copyright's confines

---

5. Anushka Indurkar, *Cultural Appropriation in Fashion Industry*, Fashion & L.J. (Oct. 6, 2021), https://fashionlawjournal.com/cultural-appropriation-in-fashion-industry/.

6. Alyssa Manansala, *"It's Only Art": How Art Controversy over Cultural Appropriation and Historical Trauma Can Move Toward a More Ethical Public Humanities*, John Nicholas Brown Center for Public Humanities and Cultural Heritage Blog, May 3, 2021.

7. Maria Godoy & Kat Chow, *When Chefs Become Famous Cooking Other Cultures' Food*, The Salt: NPR (Mar. 22, 2016), https://www.npr.org/sections/thesalt/2016/03/22/471309991/when-chefs-become-famous-cooking-other-cultures-food. See generally the series *Other People's Food*, The Sporkful, https://www.sporkful.com/tag/other-peoples-food/.

8. Jeremy Ullmann, *Writing the Other: Can Literature Escape the Criticism of Cultural Appropriation?*, Media Diversity Inst. (Dec. 9, 2020), https://www.media-diversity.org/writing-the-other-can-literature-escape-the-criticism-of-cultural-appropriation/.

9. *Black Musical Traditions and Copyright Law: Historical Tensions*, 10 Mich. J. Race & L. 463, 464–65 (2005).

[5]. *See* David Brackett, Interpreting Popular Music 127–156 (2000) (quoting Black studies scholar Henry Louis Gates).

do not reward this specific type of composition, however, since it rewards musical works of minimum creativity, minimum originality, and those works fixed in a "tangible medium of expression."[6] Moreover, copyright acts to the detriment of those who create new works out of the old by granting the author of the original work a monopoly on the creation of such "derivative" works. Hence, the modern day Public Enemy resembles the frustrated blues singer of the 1930's who stopped performing because he could not earn a livable wage for his work, or the stymied early R&B singer who could not produce and promote his hits fast enough to compete with the rock 'n' roll imitation of his own work.

The body of copyright law, with its vast revisions and amendments, was originally intended to encourage creativity and protect creators work. Yet the Black musical idiom has been and continues to be excluded from such benefits because it does not fit into copyright law's construction of ownership and composition. Copyright's requirements have stood in the way of Black musicians' integrity as artists and their economic reward, since copyright law has historically granted a limited ownership to those who can conform a musical work into standard musical notation. Copyright's notions of authorship and composition undermine the Black musical customs of (1) community composition; as exemplified by oral tradition and call-and-response; (2) rhythmic and musical complexity; and (3) improvisation.[7] The combination of this cultural clash and America's history of racism has prevented Blacks from receiving recognition for their musical contributions or copyright's promises of compensation.

Additionally, by failing to incorporate the Black musical idiom, copyright law heightens Black musicians' vulnerability to exploitation in a social milieu already accustomed to exploiting Black Labor....

---

[6]. 17 U.S.C. § 102(a) (2000).

[7]. *See* Ortiz Walton, Music: Black, White & Blue: A Sociological Survey of the Use and Misuse of Afro-American Music 2 (1972).

Knowing the context in which the federal copyright rules were enacted will be important as you think about the policy considerations underlying various decisions. The copyright eligibility requirement that the artistic expression be "affixed" to a tangible medium is a major challenge for Black creators whose work already has a history of being appropriated, as the article above notes. Countervailing policy considerations, however, include administrative concerns about enforcement. A system of registration of copyright is important for enforcing associated property rights, and it would be incredibly difficult to have such a system without some evidence of the work or creator. As courts, legislators, and effective social activists know, consideration of all surrounding policy considerations leads to informed outcomes.

But it is important to remember that, particularly when questions about cultural and racial identity are at stake, as there can be when statutes and regulations are facially neutral, not only is each individual and community distinct, but that the same community can change over time. The essential task is to practice having discussions about race, so that when (imperfect) law or policy does take effect, we know that it is at least informed by relevant perspectives.

Trademark and Hate Speech: *Matal v. Tam*[10]

A trademark is used to identify a brand. These "marks" may be registered with the United States Patent and Trademark Office (USPTO). The registration process includes a review to ensure that the mark is neither identical to/too similar to an already registered mark, nor inappropriate. In this way, vested in the USPTO is the responsibility to make culturally responsive decisions about trademarks that will be associated with brands that may be closely tied to the identity of individuals or groups. Consider the following case involving Simon Tam, the leader of a band whose members are Asian, who tried to reclaim a derogatory term by naming his band "The Slants."

10. 582 U.S. 218 (2017).

MATAL V. TAM

582 U.S. 218 (2017)

Justice Alito announced the judgment of the Court and delivered the opinion of the Court....

This case concerns a dance-rock band's application for federal trademark registration of the band's name, "The Slants." "Slants" is a derogatory term for persons of Asian descent, and members of the band are Asian-Americans. But the band members believe that by taking that slur as the name of their group, they will help to "reclaim" the term and drain its denigrating force.

The Patent and Trademark Office (PTO) denied the application based on a provision of federal law prohibiting the registration of trademarks that may "disparage ... or bring ... into contemp[t] or disrepute" any "persons, living or dead." 15 U.S.C. § 1052(a). We now hold that this provision violates the Free Speech Clause of the First Amendment. It offends a bedrock First Amendment principle: Speech may not be banned on the ground that it expresses ideas that offend.

I

"The principle underlying trademark protection is that distinctive marks—words, names, symbols, and the like—can help distinguish a particular artisan's goods from those of others." *B&B Hardware, Inc. v. Hargis Industries, Inc.*, 575 U.S. 138, 142 (2015); *see also Wal-Mart Stores, Inc. v. Samara Brothers, Inc.*, 529 U.S. 205, 212 (2000). A trademark "designate[s] the goods as the product of a particular trader" and "protect[s] his good will against the sale of another's product as his." *United Drug Co. v. Theodore Rectanus Co.*, 248 U.S. 90, 97 (1918); *see also Hanover Star Milling Co. v. Metcalf*, 240 U.S. 403, 412–413 (1916). It helps consumers identify goods and services that they wish to purchase, as well as those they want to avoid. *See Wal-Mart Stores, supra*, at 212–213; *Park 'N Fly, Inc. v. Dollar Park & Fly, Inc.*, 469 U.S. 189, 198 (1985).

"[F]ederal law does not create trademarks." *B&B Hardware, supra*, at 142. Trademarks and their precursors have ancient origins, and trademarks were protected at common law and in equity at the time of the founding of our country. 3 J. McCarthy, Trademarks and Unfair Competition § 19:8 (4th ed. 2017) (hereinafter McCarthy); 1 *id.*, §§ 5:1, 5:2, 5:3; Pattishall, The Constitutional Foundations of American Trademark Law, 78 Trademark Rep. 456, 457–458 (1988); Pattishall, Two Hundred

Years of American Trademark Law, 68 Trademark Rep. 121, 121–123 (1978); *see Trade-Mark Cases*, 100 U.S. 82, 92 (1879). For most of the 19th century, trademark protection was the province of the States. *See Two Pesos, Inc. v. Taco Cabana, Inc.*, 505 U.S. 763, 780–782 (1992) (Stevens, J., concurring in judgment); *id.*, at 785 (Thomas, J., concurring in judgment). Eventually, Congress stepped in to provide a degree of national uniformity, passing the first federal legislation protecting trademarks in 1870. *See* Act of July 8, 1870, §§77–84, 16 Stat. 210–212. The foundation of current federal trademark law is the Lanham Act, enacted in 1946. *See* Act of July 5, 1946, ch. 540, 60 Stat. 427. By that time, trademark had expanded far beyond phrases that do no more than identify a good or service. Then, as now, trademarks often consisted of catchy phrases that convey a message.

Under the Lanham Act, trademarks that are "used in commerce" may be placed on the "principal register," that is, they may be federally registered. 15 U.S.C. § 1051(a)(1). And some marks "capable of distinguishing [an] applicant's goods or services and not registrable on the principal register ... which are in lawful use in commerce by the owner thereof" may instead be placed on a different federal register: the supplemental register. § 1091(a). There are now more than two million marks that have active federal certificates of registration. PTO Performance and Accountability Report, Fiscal Year 2016, p. 192 (Table 15), https://www.uspto.gov/sites/default/files/ documents/USPTOFY16PAR.pdf (all Internet materials as last visited June 16, 2017). This system of federal registration helps to ensure that trademarks are fully protected and supports the free flow of commerce. "[N]ational protection of trademarks is desirable," we have explained, "because trademarks foster competition and the maintenance of quality by securing to the producer the benefits of good reputation." *San Francisco Arts & Athletics, Inc. v. United States Olympic Comm.*, 483 U.S. 522, 531 (1987) (internal quotation marks omitted); *see also Park 'N Fly, Inc., supra*, at 198 ("The Lanham Act provides national protection of trademarks in order to secure to the owner of the mark the goodwill of his business and to protect the ability of consumers to distinguish among competing producers").

B

Without federal registration, a valid trademark may still be used in commerce. *See* 3 McCarthy § 19:8. And an unregistered trademark can be enforced against would-be infringers in several ways. Most important, even if a trademark is not federally registered, it may still be enforceable under § 43(a) of the Lanham Act, which creates a federal cause of action for trademark infringement. *See Two Pesos, supra*, at 768 ("Section 43(a) prohibits a broader range of practices than does § 32, which applies to registered marks, but it is common ground that § 43(a) protects qualifying unregistered trademarks" (internal quotation marks and citation omitted)). And an unregistered trademark can be enforced under state common law, or if it has been registered in a State, under that State's registration system. *See* 3 *id.*, § 19:3, at 19–23 (explaining that "[t]he federal system of registration and protection does not preempt parallel state law protection, either by state common law or state registration," and "[i]n the vast majority of situations, federal and state trademark law peacefully coexist"); *id.*, § 22:1 (discussing state trademark registration systems).

Federal registration, however, "confers important legal rights and benefits on trademark owners who register their marks." *B&B Hardware*, 575 U.S., at 142 (internal quotation marks omitted). Registration on the principal register (1) "serves as 'constructive notice of the registrant's claim of ownership' of the mark," *ibid.* (quoting 15 U.S.C. § 1072); (2) "is 'prima facie evidence of the validity of the registered mark and of the registration of the mark, of the owner's ownership of the mark, and of the owner's exclusive right to use the registered mark in commerce on or in connection with the goods or services specified in the certificate,' " *B&B Hardware*, 575 U.S. 142–143 (quoting § 1057(b)); and (3) can make a mark "'incontestable'" "once a mark has been registered for five years," *id.*, at 143 (quoting §§ 1065, 1115(b)); *see Park 'N Fly*, 469 U.S., at 193. Registration also enables the trademark holder "to stop the importation into the United States of articles bearing an infringing mark." 3 McCarthy § 19:9, at 19–38; *see* 15 U.S.C. § 1124.

C

The Lanham Act contains provisions that bar certain trademarks from the principal register. For example, a trademark cannot be registered if it is "merely descriptive or deceptively misdescriptive" of goods, § 1052(e)(1), or if it is so similar to an already registered trademark or trade name that it is "likely ... to cause confusion, or to cause mistake, or to deceive." § 1052(d).

At issue in this case is one such provision, which we will call "the disparagement clause." This provision prohibits the registration of a trademark "which may disparage ... persons, living or dead, institutions, beliefs, or national symbols, or bring them into contempt, or disrepute." § 1052(a). This clause appeared in the original Lanham Act and has remained the same to this day. *See* § 2(a), 60 Stat. 427.

When deciding whether a trademark is disparaging, an examiner at the PTO generally applies a "two-part test." The examiner first considers "the likely meaning of the matter in question, taking into account not only dictionary definitions, but also the relationship of the matter to the other elements in the mark, the nature of the goods or services, and the manner in which the mark is used in the marketplace in connection with the goods or services." Trademark Manual of Examining Procedure § 1203.03(b)(i) (Apr. 2017), p. 1200–150, http://tmep.uspto.gov. "If that meaning is found to refer to identifiable persons, institutions, beliefs or national symbols," the examiner moves to the second step, asking "whether that meaning may be disparaging to a substantial composite of the referenced group." *Ibid.* If the examiner finds that a "substantial composite, although not necessarily a majority, of the referenced group would find the proposed mark ... to be disparaging in the context of contemporary attitudes," a prima facie case of disparagement is made out, and the burden shifts to the applicant to prove that the trademark is not disparaging. *Ibid.* What is more, the PTO has specified that "[t]he fact that an applicant may be a member of that group or has good intentions underlying its use of a term does not obviate the fact that a substantial composite of the referenced group would find the term objectionable." *Ibid.*

D

Simon Tam is the lead singer of "The Slants." *In re Tam*, 808 F. 3d 1321, 1331 (CA Fed. 2015) (en banc), as corrected (Feb. 11, 2016). He chose this moniker in order to "reclaim" and "take ownership" of stereotypes about people of Asian ethnicity. *Ibid.* (internal quotation marks omitted). The group "draws inspiration for its lyrics from childhood slurs and mocking nursery rhymes" and has given its albums names such as "The Yellow Album" and "Slanted Eyes, Slanted Hearts." *Ibid.*

Tam sought federal registration of "THE SLANTS," on the principal register, App. 17, but an examining attorney at the PTO rejected the request, applying the PTO's two-part framework and finding that "there is . . . a substantial composite of persons who find the term in the applied-for mark offensive." *Id.*, at 30. The examining attorney relied in part on the fact that "numerous dictionaries define 'slants' or 'slant-eyes' as a derogatory or offensive term." *Id.*, at 29. The examining attorney also relied on a finding that "the band's name has been found offensive numerous times"—citing a performance that was canceled because of the band's moniker and the fact that "several bloggers and commenters to articles on the band have indicated that they find the term and the applied-for mark offensive." *Id.*, at 29–30.

Tam contested the denial of registration before the examining attorney and before the PTO's Trademark Trial and Appeal Board (TTAB) but to no avail. Eventually, he took the case to federal court, where the en banc Federal Circuit ultimately found the disparagement clause facially unconstitutional under the First Amendment's Free Speech Clause. The majority found that the clause engages in viewpoint-based discrimination, that the clause regulates the expressive component of trademarks and consequently cannot be treated as commercial speech, and that the clause is subject to and cannot satisfy strict scrutiny. *See* 808 F. 3d, at 1334–1339. The majority also rejected the Government's argument that registered trademarks constitute government speech, as well as the Government's contention that federal registration is a form of government subsidy. *See id.*, at 1339–1355. And the majority opined that even if the disparagement clause were analyzed under this Court's commercial speech cases, the clause would fail the "intermediate scrutiny" that those cases prescribe. *See id.*, at 1355–1357.

Several judges wrote separately, advancing an assortment of theories. Concurring, Judge O'Malley agreed with the majority's reasoning but added that the disparagement clause is unconstitutionally vague. *See id.*, at 1358–1363. Judge Dyk concurred in part and dissented in part. He argued that trademark registration is a government subsidy and that the disparagement clause is facially constitutional, but he found the clause unconstitutional as applied to THE SLANTS because that mark constitutes "core expression" and was not adopted for the purpose of disparaging Asian-Americans. *See id.*, at 1363–1374. In dissent, Judge Lourie agreed with Judge Dyk that the clause is facially constitutional but concluded for a variety of reasons that it is also constitutional as applied in this case. *See id.*, at 1374–1376. Judge Reyna also dissented, maintaining that trademarks are commercial speech and that the disparagement clause survives intermediate scrutiny because it "directly advances the government's substantial interest in the orderly flow of commerce." *See id.*, at 1376–1382.

....

II

Before reaching the question whether the disparagement clause violates the First Amendment, we consider Tam's argument that the clause does not reach marks that disparage racial or ethnic groups. The clause prohibits the registration of marks that disparage "persons," and Tam claims that the term "persons" "includes only natural and juristic persons," not "non-juristic entities such as racial and ethnic groups." Brief for Respondent 46.

....

... We thus begin by explaining why Tam's argument about the definition of "persons" in the Lanham Act is meritless.

As noted, the disparagement clause prohibits the registration of trademarks "which may disparage ... persons, living or dead." 15 U.S.C. § 1052(a). Tam points to a definition of "person" in the Lanham Act, which provides that "[i]n the construction of this chapter, unless the contrary is plainly apparent from the context ... [t]he term 'person' and any other word or term used to designate the applicant or other entitled to a benefit or privilege or rendered liable under the provisions of this chapter includes a juristic person as well as a natural person." § 1127. Because racial and ethnic groups are neither natural nor "juristic" persons, Tam asserts, these groups fall outside this definition. Brief for Respondent 46–48.

Tam's argument is refuted by the plain terms of the disparagement clause. The clause applies to marks that disparage "persons." A mark that disparages a "substantial" percentage of the members of a racial or ethnic group, Trademark Manual § 1203.03(b)(i), at 1200–150, necessarily disparages many "persons," namely, members of that group. Tam's argument would fail even if the clause used the singular term "person," but Congress' use of the plural "persons" makes the point doubly clear.

Tam's narrow reading of the term "persons" also clashes with the breadth of the disparagement clause. By its terms, the clause applies to marks that disparage, not just "persons," but also "institutions" and "beliefs." 15 U.S.C. § 1052(a). It thus applies to the members of any group whose members share particular "beliefs," such as political, ideological, and religious groups. It applies to marks that denigrate "institutions," and on Tam's reading, it also reaches "juristic" persons such as corporations, unions, and other unincorporated associations. *See* § 1127. Thus, the clause is not limited to marks that disparage a particular natural person. If Congress had wanted to confine the reach of the disparagement clause in the way that Tam suggests, it would have been easy to do so. A neighboring provision of the Lanham Act denies registration to any trademark that "[c]onsists of or comprises a name, portrait, or signature identifying a *particular living individual* except by his written consent." § 1052(c) (emphasis added).

Tam contends that his interpretation of the disparagement clause is supported by its legislative history and by the PTO's willingness for many years to register marks that plainly denigrated African-Americans and Native Americans. These arguments are unpersuasive. As always, our inquiry into the meaning of the statute's text ceases when "the statutory language is unambiguous and the statutory scheme is coherent and consistent." *Barnhart v. Sigmon Coal Co.*, 534 U.S. 438, 450 (2002) (internal quotation marks omitted). Here, it is clear that the prohibition against registering trademarks "which may disparage ... persons," § 1052(a), prohibits registration of terms that disparage persons who share a common race or ethnicity.

Even if resort to legislative history and early enforcement practice were appropriate, we would find Tam's arguments unconvincing. Tam has not brought to our attention any evidence in the legislative history showing that Congress meant to adopt his interpretation. And the practice of the PTO in the years following the enactment of the disparagement clause is unenlightening. The admitted vagueness of the disparagement test and the huge volume of applications have produced a haphazard record of enforcement. (Even today, the principal register is replete with marks that many would regard as disparaging to racial and ethnic groups.) Registration of the offensive marks that Tam cites is likely attributable not to the acceptance of his interpretation of the clause but to other factors—most likely the regrettable attitudes and sensibilities of the time in question.

III

Because the disparagement clause applies to marks that disparage the members of a racial or ethnic group, we must decide whether the clause violates the Free Speech Clause of the First Amendment. And at the outset, we must consider three arguments that would either eliminate any First Amendment protection or result in highly permissive rational-basis review. Specifically, the Government contends (1) that trademarks are government speech, not private speech, (2) that trademarks are a form of government subsidy, and (3) that the constitutionality of the disparagement clause should be tested under a new "government-program" doctrine. We address each of these arguments below. . . .

NOTES ON *MATAL V. TAM*

1. So, What Happened? The Court went on to decide that trademarks are private speech, not government speech, and also that they are not a form of government subsidy or a "government program." Accordingly, the Court's next step was to determine whether the commercial nature of the speech (because of the impact trademarks have on commerce) was subject to a more relaxed standard of scrutiny. Ultimately, the Court decided that the language of the disparagement clause was too broad and therefore did not comport with the principles of free speech in the First Amendment. As a result, even though Simon Tam's argument about the application of the disparagement clause—that it does not reach trademarks that disparage racial or ethnic *groups*—was not well received by the Court, he ultimately prevailed when the clause was held to be too broad to survive. The name "The Slants" remained.

2. Reclamation of Offensive Marks. Reclaiming hate speech is difficult, and so speaking about this case in class can be extremely difficult. It should be noted, however, that over years of teaching this case, both students and professors have flinched a great deal less at using "The Slants" than other hate-speech terms that have come up in class. Consider how "racial differentializing" may have an impact on the way that we practice making culturally informed legal arguments, particularly surrounding hate speech.

Simon Tam's lawyers were not Asian, and neither were the judges and appeals officers who decided this case. Note that the Court went to the trouble of naming the judges and their opinions—perhaps it feels safer to try, in some small way, to identify individuals' racial backgrounds when writing about these issues. Though it can be uncomfortable and difficult to address hate speech, we must do so in the classroom—otherwise it will only be dealt with in the realms of anger and violence. Consider the ways in which your identity as an attorney, appeals officer, or judge might impact the way that you decide on what is derogatory in a community and when a reclamation is appropriate. These issues are nuanced and personal, and there may be differing views even within a community. There are no good answers here, and when that is the case, discussing these issues in the classroom becomes vitally important.

3. Ramifications, Redskins, and Cultural Appropriation. Simon Tam has spoken publicly about his complicated feelings about the outcome of this appeal. While *Matal v. Tam* was making its way through the courts, a public conversation was happening at the national level regarding team mascots based on caricatures of Indigenous people. In particular, the owners of the Washington Redskins were using a name, imagery, and logo that had become the subject of fierce debate. In *Tam*, there was some discussion about the ways in which an individual could not speak for a community, but that discussion only touched on the complexities of how cultural communities relate to their heritage and property. While the ruling in *Tam* meant that the Washington Redskins could continue to use their name and logo, the court of public opinion (and economic pressure) resulted in their retiring them—they temporarily changed their name to the Washington Football Team in 2020 before settling on their permanent new name, the Washington Commanders, in 2022. Also in 2022, the Cleveland Indians changed their name, becoming the Cleveland Guardians. It appears that our cultural paradigm has shifted.

However, uncomfortable questions about cultural appropriation remain unresolved. Difficult even to define in practice, cultural appropriation relates to the adoption, and often exploitation, of one culture by another. And often overlooked in this definition are the power dynamics and hierarchies inherent in these questions. Property is at stake here: commerce revolves around cultural appropriation, and the race to be "authentic" drives value. Who may represent and profit from a culture is a difficult question to address, but is one that is better discussed than not.

Introduction to Critical Race Theory[11]

Throughout this work, the law of property has been explained through the lens of American legal history. It is only after completing the first year of law school that it is appropriate to begin the study of a new doctrine: critical race theory (CRT).

In recent elections and the current national discourse, critical race theory has become a hot-button political issue. It is a relatively new doctrine, one which sprang from the minds of legal scholars in the 1970s. At a famous conference in Wisconsin (of all places!) in 1989, the first workshop on critical race theory was held. Professor Derrick Bell, widely considered to be the movement's intellectual father figure, authored many of the foundational texts on the doctrine and established the theory of interest convergence based on his experience as a civil rights litigator.

Though it tends to lack bright lines and clearly defined elements, CRT does have a number of generally agreed-upon tenets. Introducing a few of its often-discussed tenets seems a fitting conclusion to this work on property and legal history.

Ordinary Racism: One of the first assumptions underlying CRT is "that racism is ordinary, not aberrational—'normal science,' the usual way society does business, the common, everyday experience of most people of color in this country ... [—and] that our system of white-over-color ascendancy serves important purposes, both psychic and material."[12] If this seems difficult to take in, you are not alone. It is this very "ordinariness" that makes racism "difficult to cure or address" because it is not acknowledged. To echo what Professor Harris, one of the founders of CRT, wrote in her work *Whiteness as Property*:[13] it is the normative centering of whiteness that puts it at the center of our society. The way in which individuals of all races have accepted that paradigm is what is expressed by this first tenet of CRT.

Interest Convergence/Material Determinism: The theory of interest convergence, or material determinism, which was established and made famous by Professor Derrick Bell, takes into account the various self-interests of different racial groups to help explain racial progress (or re-

---

11. This section quotes heavily from Richard Delgado & Jean Stefancic, *Critical Race Theory: An Introduction* (2017).

12. *Id.* at 7.

13. Harris, *supra* note 1.

gression). According to this theory, the greatest civil rights advances occur when they are in the interest of the dominant (white) group. As Professor Bell reflected on the Supreme Court's decision in *Brown v. Board of Education*, his hindsight brought him the perspective that the interest of all parties "converged" at that moment, making the decision in Brown inevitable. As Professor Bell continued his career, he realized that racial dynamics across the country would diminish that convergence of interests and make integration less feasible.[14]

Social Construction Theory: Somewhat similar to the ideas Justice Sutherland expressed in his opinion in *Thind*, the social construction theory posits that race is not biologically fixed but is instead a creation of society. It is closely related to the concept of differential realization, which "calls attention to the ways in which the dominant society racializes different minority groups at different times, in response to shifting needs, such as the labor market" or geopolitical forces.[15]

Intersectionality/Anti-Essentialism: Established and made popular by Professor Kimberle Crenshaw, the theory of intersectionality recognizes that belonging to/identifying with more than one minority group can compound the effects of discrimination. Professor Crenshaw had worked on the case of Emma DeGraffenreid, a Black woman who was denied employment and subsequently filed an action alleging discrimination, only to find that her race and gender together precluded her from relief: because Black men were employed on the assembly line, the employer was able to show that it did not discriminate on the basis of race, and because white women were employed as administrative support staff, the employer was able to demonstrate that it also did not discriminate on the basis of gender. Professor Crenshaw identified this plaintiff's particular problem as one resulting from her sitting at the intersection of race and gender—she was denied legal relief because of this intersectionality. Anti-essentialism is a related concept that emphasizes that no person has one single or "essential" identity.

Armed with a better knowledge of American legal history, stronger legal-analysis skills, and a working understanding of some property-law doctrine, go forth into the world and make your mark.

---

14. Bell, Derrick Jr. Brown v. Board of Education *and the Interest Convergence Dilemma*, Harvard Law Review, Vol. 93, No. 3 (January 1980).

15. Delgado & Stefancic, *supra* note 11, at 8.

Index

T